Negativity in Democratic Politics

This book explores the political implications of the human tendency to prioritize negative information over positive information. Drawing on literatures in political science, psychology, economics, communications, biology, and physiology, this book argues that "negativity biases" should be evident across a wide range of political behaviors. These biases are then demonstrated through a diverse and cross-disciplinary set of analyses, for instance: in citizens' ratings of presidents and prime ministers; in aggregate-level reactions to economic news, across seventeen countries; in the relationship between covers and newsmagazine sales; and in individuals' physiological reactions to network news content. The pervasiveness of negativity biases extends, this book suggests, to the functioning of political institutions – institutions that have been designed to prioritize negative information in the same way as the human brain.

Stuart N. Soroka is professor and William Dawson Scholar in the department of Political Science at McGill University, Montreal, Canada. He is currently a coinvestigator of the Canadian Election Study and a member of the Centre for the Study of Democratic Citizenship. Soroka's previous books are *Agenda-Setting Dynamics in Canada* (2003) and *Degrees of Democracy: Politics, Public Opinion, and Policy* (coauthored with Christopher Wlezien, 2010), the latter of which received the Seymour Martin Lipset Best Book Award from the Canadian Politics Section of the American Political Science Association. His research has also been published widely in such journals as the *Journal of Politics*, the *British Journal of Political Science*, the *American Journal of Political Science*, *Political Communication*, and *West European Politics*. Soroka is a member of the editorial boards of *Political Communication*, the *Journal of Elections, Public Opinion and Parties*, and the *Canadian Journal of Political Science*.

Cambridge Studies in Public Opinion and Political Psychology

Series Editors

Dennis Chong,
University of Southern California and Northwestern University
James H. Kuklinksi
University of Illinois, Urbana-Champaign

Cambridge Studies in Public Opinion and Political Psychology publishes innovative research from a variety of theoretical and methodological perspectives on the mass public foundations of politics and society. Research in the series focuses on the origins and influence of mass opinion; the dynamics of information and deliberation; and the emotional, normative, and instrumental bases of political choice. In addition to examining psychological processes, the series explores the organization of groups, the association between individual and collective preferences, and the impact of institutions on beliefs and behavior.

Cambridge Studies in Public Opinion and Political Psychology is dedicated to furthering theoretical and empirical research on the relationship between the political system and the attitudes and actions of citizens.

Books in the series are listed on the page following the Index.

Negativity in Democratic Politics

Causes and Consequences

STUART N. SOROKA

McGill University

CAMBRIDGE
UNIVERSITY PRESS

32 Avenue of the Americas, New York, NY 10013-2473, USA

Cambridge University Press is part of the University of Cambridge.

It furthers the University's mission by disseminating knowledge in the pursuit of education, learning, and research at the highest international levels of excellence.

www.cambridge.org
Information on this title: www.cambridge.org/9781107636194

© Stuart N. Soroka 2014

First published 2014

Printed in the United States of America

A catalog record for this publication is available from the British Library.

Library of Congress Cataloging in Publication Data
Soroka, Stuart Neil, 1970–
Negativity in democratic politics : causes and consequences / Stuart N. Soroka.
    pages cm
Includes bibliographical references and index.
ISBN 978-1-107-06329-7 (hardback) – ISBN 978-1-107-63619-4 (paperback)
1. Political culture.   2. Political participation.   3. Political psychology.   4. Political sociology.
I. Title.
JA75.7.S675   2014
320.01'9–dc23   2013038845

ISBN 978-1-107-06329-7 Hardback
ISBN 978-1-107-63619-4 Paperback

Contents

Figures

Tables

Preface

One mouse dropping ruins the whole pot of rice porridge.

– Chinese proverb

Modern politics is overwhelmingly negative in tone. Everyday political reporting focuses on conflicts in the legislature, on major policy issues that have thus far been ignored, on political problems at home and abroad. It is accepted wisdom that following a brief post-election "honeymoon," governing parties and candidates tend to suffer a gradual decline in approval. (It is apparently nearly impossible to both govern and maintain support for governing.) Campaigns are regularly strewn with attack ads, and even when they are not, journalists debate whether or when the campaign will "go negative."

Why is modern politics so negative? And what are the consequences of that negativity? These are the two questions driving the work in this book. The answers have at their root theories drawn from disparate fields in the social and physical sciences – theories that try to describe and explain the negativity biases that seem to be so prevalent in social, economic, and political interactions. But the application of these theories is, in this case, entirely focused on politics.

The discussion should begin, however, with a clear statement of what exactly a negativity bias is. What follows is not a definition, but rather a short illustrative story. This is, for me at least, a useful illustration of the kind of negativity biases I wish to examine:

> Elizabeth is a 35-year-old interior designer, invited to a party where she makes a new acquaintance, Sara. When Elizabeth meets new people she immediately (and largely unconsciously) ranks them on four dimensions. Each of those dimensions ranges from −10 to +10, where zero is neutral, −10 is entirely negative, and +10 is entirely positive. There is no particular reason to believe that Sara will be a bad person, and Elizabeth is initially optimistic. She enters the room assuming that Sara is roughly +2 on all four dimensions.

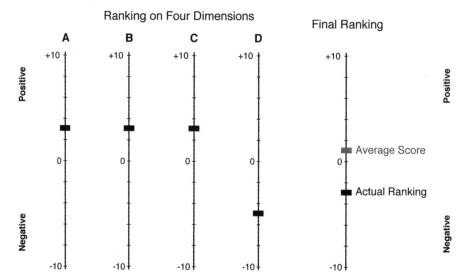

FIGURE 0.1. Impression Formation

Having spoken for several minutes, Elizabeth begins to revise her assessments of Sara. Sara is, as it turns out, a +3 on three of the four dimensions: she dresses well (dimension A), she is polite (dimension B), and she is clearly very knowledgeable about art and design (dimension C). But in the course of conversation Sara declares that she only drives foreign cars. Elizabeth's entire family works for General Motors. On this – support for the North American automotive industry (dimension D) – Elizabeth's assessment of Sara drops to −5.

What is Elizabeth's overall assessment of Sara? The obvious answer is that it is an average of Sara's scores on all four dimensions: +3, +3, +3, and −5. Overall, then, an average score is +1. (See Figure 0.1.) But Elizabeth's overall assessment of Sara is actually −3, because Elizabeth has a stronger reaction to negative information than to positive information. The three scores of +3 thus have a smaller impact on her overall assessment than does the one score of −5. And while all this numerical rating of Sara is largely unconscious (Elizabeth does not actually tally numbers in her head as she meets people), the rating itself has real-world behavioral consequences. Elizabeth is not a big fan of Sara. In spite of Sara being well dressed, polite, and knowledgeable, she drives a Volkswagen. So Elizabeth makes an excuse and moves to the other side of the room.

The real strength of this story in illustrating the negativity bias is that it will ring true for almost all of us – not support for the American automotive industry, perhaps, but the tendency to allow a single bad trait to weigh heavily on our overall assessment of others, and more generally the propensity to react more strongly to negative information than to positive information. These tendencies have certainly been well demonstrated in psychology research on "impression formation"; and this is by no means the only domain in which negative information seems to carry greater weight than positive information. A negativity bias has been evident across a wide range of social and natural sciences, from psychology and economics to anthropology, physiology, and evolutionary biology.

This book presents the argument that this negativity bias has potentially important implications for politics. Political attitudes and assessments regularly involve considerations of positive and negative information, after all. We assess political candidates, parties, policies, and policy outcomes in roughly the same way as the hypothetical Elizabeth assessed Sara. And in politics, as in impression formation, negative information carries more weight.

Note that what emerges in the chapters that follow is not an argument against a focus on negative information in the political sphere. It is, rather, an explanation for why media content, public opinion, and even the design of political institutions tend to be focused on negative information. Each of these is related – more or less directly – to the design and functioning of the human brain. That our brains show this tendency is understandable, and indeed often advantageous. But the negativity bias may also produce systematic inaccuracies in the ways people and governments receive or process information. For instance, negativity biases may allow citizens to monitor the economy effectively; they may alternatively lead citizens to overreact to comparatively small negative shifts in the economy. Governments may similarly do a great job of monitoring even minor concerns among their constituents, or they may overreact to small negative shifts in public opinion and produce inefficient and misdirected policy as a result. In short, there may be both positive and negative consequences of negativity in the political sphere. And while weighing the actual costs and benefits of negativity will require more research, this book takes one additional step, at least, toward better understanding the sources and effects of the negativity biases that characterize both political behavior and political institutions.

Chapter 1 gets the ball rolling by cataloging the rather overwhelming evidence of a negativity bias across a wide range of disciplines. Pulling this literature together not only helps make the case that a negativity bias exists; it provides an explanation for how and why the negativity bias got there. It also sets the stage for the chapters that follow – chapters that trace out the facts and consequences of asymmetric responsiveness to negative versus positive information in the political sphere.

Chapter 2 then reviews similar findings regarding the relative strength of negativity in the political sphere. Political scientists have not yet embraced asymmetry in the same way psychologists and economists have, but there is an accumulating body of evidence throughout the discipline that suggests a similar dynamic. This chapter reviews these rich but thus far somewhat scattered findings.

Chapter 3 turns to data analysis. This chapter presents a relatively simple analysis of U.S. presidential evaluations, built on models in the psychological

xvi
Preface

literature on impression formation. As past work in psychology suggests, negative domain-specific evaluations matter more to overall presidential evaluations than do positive domain-specific evaluations. The same is true outside the United States; here, ratings of Australian prime ministers serve as a test case. And U.S. election study data offer opportunities to examine additional issues as well, including individual-level heterogeneity in the negativity bias and the difficulty of identifying the difference between positive and negative in interval-level measures.

Chapter 4 then turns to aggregate-level survey data and an analysis of economic voting models across a wide range of advanced industrial democracies. Asymmetries are demonstrated across the developed world, and time series are used to consider not just the asymmetric impact of negative versus positive information but also the possibility that the asymmetry varies over time.

Chapter 5 focuses on media content. People are asymmetric in their attentiveness, so it should come as no surprise that mass media are as well. Analyses here suggest a bias in which news gets selected for publication, starting with a comparison of daily crime statistics (drawn directly from a police database) and news stories in Bloomington, Illinois. Analyses then turn to distributions of information in the real world and in media content on the economy and on foreign affairs.

Chapter 6 then connects findings in public opinion with findings in media. The chapter uses data from weekly newsstand sales of *Time* and *Maclean's*, alongside content analyses of covers, to show that negative covers sell more magazines – more to the point, that people *choose* negative over positive information. These findings are supported by results from psychophysiological experiments suggesting that viewers are highly activated by negative news content and barely activated by equivalently positive content.

Chapter 7 both reviews the preceding findings and tries to connect them with the design of representative political institutions. Media can be seen as catering to the way in which the human brain works – we are more interested in negative information, so audience-seeking media tend to provide more negative information. But media can also be viewed as behaving *like* the human brain. Our own minds are hardwired to focus on negative information; we have designed a mass media hardwired in roughly the same way. The mass media are not unique in this regard, however. This chapter argues that a wide range of political institutions are designed in exactly the same way – to largely ignore positive information but to react very strongly (and publicly) to negative information. Indeed, negative feedback and error correction are perhaps the principal means by which modern representative democratic institutions function.

The end result of all of this, I hope, is a view of the political process that is (ironically) less negative. A common account of politics today, certainly in the United States and Canada but elsewhere as well, is that it is consumed with negativity. Media reports are increasingly negative; politicians (and their campaigns ads) are increasingly negative; and publics are increasingly negative in their treatment of politicians, their assessments of policy, and their views of the political system more generally. Politics is, this account goes, slowly descending into a bottomless pit of negativity.

The account offered in the chapters that follow provides a rather more optimistic, or at least more tempered, interpretation. First, evidence suggests that we are not destined to fall further and further into negativity, ad infinitum; indeed, the same (psychological or political) system that leads to a negativity bias in the first place likely also contains the mechanisms that constrain that negativity. But, second, even though politics may almost always be a predominantly negative endeavor, that may be for good reason. More to the point, given the common account, negativity in politics is not (entirely) the product of a few bitter and malicious individuals. It is, rather, a product of a general human tendency to prioritize negative information – a tendency that has been purposefully built into political institutions, and may well be a relatively effective way to manage large representative democratic governance.

None of this is to say that there are not costs to negativity in politics. A focus on negativity, as we shall see, may well produce all kinds of biases in politics. But in the case of this book, at least, it is not all bad news. There may be reasonable causes, and sometimes even positive consequences, of negativity in modern politics. It is to those causes and consequences, both positive and negative, that we turn in the chapters that follow.

Acknowledgments

This book is a product not just of my own work, but of a series of very helpful reactions from colleagues and friends. I am first and foremost grateful to Patrick Fournier, whose first read of the full manuscript was the ideal combination of harsh and helpful. (Indeed, given the quality of the review, it is very likely that any remaining weaknesses are his fault.) I am grateful to other collaborators as well: to Christopher Wlezien, who provided some very influential comments on the manuscript and a great deal of helpful advice along the way as well, and to both Stephen Farnsworth and Stefaan Walgrave, whose comments on the penultimate draft made a huge difference to the final product.

I have had the good fortune of working at a university full of helpful colleagues. I am grateful to Arash Abizadeh, Darin Barney, Jim Engle-Warnick, John Galbraith, Erik Kuhonta, Jacob Levy, Filippo Sabetti, Blema Steinberg, Dietlind Stolle, and Christina Tarnopolsky, each of whom has offered helpful reactions to parts of what follows; and to Elisabeth Gidengil, who as the founding director of the Centre for the Study of Democratic Citizenship (CSDC) played a crucial role in developing the lab in which my physiological experiments were run. Those experiments were the product of a collaboration with another McGill colleague, Stephen McAdams, and a second round of experiments was done in collaboration with Penelope Diagnault and Thierry Giasson at Laval University. The CSDC speakers' series offered a valuable opportunity to get reactions to some of this work in its penultimate form; I am grateful to my audience there, and particularly to Centre members André Blais, Henry Milner, and Elin Naurin. I was able to present this material in its near-final form at the Annenberg School for Communication at the University of Pennsylvania, at the School of Journalism and Mass Communication at the University of Wisconsin (Madison), at the Noah Mozes Department of Communication and Journalism at the Hebrew University in Jerusalem, and at the Department of Communication Studies at the University of Michigan. The final product was greatly improved by reactions at these talks, and I am very grateful to audience members for their feedback – particularly to Kathleen Hall Jamieson, Russell Neuman, Lilach Nir, and Mike Traugott. There were many others who have commented on precursors to and/or parts of what follows, either formally or informally. I am very grateful for their help, particularly to Toril Aalberg, Keith Banting, Amanda Bittner, Fred Cutler, Jamie Druckman, John Geer, Shanto Iyengar, Richard Johnston, Bryan Jones, Michael Mitchell, and Andrew Owen.

Current and former students have played a crucial role in this work as well. Lori Young took the lead in developing the Lexicoder Sentiment Dictionary; my work with Lori was absolutely critical to the chapters on media content. Blake Andrew also helped develop many of the ways in which I and my students now look at media data. Marc Bodet helped work on campaign-period analyses that inform the work that follows and reacted to many of the ideas in their early stages. Mark Daku programmed Lexicoder. I have also benefited from a number of very good research assistants who have helped with experiments, proofreading, and data gathering on this project. They include Quinn Albaugh, Sheena Bell, Clare Devereux, Nicole Gileadi, Matthias Heilke, Andrea Lawlor, Adam Mahon, Dominic Stecula, and Marc Trussler. I also am indebted to Carl Fever, crime analyst for the Bloomington, IL, Policy Department, who provided the crime database used in Chapter 5, and to Ken Whyte, who as editor and publisher of *Maclean's* magazine at the time both reacted to some early analyses and provided access to the data on covers and newsstand sales used in Chapter 6.

Finally, I am very grateful for my family's support and tolerance for stories about negativity biases – evident in the movement of sheep's ears (Reefmann et al. 2009), or the faces of Lego figurines (Bartneck and Obaid 2013), or . . . ! My parents Anne and Lewis have been encouraging; my daughters Sara and Ellie have been both understanding and supportive, not to mention the subjects of innumerable small field experiments; and my wife Kim has been all of this and more. I am so surrounded by positive feedback, it is no wonder I am so hyperattentive to negative information.

I

On Negativity

You can't have a light without a dark to stick it in.

– Arlo Guthrie

A December 2012 op-ed in the *Moscow Times* described State Duma Deputy Oleg Mikheyev's proposal to force Russian media to report more good news. Mass media would have to shift the amount of positive information to 70 percent and restrict bad information to the remaining 30 percent. Too much bad information was said to damage the human psyche – indeed, it "weakens their ability to think and lowers their creative powers." Michael Bohm, opinion editor of the *Times*, was of course critical of Mikheyev's (preposterous) bill. Among his reasons, Bohm wrote, "Mikheyev has got the cause-effect relationship of negative information all wrong. The media is much less a cause of society's ills than it is a mirror image of those ills."

Media are certainly as much a reflection as they are a driver of public attitudes. For the most part, media do not make us negative – they reflect our negativity. But whether that negativity is an "ill" is another matter. Focusing on negative information may be a perfectly reasonable means for citizens to monitor their environment, and particularly their governments. Ongoing negativity in politics and political communication may be a problem, but it may also be effective and advantageous.

At a minimum, negativity in politics and political communication may be understandable. Exploring the scope of, and reasons for, this negativity is the purpose of the chapters that follow. In short, this book is about the importance of negative information in modern politics. The argument has three parts. First, negativity biases are readily apparent across a wide range of political behaviors. Second, similar biases are evident in the design and functioning of political institutions. Third, it is not yet clear whether these negativity biases are efficient

or fundamentally flawed. We cannot yet tell whether our heightened attentiveness to negative information is a boon or a curse for modern democratic
politics.

That said, the argument presented here need not apply just to modern politics; indeed, it need not be about politics at all. The strength of the argument
is not derived from what we know about politics and political behavior nearly
so much as from what we know about humans and human behavior. This
broader body of evidence is the subject of this first chapter. The chapter begins
by reviewing the literatures in psychology on the tendency for negative information (or events, or assessments) to have a greater effect on attitudes and
behaviors than their positive equivalents. These bodies of literatures are, as we
shall see, vast. They make it rather difficult to believe that asymmetry does
not exist. That said, the evidence does not end with psychology. Subsequent
sections draw on economics, on physiology and neurology, on evolutionary
biology, and on anthropology. We start with the subject of the Preface: impression formation.

The Psychology of Negativity

There is evidence of a negativity bias – or, more broadly, the relative strength
of negative over positive – throughout psychology. Indeed, the overwhelming
evidence of a negativity bias has been the subject of several very valuable meta-
reviews (e.g., Baumeister et al. 2001; Cacioppo and Gardner 1999; Rozin and
Royzman 2001). Those reviews cover the literature far more thoroughly than
will be attempted here. That said, this section provides a brief but (hopefully)
convincing account of the negativity bias in the psychology literature.

We begin with "impression formation," one of the domains in which a
negativity bias was first observed, and the one in which the phenomenon has
been most explored and analyzed. The story of Elizabeth and Sara in the Preface
draws directly on this literature, and especially on Anderson's (1965) early
description of a mathematical approach to impression formation. Anderson
was interested in (and found evidence of) a primacy effect: in a list of adjectives
describing a person, those at the beginning of the list matter more to an overall
evaluation of that person than do those toward the end. He suggested several
possible models for this effect, including a "weighted-average model" in which
the effect of any single adjective was weighted according to its position on the
list, and in this case, those at the beginning received a greater weight.

A good deal of work has since drawn on Anderson's weighted-average
model of impression formation, suggesting not just that weights vary with
primacy, but that that unfavorable information has a greater impact on overall
impressions than does favorable information. (For early work, also see Feldman
1966; Hodges 1974; Hamilton and Huffman 1971. For more recent work see,
e.g., Fiske 1980, Ronis and Lipinski 1985; Singh and Teoh 2000; Van der Pligt

and Eiser 1980; Vonk 1993, 1996.) To be clear, this work suggests that the relative weight in which a single dimension is given an overall assessment varies systematically with the negativity of that dimension.[1]

Several explanations have been given for the apparently greater weights attached to negative information in impression formation. Most work suggests that impressions are formed based on an expectation, or reference point. These impressions can vary based on experience; however, individuals tend to be mildly optimistic, so the reference point tends to be, on average, slightly positive. (I shall return to the subject of this positive reference point in later sections.) In one conception, this simply means a shift in perspective: −4 looks much worse from an expectation of +2 than it does from an expectation of 0, and +4 is not especially impressive when it is only a little better than what you expected (e.g., Helson 1964; Sherif and Sherif 1967). An alternative theory suggests that the asymmetry is driven by cognitive weighting: more attention is given to information that is regarded as unique or novel, which tends to be information that is more extreme (e.g., Fiske 1980). So similarly, −4 is more extreme (and thus is given greater weight) if the expectation is +2 rather than 0.

This difference between what Skowronski and Carlston (1989) refer to as "expectancy-contrast" and "frequency-weight" theories is subtle but important. Expectancy-contrast theories suggest that the negativity bias is a product of how we perceive negative versus positive information: a rating close to our expectation, +2, is accurately perceived, while a rating far from our expectation, −4, is misperceived, and that misperception tends to lead to an estimate that is even further away from our expectation. So a rating that by some objective, neutral standard should be a −4 is perceived to be a −6. Negative ratings thus play an especially important role because we tend to misperceive the degree to which they vary from our expectations.

Frequency-weight theories, in contrast, assume that we have accurate perceptions; we just tend to give greater weight to information that is further from expectations because we believe it is more valuable when trying to differentiate between people (or things). So we accurately perceive the −4 but give it greater weight than figures closer to our expectation of +2. These frequency-weight theories fit more easily with the story in the Preface (and the literature on "loss

---

[1] Borrowing directly from Anderson's model, the overall assessment A represents a weighted average of k number of dimensions D, $A = \frac{\sum \omega_k D_k}{\sum \omega_k}$, where the weight ω_k for each dimension D_k is a function of the negativity of that dimension, N_k, $\omega = \alpha + \beta N_k$. The constant α and coefficient β will vary from case to case, but the general idea here is that the weight begins at α and then increases at some interval β with one-unit increases in negativity N. The greater the negativity (the value of N_k), then, the greater the weight attached to D_k. And the effect of negativity on the weight of a given dimension need not increase linearly. The correct model might be an exponential one, for instance, where $\omega_k = \alpha + \beta N_k^2$.

aversion" in economics, reviewed later), and find somewhat more support in the experimental literature.[2]

Either way, our impressions of people are especially susceptible to the effects of negative rather than positive assessments. And evidence supporting a negativity bias has been found in many other domains of psychology as well. Consider, for instance, the body of research on information processing, which suggests that people devote more cognitive energy to thinking about bad things than to thinking about good things (e.g., Abele 1985). In an experiment in which people were asked to form impressions of various photographs, for instance, participants spent longer looking at photos depicting negative behavior than at photos depicting positive behavior (Fiske 1980). Work on attributional processing – the process of trying to find explanations or meaning for events – suggests a similar asymmetry (e.g., Taylor 1983). In one experiment, participants bet on sports events. When settling their bets with the experimenter, those who lost spent a greater amount of time discussing the game than did those who won (Gilovich 1983).[3]

Not only does negative information induce a greater degree of processing; *all* information is subject to more processing when the recipient is in a bad mood. Put more precisely, different affective states are associated with different styles of information processing (e.g., Bless, Hamilton, and Mackie 1992; Scharz 1990). Information processing while in positive affective states tends to be characterized by a greater degree of "clustering" – the tendency to identify themes, or clusters, across otherwise separate pieces of information. People in negative affective states do not show the same tendency to "cluster," but rather are more inclined to pay careful attention to details. Some work suggests that a positive mood allows for a more complex cognitive context, so individuals are more able to see things as related (Isen 1987). But the body of evidence leans toward the hypothesis that those in positive moods are more inclined to simplify, and thus miss information (Isen et al. 1987). Those in negative moods – less likely to use shortcuts, or "heuristics" – do not.

The implication is that there will be an especially large degree of information processing when someone in a bad mood receives bad news. Forgas (1992) finds as much: he examines information processing by people in various affective states, in reaction to people who either conform or do not conform to stereotypes. A bad mood combined with atypical (more complex) information produces the greatest degree of information processing.

Indeed, there are vast literatures cataloging the many different ways in which negative information matters more than positive information. Related to impression formation, research in "person memory" – who we remember, and what we remember about them – finds that we tend to remember negative

[2] Some authors have suggested alternative accounts for the mental process through which the negativity bias exists. See esp. Skowronski and Carlston's (1989) "category diagnosticity approach."
[3] Similar differences have been found across other domains. For a review, see Weiner 1985.

behaviors more than we do positive behaviors (e.g., Ybarra and Stephan 1996). Work on performance evaluations of employees and students, in which assessors regularly provide both numerical skill- or attribute-specific evaluations as well as an overall summary evaluation, suggest that negative rankings weigh more heavily on the overall evaluation than do positive rankings (Ganzach 1995; Rowe 1989; for a review, see DeNisi et al. 1984). Relatedly, learning, by both children and adults, tends to occur faster through punishment as opposed to reinforcement (Constantini and Hoving 1973; Meyer and Offenbach 1962; Penney and Lupton 1961; Penney 1968; Spense and Segner 1967; Tindall and Ratliff 1974).[4] In addition, bad feedback from teachers tends to be regarded as a more credible indicator of teachers' assessments than does positive feedback (Coleman, Jussim, and Abraham 1987), and when participants are presented with videotaped evaluations from another person, they monitor the negative evaluations for significantly more time than the positive evaluations (Graziano, Brothen, and Berscheid 1980).

The relative strength of negativity is also apparent in work on the effects of positive versus negative events. The loss of resources, social, behavioral, objective, or otherwise (see, e.g., Hobfoll 1988), has a greater and more long-lasting impact on psychological distress (e.g., stress or depression) than does the equivalent gain in resources (e.g., Wells, Hobfoll, and Lavin 1999). Negative events have a more powerful effect on daily "mood" than do positive events (e.g., David et al. 1997). Bad days have an effect that often carries over to the next day, whereas positive days show no such effect (Sheldon, Ryan, and Reis 1996; Marco and Suls 1993). "Adaptation-level" theories (Helson 1964) suggest a related dynamic: long-term happiness tends to be stable, because the effects of all events wear off; but the effects of bad events wear off more slowly than do the effects of good events (see, e.g., Brickman, Coates, and Janoff-Bulman 1978; also Taylor 1983).[5]

Prospective and retrospective evaluations of events reflect an asymmetry as well. When looking back over the day, people tend to underestimate the frequency of positive affect and overestimate the frequency of negative affect (Thomas and Diener 1990). (But note that long-term memory shows a positivity bias – this is discussed further later in the text.) Affective forecasting – the prediction of the emotional consequences of events – tends also to be biased

---

4 But note that punishment has other consequences. And it may be that the textbook assertion that reward is better than punishment is motivated not so much by evidence of the effectiveness of reward per se, but by the potential negative side-effects of punishment. See Baumeister et al. 2001: 335.

5 Helson's (1964) "adaptation level" theory suggests that the impact of any event is temporary – that people react more to change than stasis, and that their reaction to change wears off over time. This led to Brickman and Campbell's (1971) discussion of the "hedonic treadmill," whereby long-term happiness remains roughly constant because the effect of all events eventually wears off, and so to stay happy we need a constant supply of positive change. And it was testing of this hedonic treadmill that suggested the longer durability of negative effects.

toward the negative. That is, we are more likely to overestimate the duration of negative affect as opposed to positive affect (Gilbert et al. 1998). It is little wonder, then, that according to work on "self-regulation," people have developed many more techniques for escaping bad moods than for inducing good ones (Baumeister, Heatherton, and Tice 1994).

Relatedly, the presence or absence of negative behaviors is more predictive of the quality of married relationships than is the presence of absence of positive behaviors (Gottman 1979). Indeed, Gottman's (1994) work suggests that for a relationship to succeed, positive interactions must outnumber negative ones by a ratio of five to one. (See also Huston et al. 2001; Huston and Vangelisti 1991; Rusbult et al. 1986.) On an entirely different subject, negative feelings about organ donation weigh more heavily on the decision (to donate or not) than do positive feelings (Cacioppo & Gardner 1993). And unsurprisingly given the preceding evidence, an early content analysis of 172 introductory psychology textbooks found not just a focus on negative feelings over positive ones but a rise in this negative bias over the period of study (Carlson 1966; for a similar study on journal articles, see Czapinski 1985). There is, in short, a voluminous body of work in psychology finding evidence of a negativity bias, across a wide range of situations, events, and behaviors.

Negativity in Microeconomics

Work in behavioral economics (albeit much of it by two cognitive psychologists) suggests a similarly asymmetric story. Prospect theory (Kahneman and Tversky 1979; Tversky and Kahneman 1991) is a theory of choice under uncertainty, which includes a feature called loss aversion. Simply put, people care more strongly about a loss in utility than they do about a gain of equal magnitude. Prospect theory bears a close resemblance to "frequency-weight" accounts of impression formation in psychology – it too is a product of differential reactions to (accurately observed) negative and positive information.

The relative power of negative over positive is perhaps best (and most famously, at least for those political scientists interested in policy framing) captured in Kahneman and Tversky's (1984) experiment on policy choice. The policy choice is framed as follows:

> Imagine that the US is preparing for the outbreak of an unusual Asian disease, which is expected to kill 600 people. Two alternative programs to combat the disease have been proposed. Assume that the exact scientific estimates of the consequences of the programs are as follows:

One group is given these two options:

> If Program A is adopted, 200 people will be saved.

> If Program B is adopted, there is 1/3 probability that 600 people will be saved, and 2/3 probability that no people will be saved.

Another group is given these two options:

> If Program C is adopted, 400 people will die.
>
> If Program D is adopted, there is 1/3 probability that nobody will die, and 2/3 probability that 600 people will die.

Programs A and C are exactly equivalent, of course: under one 200 of 600 are saved, and under the other 400 of 600 die. Programs B and D are also identical. But while more than two-thirds of respondents select A over B, two-thirds also select D over C. When the first option is about being saved, in short, it seems much more attractive than when it is about dying. Put differently, the riskier option (B or D) received greater consideration when pitched against sure losses (deaths) rather than sure gains (lives); negative information is a stronger motivator (toward risky behavior) than is positive information.

Prospect theory is an extension of more standard expected utility theorems, in which the preferences of individuals for various outcomes reflect a simple (and symmetric) combination of the utility of outcomes and their respective probabilities. In prospect theory, people assess the utility of an outcome based on not the final status (as in normal expected utility theorems), but rather based on a reference point, often the status quo (as in the experiment discussed earlier). In addition, people have different attitudes about risk when they are facing gains versus losses: they are loss averse, that is, they care more about losses than about gains. The crux of the matter is thus not very different from what we have in psychological work on impression formation. In this case, we are not assessing individuals but rather making economic decisions. But the critical dynamic is the same: in making those economic decisions, people are expected to have stronger short-term reactions to potential losses than to potential gains.

Loss-averse behavior has been found at the individual level across a wide range of decision-making environments, both in the lab and in the real world. (The literature is vast, but see, e.g., Tversky, Slovic, and Kahneman 1990; Kahneman and Thaler 1991; Shoemaker and Kunreuther 1979; Arkes and Blumer 1985; Diamond 1988. For a partial review, see Edwards 1996.) It has also been evidenced in aggregate-level macroeconomic dynamics. For instance, consumption tends to drop more when the economy contracts than rise when the economy expands (Bowman, Minehart, and Rabin 1999). Bowman and colleagues suggest the following explanation: because people are averse to losses, they fail to cut back on expenditures immediately following news that economic performance is expected to decline, which forces them to cut back more sharply when the poor economic outcome is actually realized. Because people are not averse to gains, their immediate increase in consumption following good news means that there is not a steep increase in consumption once the good outcome is realized. The net result is that current increases in income have an incremental (positive) effect on current consumption, whereas current decreases have quite a dramatic (negative) effect. (For other applications in macroeconomics, see Rosenblatt-Wisch 2008 and Vogel et al. 2009.)

Work on endowment effects (e.g., Thaler 1980; Kahneman, Knetsch, and Thaler 1990; Carmon and Ariely 2000) provides further evidence of loss-averse behavior in a wide variety of contexts. Also known as "divestiture aversion," research in this domain shows that people tend to place a higher value on things they own than things they do not. That is, once you own something, you attach more value to it than you would have before you owned it; put differently, you assess the loss of something as greater than you would assess the gain of that same thing. I revisit endowment effects later, where they provide some supporting evidence for the argument that the negativity bias is a product of evolution. Before we jump to evolution, however, I review the recent evidence from neurology.

Negative Brains and Bodies

In line with what we have seen in experimental environments in both psychology and economics, there is a growing body of evidence that neurological processes are greater for negative than positive events. In lab experiments, for instance, Smith et al. (2003) find that unpleasant pictures elicit more brain activity than pleasant pictures, suggesting that negative stimuli garner greater attention than do positive stimuli.

Research also points toward a brain mechanism the role of which is specifically to detect self-generated errors. Neurologists believe that the anterior cingulate in the frontal lobe of the brain plays an important role in pain perception and self-regulation, including the monitoring of error responses. (For a review, see Luu, Collins, and Tucker 2000.) Capturing electrophysiological responses in the brain using an electroencephalogram (EEG), a growing body of work has identified something referred to as error-related negativity (ERN) – negativity in the electrical activity at the front of the head associated with respondents giving incorrect responses (e.g., Dehaene, Posner, and Tucker 1994; Gehring et al. 1993; Luu et al. 2000; Miltner, Braun, and Coles 1997). This marked, identifiable neurological reaction to negative responses has no equivalent where correct responses are concerned.

This asymmetry in neurological reactions is paralleled by asymmetries in physiological reactions. For instance, the fight-or-flight reaction to negative events, leading to heightened heart rate, blood pressure, and perspiration, prepares the organism for either fighting or fleeing (Cannon 1932). There is no positive equivalent. And physiological research on stress and arousal has focused almost exclusively on negative stimuli. As Taylor (1991) notes, "the overwhelming majority of current laboratory-based stress work continues to make use of negative stressors, such as electric shock, cold pressor tests, and the like, thereby perpetuating the assumption that negative events and physiological arousal are more clearly linked than positive events and physiological arousal." The assumption may be well founded.

Rozin and Royzman's (2001) review of the literature provides a particularly cogent description of the negativity bias in our experience of sensations: "With the exception of positive sensations arising in muscles (as in massage), the inside of the body is basically a source of evaluatively negative input" (301). Even on the body exterior, these authors suggest, there is a wider distribution of pain; that is, pain can be produced anywhere, while the centers for pleasure are much more limited.

Why Are We So Negative?

It seems very likely that we are so negative because evolution favors animals that exhibit a combination of mildly optimistic and loss-averse behaviors. You have to be willing to try new food sources. But if your friend gets eaten while you are there, you need to be the animal that *never goes back*.

Put a little more scientifically, work on "orienting responses" suggests that evolution has produced animals with attentional systems that give preference to stimuli with adaptive significance (Öhman et al. 1998; Hunt and Campbell 1997). Foremost among those stimuli are signs of danger. And "[b]ecause it is more difficult to reverse the consequences of an injurious or fatal assault than those of an opportunity unpursued, the process of natural selection may also have resulted in the propensity to react more strongly to negative than to positive stimuli" (Cacioppo & Gardner 1999; see also the discussion in Herwig et al. 2007).[6]

This evolutionary account is supported by a body of work finding evidence of a negativity bias in animals other than humans. Miller's early work with rats – in which fear of shock was clearly more motivating than hunger – is one early example (Miller 1961; see also Garcia and Koelling 1966; and for earlier work, see Hodge and Stocking 1912; Warden and Aylesworth 1927). Just like humans, rats tend to learn faster in response to punishment rather than reinforcement (though ideally both; see earlier discussion). The fight-or-flight reaction noted in the preceding section has similarly been identified in animals (e.g., Mahl 1952). And this behavioral evidence is buttressed by neurological research on rats and monkeys, which finds that fear-inducing events leave indelible memory traces in the brain, whereas there is no similar impact of very positive events (LeDoux, Romanski, and Xagoraris 1989; Quirk, Repa, and LeDoux 1995; Sanghera, Rolls, and Roper-Hall 1979).

Economics experiments with animals provide further support for the evolutionary account for the negativity bias. Knetch's (1989) paradigmatic endowment effect experiment – for humans – proceeded as follows: One group

---

[6] The idea that a negativity bias may be a product of evolution is by no means recent. See Darwin (1872), and a useful discussion of Darwin's work in Fridlund (1991).

of students received a mug and was then offered the chance to trade that mug for a chocolate bar. A second group was presented with the opposite possibility, that is, trading chocolate bars for mugs. And a third group, as they arrived, were able to simply take either a mug or a chocolate bar. This last group revealed students' preferences for mugs versus candy bars, in the absence of any endowment effect. In this case, 56 percent took mugs, 44 percent chocolate bars. But the preferences revealed by the first two groups were systematically different. Fewer students traded mugs for chocolate bars than we would have predicted given the third group's preferences; and fewer students traded chocolate bars for mugs as well. Indeed, 89 percent of students kept their mug and 90 percent of students kept their chocolate bar. Preferences were not independent of ownership effects.

The same is true, it turns out, for chimpanzees. Brosnan et al. (2007) replicated the Knetch experiment using chimpanzees, and both food and nonfood items (frozen juice stick versus PVC pipe filled with peanut butter, and bone versus rope). Trades were very common for the nonfood items, suggesting to the researchers that the interaction with the experimenter may have value over the item itself. For food items, however, trades were fewer and endowment effects were clear. To be clear: a chimpanzee attaches more value to a PVC pipe filled with peanut butter once they believe that they own it.

This work on negativity biases and endowment effects in animals supports the notion that the negativity bias in humans has a neurological or physiological source, and that this source is in all likelihood the consequence of evolution. This is not to say that a negativity bias is a good thing – that is an entirely different matter, and one that will come up repeatedly over the next few chapters. But evolution need not produce outcomes that are normatively good; it should produce outcomes that are empirically effective, at least where survival is concerned. One possible product, or perhaps a side effect, of evolution is a tendency to devote more attention, and react more, to negative information than to positive information. This is because focusing on negative information, even at the expense of positive information, may increase chances for survival. In short, "[t]he individual remains alive after several years only if he or she managed to survive every single day, and no degree of optimal experience on any given day can offset the effects of failing to survive on another" (Baumeister et al. 2001: 358).[7]

Does Positive Never Win?

Is there really no domain in which positive outweighs negative? Actually, in many if not most domains, there are more positive events than negative ones.

---

[7] See Weinberg's (1975) work on "general systems thinking" and its application to evolution for a particularly cogent description of how no single part of a system can ensure the system's success, but any single component can ensure the system's failure.

This is apparent in psychology studies of "event recall" – even as participants are affected more by negative events, they can recall more positive ones. (It is also apparent in macro-level measures, economic and otherwise, as we shall see in later chapters.)

Taylor's (1991) work on the "mobilization-minimization" hypothesis is particularly instructive here. Taylor reviews work suggesting both that (a) there is a marked short-term impact of negative events on arousal, attentiveness, and so forth; and (b) there may be offsetting effects once the negative event is over. Put differently, "[f]ollowing the occurrence of a negative event and the organism's concerted response to it, opposing responses set in that seem to damp down, mute, and even erase its existence" (p. 72). So we are initially highly mobilized by negative information, but the role that information plays over the long term tends to be minimized.

This time-varying version of asymmetries in the impact of negative information helps account for why there can be a large body of work finding negativity biases alongside research that suggests a human tendency to have generally positive expectations. This tendency toward positive expectations has been referred to as the "pollyanna principle"; the critical work is by Matlin and Stang (1978). Positive events, these authors find, are more easily recalled than negative events. Work on autobiographical memory provides supporting evidence (e.g., Thompson 1985; Wagenaar 1986; White 1982; but, again, there is some disagreement here: see, e.g., Banaji and Hardin 1994; Skowronski and Carlston 1987). The more easy recall of positive events may be a product of those events having been more effectively encoded: we are better able to recall events when they have been associated with other events, so the higher frequency of positive events means that they have an advantage where memory and recall are concerned (see Isen 1984).

A similar kind of positive default is evident in the evolutionary account of the negativity bias – an account that is dependent not just on loss aversion in the presence of danger, but on initial optimism, to try new food sources, for instance. Cacioppo and Gardner (1999) refer to this as the "positivity offset," "the tendency for there to be a weak positive (approach) motivational output at zero input." Without initial positivity we would lack the exploratory behavior critical to survival. This positivity is reflected in research dealing with people's assessments of unknown people and future events (e.g., Brinthaupt et al. 1991; Klar and Giladi 1997; Regan et al. 1995; Sears 1983).[8]

---

[8] The relative frequency of positive events over negative ones is nicely reflected in work on languages. In a comparative study of seventeen different languages, Rozin and Royzman (2001) find that the number of positive words is consistently greater than the number of negative words. (Although there is some disagreement on this issue. See Averill 1980; see Van Goozen and Frijda 1993 for similar comparative findings; also Clore and Ortony 1988; Russell et al. 1995.) Relatedly, Matlin and Stang (1978) note that most negative words begin with a positive root, made negative through a prefix. The starting point is positive.

That said, the tendency to recall more positive than negative events is likely also linked to the fact that in most domains there simply are more positive than negative events. Think about a regular day, in which you successfully eat breakfast, get to work, talk to friends, and so on. Most of these are positive (albeit often only marginally positive) events; and, for most people most of the time, these simple, positive events tend to outnumber negative events.

This difference in the relative frequency of positive versus negative events is critical. Recall the "frequency-weight" account of the negativity bias in impression formation: negative information is given more weight because it is further away from the usual. It is, some work suggests, the novelty or unusualness of negative information that makes us pay more attention to it (see esp. Fiske 1980). *The relative frequency of positive over negative events is thus not counter to the negativity bias – it may be the reason for the negativity bias.* (This testable proposition is taken up in some detail in Chapter 4.) Note that from this perspective, the negativity bias is itself the evidence that things are, on the whole, relatively positive.

Alternatively, we might view negative and positive not so much as opposite ends of the same spectrum, but rather two quite distinct traits/feelings. The strength of negativity does not in this view necessarily mean the weakness of positivity – it is not a zero-sum game. There is some evidence that negative and positive processes may be independent, both in psychology (e.g., Diener et al. 1985; Watson and Tellegen 1985) and neurology (e.g., George et al. 1995; Lane et al. 1997). Cacioppo and Berntson (1994) review the relevant literature and discuss a bivariate evaluative plane, whereby information is evaluated on separate positive and negative dimensions (rather than a bipolar perspective, where positive and negative are at opposite ends of a single dimension). This perspective fits well with the observation that certain stimuli appear to produce both pleasure and pain simultaneously. Even so, and most critically for the current discussion, while positive events may outnumber negative ones, or while the relative strength of negative emotion need not come at the direct cost of positive emotion, the following seems to be clear: we are over the long term relatively optimistic, and we tend to be able to better recall positive events – even as, over the short term, we have a tendency to be more reactive to negative information.

Negative Institutions

Given the many psychological, economic, and physiological domains in which a negativity bias is evident, it should come as no surprise that similar dynamics are apparent in the functioning of a wide range of social and cultural institutions. This is one of the principle implications of our negative brains. In short, institutions reflect the same biases as the humans that created them.

Political institutions are the subject of subsequent chapters, but the argument that institutions exhibit a negativity bias can be drawn for extra-political institutions as well. Religions may be foremost among these, Judeo-Christian and otherwise. Some authors suggest no negativity bias in religions – indeed, even a positivity bias. Religions devote a considerable amount of time to salvation (Eliade 1982, 1985), and modern belief in heaven exceeds believe in hell (Àries 1981). (The latter may reflect the "positivity offset" noted in the preceding section.) But it is nevertheless true that for most religions, becoming possessed by a malevolent force is relatively easy (Oesterreich 1974), whereas getting rid of that force is quite difficult. Becoming a saint requires a lifetime of good acts; failing to become a saint requires just a few immoral acts (Rozin and Royzman 2001). The relative strength of a given unit of negativity is clearly greater than a given unit of positivity.

Cultural and social institutions reflect the same asymmetry. In the Indian caste system, for instance, people of higher castes are easily contaminated by contact with people from lower castes. The dynamic does not work in the other direction. And this belief is by no means exclusive to India.[9] The "Code Noir" of 1685, defining the conditions of slavery in the French empire, and concerned with the purity of the white race, maintained that "any known African ancestry renders one black" (Haney López 1996: 27). The colony of Maryland provided in 1664, "That whatsoever free-born [English] woman shall intermarry with any slave ... shall serve the master of such slave during the life of her husband; and that all the issue of such free-born women, so married shall be slaves as their fathers were." The Nuremburg laws produced a similar definition for Jewishness.

Rozin and Royzman (2001) link these various social phenomena to the notion of "contagion," initially laid out in anthropological accounts of magical and ritual practices in ancient cultures (Frazer [1890] 1959; Mauss [1902] 1972). According to the law of contagion, things that have been in contact can continue to affect each other even after the contact has ceased. The "law" appears to hold in modern times as well: Rozin and colleagues find experimental evidence of contagion effects, though notably more often negative ones (Rozin and Nemeroff 1990; Rozin et al. 1986; Rozin et al. 1989).

Whether "contagion" matters in politics is not clear (but it is clearly an interesting line of analysis for future work). What is most critical here is that there are considerable bodies of work, across many fields in the social and physical sciences, finding evidence of negativity biases in humans and in human-designed social and cultural institutions. Note that this does not necessarily point to a steady downward spiral into increasingly more negative behaviors and environments. The effects of all events, even negative ones, decay over time; moreover, there are in most domains more positive events than negative ones. As noted earlier, it may be the frequency of positive events that makes the

---

[9] Meigs's (1984) work suggests a similar dynamic among the Hua in the Papua New Guinea Highlands, for instance.

negative more salient, and were the proportion of positive events to decrease, the relative salience of negative events might well decrease.

For the time being, suffice it to say that the principal consequence of the negativity bias is rather obvious but important: across a wide range of subjects and contexts, negative information matters more than positive information does. This chapter has traced this asymmetry in psychology, economics, physiology and neurology, and biology and anthropology. The next chapter focuses on politics.

2

Negativity in Politics

Nothing travels faster than light, with the exception of bad news, which follows its own rules.

— Douglas Adams

Is a negativity bias evident in work on politics as well? Yes, although the observation that negative information carries more weight in political decision making has been somewhat dispersed and spread across several subfields. There are some domains in which negativity has clearly received a good deal of attention, of course; for instance, there is a considerable body of work on negative campaign advertising. As a discipline, however, political science has been rather slow to come around to the idea that negative information may matter more than positive information does. This is somewhat ironic, given that one does not have to look very far to find critiques arguing that politics and news media are too focused on the negative. Nevertheless, the incorporation of a negativity bias into political scientists' views of political behavior, of political communication, or of electoral and legislative politics more generally has yet to happen.

This chapter gets the ball rolling by pulling together a disparate but, as we shall see, relatively consistent body of work concerned with a negativity bias in politics. The chapter reviews work on evaluations of political leaders, political economy, political advertising, and political communications. Much of the chapter is a review of existing work – a state of the discipline, where observations of negativity biases are concerned. The chapter ends with a new observation, however: it proposes that the negativity bias is evident in the design of political and legal institutions. More specifically, the chapter includes an introduction to the argument that a wide range of political and legal institutions has been designed to process information like the human brain, focusing far more on negative information than on positive information. (That said, this chapter includes just an introduction to this topic; the link between evidence in subsequent chapters and the design of political institutions is given further attention in Chapter 7.) First, however, I begin with early work in political behavior.

The Negativity Bias in Political Behavior

Nehemiah Jordan was among the first to feature the argument that, in public opinion surveys on political issues, negative attitudes may matter more than positive attitudes do. Jordan's (1965) paper reviewed some work on the issue by psychologists and urged political scientists to follow their lead. The first paragraph of Jordan's discussion is relatively clear:

Discussion

> Actually, there is no need for a discussion. Enough data have been presented to show that the "asymmetry" between "liking" and "disliking" does exist in enough cases and has a striking enough effect to question the simple "push-pull" model of attitudes and opinions inherent in the contemporary scales we use to measure them; consequently, it merits – in fact, demands – further reflection and research. (Jordan 1965: 322)

Jordan may well have been the clearest on the matter, but he was not the only one to make such an observation around that time. Campbell, Converse, Miller, and Stokes noted in their seminal book, *The American Voter*, that "changes in the party balance are induced primarily by negative rather than positive attitudes toward the party controlling the executive branch of federal government" (Campbell et al. 1960: 554–55), for instance. Nevertheless, a rather limited number of political scientists have since taken up Jordan's task.

That said, those who have searched for a negativity bias in political behavior have tended to find it. Perhaps the best place at which to leap into the political science literature is with the work that most clearly parallels what we have already seen in psychology: work on impression formation. Klein has applied impression formation theories to survey data on U.S. presidential evaluations. A 1991 paper finds that traits (such as inspiring, strong, intelligent, etc.) on which a respondent ranks 1984 and 1988 presidential candidates lower matter more to their overall assessment of those candidates. A subsequent paper (Klein 1996) confirms the dynamic for the 1992 presidential candidates.

This role of negativity in respondents' perceptions of presidential candidates has been identified using a variety of different survey instruments. For instance, Richard Lau's (1982) early paper covers several approaches across twelve years of U.S. elections. Lau looks first at the asymmetric effects of presidential approval versus disapproval on turnout and defection. He then looks at the effects on voting decisions from responses to, "Now I'd like to ask you about the good and bad points of the Democratic and Republican candidates for Presidents. Is there anything in particular about <candidate's name> that might make you want to vote for him?" The survey captures up to five possible answers, and a subsequent question asks about reasons to vote against the candidate. Analysis suggests that the negative mentions matter more to the voting decision than positive mentions do.[1] Finally, Lau looks at the relationship between voting and responses to a checklist of seven different traits (both positive and negative) voters may have felt a candidate possesses. Again, negative traits have more predictive power than positive traits do.[2]

Relatedly, Kernell (1977) was among the first to suggest not just that midterm congressional elections were partly a referendum on the popularity of the current president, but that unpopularity has a much greater effect on voting decisions than does popularity. These "negative voting" results have been contested by other authors, suggesting alternative hypotheses that account for the regularity with which presidents' parties lose seats in midterm elections (e.g., Hinckley 1981; Cover 1986; Born 1990). Recent work suggests a story more in line with Kernell but based on a prospect theory account that emphasizes the relationship between disappointment with the current presidential administration and electoral turnout (Patty 2006). Aragones's (1997) work suggests a related negative-reaction account for declining popularity the longer a candidate stays in office.

There is an accumulation of similar findings in work on economic voting as well. Early work linking economic conditions to support for the incumbent government met with varying results: some studies found evidence of a link between the economy and government support, others did not. Bloom and Price's (1975) effort to resolve the issue led to the realization that economic downturns have a powerful effect on U.S. House elections, but economic prosperity does not. Their findings reflect observations in several earlier studies, including Campbell et al.'s (1960) work on electoral behavior and Mueller's (1973) study of U.S. foreign policy. Subsequent work on economic voting confirmed that negative economic swings had a greater effect on parties' and presidents' vote shares than did the positive equivalents (e.g., Kiewet 1983; Claggett 1986). Similar results were found elsewhere – for instance, in the United Kingdom (Headrick and Lanoue 1991; Soroka 2006) and in Denmark (Nannestad and Paldam 1997).

Two recent studies in political behavior are particularly notable, not just for the finding that negative information matters more than positive, but for the argument – in line with what we have seen in psychology – that optimism (a positive reference point) is at the heart of the negativity bias. Niven (2000) argues that declining trust in government is partly a consequence of citizens'

---

[1] This finding is evidenced further in recent work by Holbrook et al. (2001), using a model allowing for both asymmetry and nonlinearity in the effects of positive versus negative traits.

[2] In a subsequent paper dealing with similar data, Lau (1985) contrasts psychological and economic accounts for the apparent asymmetry.

(perhaps unrealistically) high expectations. Drawing on earlier work suggesting that high expectations are at the heart of decreasing confidence (Craig 1993; Miller 1974; Citrin and Green 1986), Niven finds a strong relationship between measures of optimism (in life generally) and levels of trust or confidence in government. That is, people who are more optimistic, and thus have a high expectations of governments, tend to react more strongly to political disappointments. Relatedly, using an online survey experiment, Owen (2008) finds that candidate evaluations are more strongly affected by negative policy change than by positive policy change. This on its own is a demonstration of the kind of asymmetry detailed through this and the previous chapter. But Owen also finds that assessments in situations when there is no policy change are very close to those in which the change is negative. He suggests that the negativity bias may thus be a product of positive expectations. To be clear: the expectation of positive policy change means that respondents react only marginally to positive change but quite strongly to both no change and negative change.

Negativity in Political Advertising

The area of research in political science that has undoubtedly seen the most consideration, and reconsideration, of negativity effects is political advertising. One thing is clearly not disputed: over the postwar era, and particularly over the past two decades, there has been a steady increase in negative advertising in the United States (Geer 2006; Fridkin and Kenney 2004). Campaign strategists believe that negative advertising works, especially in competitive races (Abbe et al. 2001; Goldstein et al. 2001). And negative ads are commissioned, and aired, accordingly.

Whether negative ads have the intended effect is another matter, and on this there is a good deal of disagreement in the literature. There are at least two general themes: (1) Does negative advertising win or lose votes? (2) Does negative advertising attract or repel voters? The first is an issue of vote intentions; the second is concerned with efficacy and/or whether people choose to vote at all. Results, many of which are incorporated into a meta-analysis by Lau et al. (1999), are rather divided for both issues. Some studies suggest that negative advertising is successful in winning votes (e.g., Bullock 1994), whereas others suggest that negative advertising by one candidate actually alienates voters and causes them to switch to the other candidate (e.g., Hitchon et al. 1997; Martinez and Delegal 1990). The possibility that negative advertising alienates of voters has seen somewhat more attention; even here, however, some work suggests alienation and withdrawal (e.g., Ansolabehere et al. 1994; Ansolabehere and Iyengar 1995) whereas other research finds no such evidence, and perhaps even greater participation connected with greater levels of negative advertising (e.g., Freedman and Goldstein 1999; Geer and Lau 1998; Kahn and Kenney 1999).

Some of the differences across studies may be a product of very different methodologies. The argument that negative advertising leads to political disaffection, for instance, is based largely on lab-based experimental studies, while opposition to that argument draws mainly on survey data. The "external validity" (generalizability beyond the lab) of experimental studies features prominently in the early debate, then, although more recent work finds evidence on both sides of the argument, using both techniques. Lau et al.'s (1999) statistical meta-analysis of existing findings reveals no consistent effects where either turnout or voting is concerned.

That said, there are some issues for which the body of evidence is somewhat more suggestive. Of the studies investigating respondents' ability to remember ads, either positive or negative, all *survey*-based studies suggest that various aspects of (or candidates in) negative ads are more likely to be remembered than aspects of (or candidates in) positive ads (Brians and Wattenberg 1996; Lang 1991; Newhagen and Reeves 1991; Roberts 1995; Sulfaro 1998). *Lab*-based experiments with undergraduates, with only one exception (Shapiro and Rieger 1992), suggest the opposite (Hitchon and Chang 1995; King et al. 1998; Kaid, Chanslor, and Hovind 1992a; Kaid, Leland, and Whitney 1992b; Thorson, Christ, and Caywood 1991). The difference may have to do with the timing involved – lab experiments clearly involve much less time than do survey-based analyses. But the bulk of the survey-based evidence here at the very least raises some questions about the external validity of the lab experiments; at the most, it confirms what we would expect given the literature in psychology and elsewhere: people are more attentive to negative ads.

Also in line with what we know from work in psychology, the information conveyed in negative ads is more likely to be remembered than the information conveyed in positive ads (e.g., Babbitt and Lau 1994; Kahn and Kenney 1998b). Indeed, this may be the one finding about which there is no evidence to the contrary. And this fits with the fact that the volume of negative advertising has been and continues to increase, in the United States and perhaps elsewhere as well.

Elsewhere in (Political) Communication

Advertising is by no means the only communications domain in which there is a good degree of negative content. The same trend is apparent throughout media, both print and television. There exist content analyses showing the relatively high proportion of news content that is sensationalistic, certainly (e.g., Davie and Lee 1995; Harmon 1989; Hofstetter and Dozier 1986; Ryu 1982), and a good deal of work documenting a tendency toward negative stories (e.g., Diamond 1978; Fallows 1997; Just et al. 1996a; Kerbel 1995; Lichter and Noyes 1995; Niven 2000; Patterson 1994; Robinson and Levy 1985; Sabato 1991).

What accounts for the apparent negativity in media content? Explanations include the administrative or financial structure of news organizations, the biases of editors or audiences, the behavior and priorities of journalists as a profession, and so on. The media gatekeeping literature has been particularly useful here. Gatekeeping "is the process by which the billions of messages that are available in the world get cut down and transformed into the hundreds of messages that reach a given person on a given day" (Shoemaker 1991: 1). The original idea of gatekeeping is derived from Lewin's (1951) work on community dynamics; White's (1950) case study of a wire editor at a small-town daily newspaper was the first to use the term in communications. Like White, early work focuses on the role of individual editors' interests and whims in gatekeeping, but later research emphasizes more systematic biases, including (1) organization-level factors such as administrative characteristics, working procedures, and cost and time constraints (e.g., Bass 1969; Berkowitz 1991; Dimmick 1974; Donohue, Olien, and Tichenor 1989; Gieber 1964; Jones et al. 1961; McCombs and Becker 1979; Shoemaker et al. 2001; Sigal 1973; Westley and MacLean 1957); (2) story-level factors such as the geographic proximity of the story, visual features (for television), clarity (ready interpretability) of the story, and story types – disasters, economics, crime, and so forth (e.g., Abbott and Brassfield 1989; Berkowitz 1990; Galtung and Ruge 1965); and (3) extra-organizational, or professional, factors such as journalistic values and norms and views of "newsworthiness" (e.g., Johnstone et al. 1972; Gans 1979).[3]

What does the gatekeeping literature tell us about negative news? As noted earlier, one of the main focuses of the literature is the tendency for news to be both sensationalist and negative; a consequence not just of the preferences of individual journalists and editors, but of the entire structure of the practice of journalism, as well as of the mediums themselves – newspapers, but especially television. Altheide's (1997) recent work is especially relevant here. He argues that media news content is increasingly presented using a "problem frame." Altheide draws on work suggesting that news content is heavily conditioned by media practices and news format, and that audience interests can over time become conditioned to expect news in certain formats (Altheide 1985; Altheide and Snow 1991; Ericson, Baranek, and Chan 1989; Meyrowitz 1985). The "problem frame," he argues, represents one means by which news can be adapted to increasingly entertainment-oriented news format. But framing all news as a problem – highlighting distress and suffering – and selecting news that tends to fit that frame more easily has consequences. Some of these, Altheide argues, include the increasing perception that life is dangerous, and an increasingly fearful population.[4]

Where does this bias in media content come from? Some popular accounts suggest, implicitly if not explicitly, that journalists or editors might just be cynical people, drawn to present negative news whenever possible. But there is,

[3] This review draws in part on Soroka 2012. For reviews of the literature, also see Shoemaker 1991, 1996; Shoemaker et al. 2001; Shoemaker and Vos 2009.
[4] Whether the news audience is indeed more fearful remains to be seen. Indeed, as we shall see in subsequent chapters, it is not necessarily the case that the ongoing prominence of negative news will lead to a long-term decline in public sentiment – individual effects do decay over time.

following from all of the work cited earlier, a much more convincing answer: journalists and editors are humans, creating content that will be consumed by other humans, and humans are more interested in negative than in positive information.

Note that this is not an argument for negativity in media content, nor does it preclude the possibility that economic incentives produce an unfortunate bias in media content. A considerable body of work explores the potentially detrimental consequences of a profit-driven media (e.g., Herman and Chomsky 1988). This work may well be correct; indeed, it may partly be driven by the asymmetric attentiveness to positive versus negative behavior detailed earlier. A media that is entirely profit-driven will provide whatever sells most, after all, and negative news sells more than positive news. This fact will be demonstrated in some detail in Chapter 5, although there is some existing work that already points to this conclusion. In a simple but telling psychology experiment, when asked if they would rather hear the good or bad news first, roughly 80 percent of participants chose bad news (Marshall and Kidd 1981). Another experiment in which participants were asked to choose between hyperlinks to different new stories about a fictional campaign suggested a similar dynamic: negative stories were consistently chosen over positive ones (Meffert et al. 2006).

There may, in short, be a link between the general tone of media content and biases in the human brain (see Shoemaker 1996a; Ju 2008). We are more interested in negative information than in positive information, and audience-seeking media provide the kind of information in which we are most interested. But the propensity for media to overrepresent negativity may be a product not just of profit maximization – it may also be a product of the very design of media as an institution. That is, it may be that media outlets' emphasis on negative news reflects one of their principle institutional functions in a democracy: holding current governments (and companies, and indeed some individuals) accountable. The notion of mass media as a "Fourth Estate" (Carlyle 1841) has been prominent both in the literature on newspapers (e.g., Merrill and Lowenstein 1971; Hage et al. 1976; Small 1972) and in the pages of newspapers themselves. Surveillance of this kind mainly involves identifying problems. We might consequently expect that media emphasize negative information in part because it is their job to do so. (Indeed, we might expect this of a wide range of political institutions; more on this in discussions that follow.)

Beyond Political Behavior and Communications

There clearly are accumulating bodies of work in political behavior and communications that point toward a bias in the ways in which individuals react to negative versus positive information in the political sphere. Prospect theory, loss aversion, and asymmetry more broadly construed have played an important role in a wide range of political science subfields. There exist several recent reviews of the literature informed by prospect theory (Levy 2003; McDermott 2004; Mercer 2005); again, I will review only a sample here. Even so, the variety of work that finds value in or evidence of theories of asymmetric responsiveness does much to support the notion that negative information matters across a wide range of political domains.

James C. Scott's (1977) well-known political-historical work on peasant societies in Burma and Vietnam in the 1930s provides one example of the appearance of negativity biases in comparative political studies. Admittedly, the work is not entirely divorced from research in political behavior – Scott's argument hinges on a theory of the behavior of peasants. But his focus is quite clearly not on the typical (in political behavior) Anglo-American voter. Scott's argument, in short, is that to explain peasants' political behavior, we need to focus of their main concern: subsistence. Contrary to the view that peasant revolts are motivated by the resources extracted by elites, Scott argues that they are driven by concerns about the resources that remain. Peasants are concerned primarily with the possibility of subsistence crises, or rather with the increased likelihood of subsistence crises given rising resource extraction by colonial powers. What is critical here is that the principle motivator in Scott's account of peasant revolts is risk; it is the fear of an inability to deal with negative situations (i.e., bad harvests) in the future that leads to revolt.

This identification of a negativity bias in the developing world is echoed in work in international relations, particularly work suggesting that countries are sometimes willing to fight to defend territories they would not have been willing to fight to acquire (e.g., Ross 1984; Schweller 1996) – a rather large-scale version of the endowment effect. But international relations has as a subfield taken particularly seriously the value of prospect theory in understanding when countries or leaders will or will not engage in risky behavior (e.g., McDermott 1994, 1998; McDermott & Kugler 2001; Schaubroeck and Davis 1994). In a review of the literature, McDermott offers a paradigmatic example:

> George H. W. Bush took an initial risk in launching military action against Saddam Hussein in the Persian Gulf war after Hussein's invasion of Kuwait. However, once American forces had repelled Iraqi forces from Kuwait, thus shifting the situation from one of losses into one of gains, Bush's risk propensity shifted from a more risky stance to a more cautious one. He forewent his chance to continue the invasion into Iraq to try to capture Baghdad and unseat Saddam Hussein from power. Once the situation had changed in his favor on the ground, Bush and his advisors stopped the war after a hundred hours, taking the cautious route to prevent any further loss of life. (McDermott 2004: 292–93)

The notion that leaders are willing to take large risks in certain circumstances but avoid those risks in others has also been echoed in work on domestic policy making as well. Weyland (2004), for instance, examines economic policy in Latin American states and suggests that major (and risky) reforms pursued by Argentina, Brazil, Peru, and Venezuela were made possible by real crisis. Facing crisis, Weyland argues, governments (and publics) are more willing to support risky reforms; in the absence of major crisis, however, they tend to be more risk averse. Negative circumstances thus can produce quite dramatic responses, whereas positive circumstances produce only incremental responses.

Similar asymmetries are evident in recent work on welfare state retrenchment, which suggests that the politics of taking away benefits are quite different than are the politics of extending them (e.g., Pierson 1994, 1996). On the one hand, Pierson argues, welfare state retrenchment involves "concrete losses on a concentrated group of voters in return for diffuse and uncertain gains" (1994: 8). The consequence is that there a specific subset of a population that has an interest in and is mobilizing in order to block welfare state retrenchment. More to the point for our purposes, however, Pierson highlights the fact that welfare retrenchment (losses) does not have the same potential political benefit as welfare expansion (gains). Politicians will highlight the latter; they will simply try to avoid blame for the former.[5]

Blame Avoidance

In fact, there is a considerable body of work on blame avoidance in government. This literature has a long lineage – it is readily evident, for instance, in Machiavelli's oft-cited suggestion that "princes should delegate to others the enactment of unpopular measures and keep in their own hands the distribution of favours" (Machiavelli 2003: 61). But the importance of blame avoidance in modern work on policy making can generally be traced to Weaver's (1986) seminal account: politicians must "be at least as interested in avoiding blame for (perceived or real) losses that they either imposed or acquiesced in as they are in 'claiming credit' for benefits they have granted" (372).

Weaver's argument is based on work suggesting a negativity bias in economics and political science – work that suggests that politicians seeking reelection are better served by blame avoidance than by claiming credit. (See the discussion of asymmetry in political behavior earlier in the chapter.) That behavior, Weaver argues, has real consequences for policy. Rather than welcome opportunities for change from the status quo when appropriate, the importance of blame avoidance encourages policy makers to often avoid that change. Their calculations are roughly as follows: while there may be credit to be taken for policy change, there may also be blame, and the potential costs of the latter are often greater than the potential benefits of the former.

Weaver's annunciation of the various situations in which blame avoiding is most likely, and the various strategies by which officials will try to avoid blame, has led to a growing body of literature on the importance of blame

---

[5] This is by no means an exhaustive list of the work featuring some form of asymmetric effects for positive versus negative information. For instance, Hansen (1985) suggests a similar call-to-action effect of negative but not positive information, this time relating to one's interest in joining an interest group. Hansen examines the Farm Bureau, the League of Women Voters, and the Home Builders in the United States and finds that external threats are a critical determinant of increases in membership.

avoiding in policy making. It clearly is an important precursor to Hood's (2002) influential work on blame avoidance, and particularly his emphasis on the growing concern with risk regulation and management in government. (Hood [2007] also notes the tension between increased transparency in government and the desire within government for blame avoidance – in short, transparency is difficult for governments in part because it reduces their ability to avoid blame.) In short, Hood's work, like Weaver's, emphasizes the important role that negative information can play in policy decisions by both elected and unelected officials.

This emphasis on negative information in policy seems well placed given the body of empirical evidence on the ways in which blame avoidance and risk have structured policy outcomes. For instance, Sulitzeanu-Kenan (2010) shows that an important motivation for the appointment of Commissions of Inquiry after crises in the United Kingdom is short-term blame avoidance. Essentially, the appointment of commissions of inquiry allows a government, temporarily at least, to extract itself from a situation and confuse, if not also shift, the attribution of blame. Similar arguments have been made about legislative processes in the United States as well (e.g., Fiorina 1982, 1986; Ellis 1994; Twight 1991; McGraw 1991). Bartling and Fischbacher's (2011) economics experiments reveal the micro-level dynamics behind these policy decisions. Their work suggests that avoiding blame is an important motivation for, and an effective outcome of, delegation of authority.

There is, in sum, a policy literature that mirrors what we have seen in work on public opinion, particularly work related to government support. Publics are more likely to penalize elected officials for errors than reward them for successes. Officials are accordingly likely to err on the side of caution; that is, they have a strong incentive to avoid responsibility in order to avoid blame, even in situations where claiming credit is possible, because the potential gains of claiming credit may pale in comparison to the costs of accepting blame. One likely result is that policy will be systematically biased toward conservativism – not in the ideological sense, but rather in the tendency to move incrementally and avoid significant change. There is of course a vast literature documenting incrementalism in policy making (e.g., Lindblom 1975; Wildavsky 1984; Baumgartner and Jones 1993; Tsebelis 2002). That literature focuses on the number of policy actors, on the structure of political institutions, and/or on limited attentiveness from policy makers as the principle culprits. But a negativity bias – in the form of penalties for errors that greatly outweigh rewards for success – may be just as important.

Altruistic Punishment and Common-Pool Resources

The vast body of work on altruistic punishment and common-pool resources reflects similar, asymmetric tendencies in human behavior. Altruistic punishment refers to a willingness to, in group settings, penalize noncooperators even though (a) the costs of inflicting penalties are suffered by a single individual, and (b) the benefits (in the form of more cooperative behavior in the future by the noncooperator) are enjoyed by the entire group. Consider the following example. Someone throws trash on the sidewalk, so you pick up the trash and confront the litterer. This comes at a cost to you – you are holding trash, and you are arguing with a stranger. And even if the confrontation leads the stranger to not litter next time, that benefit is not yours alone (if at all), but everyone's. More to the point from an evolutionary standpoint: everyone reaps the benefits, while you alone pay the costs. So evolution should produce far more shirkers (non-punishers and/or litterers) than punishers. Why then are so many people willing to engage in this kind of altruistic punishment?

Perhaps littering is not the best example – there seem to be far too many people willing to litter. But environmental management has been central to a related literature on "governing the commons," which I turn to later. And for the time being, what is critical is that altruistic punishment is – somewhat perplexingly for those focused on processes of natural selection – readily evident in a wide range of environments and species. For instance, there is a considerable body of work in experimental economics showing a willingness to punish asocial behavior, even when doing so involves clear, personal costs (e.g., Carpenter 2006; Fehr and Fischbacher 2004). This appears to be true across a wide range of cultures (Henrich et al. 2006). There is a large of body of literature documenting the same dynamic in other animals as well (e.g., Clutton-Brock and Parker 1995). (For a valuable review of the recent literature on humans, see Sigmund 2007.)

Why is this the case? Fehr and Gachter (2002) point to (humans') emotions as one likely cause: "Our results suggest that free riding causes strong negative emotions and that most people expect these emotions" (139). This suggestion is in line with findings in neurology, specifically, de Quervain et al.'s (2004) finding that "altruistic punishment provides relief or satisfaction to the punisher and activates, therefore, reward-related brain regions" (1258; also see Seymour et al. 2007). Evolutionary processes may well be a factor in the widespread tendency for altruistic punishment, then. In short, we may be hardwired to punish noncooperators.

Moreover, this may in fact be in line with, rather than contrary to, evolutionary principles. Economics experiments suggest that cooperation among participants is more likely when there is the threat of punishment for noncooperators, after all (e.g., Fehr and Gachter 2000, 2002; Gächter et al. 2008). Anthropological simulations also suggest that cooperation is more likely over the long term when a population includes a sufficient number of altruistic punishers (Boyd et al. 2003). Fowler's (2005) pathbreaking work linking evolutionary biology and politics suggests similar results. When cooperation is necessary, altruistic punishment is both a common and effective strategy. (For a recent review in political science, see Smirnov 2007.)

Perhaps most important for the current project is the fact not just that altruistic punishment is prominent and effective, but that potential punishments seem to be more effective in generating cooperation that do potential rewards. This has been seen in experimental economics (e.g., Andreoni et al. 2003; Dickinson 2001; but also see the literature reviewed in Chapter 1). In a study of the impact of reputation on the effects of rewards and punishments, Sigmund, Hauert, and Nowak (2001: 10762) summarize the state of the literature rather well: "The possibly irritating message is that for promoting cooperative behavior, punishing works much better than rewarding."

The relative effectiveness of punishment may be a product of our being particularly loss averse. But there may be other reasons for the reliance on punishments rather than rewards to produce cooperation as well. Price et al. (2002) suggest that punishment may have other evolutionary advantages – not only might punishment be effective at encouraging cooperation; it may be an effective way to decrease the health of free riders (and thus lead to more cooperators over the long term). Oliver (1980) suggests another reason for the apparent dominance of punishment over rewards. Oliver makes clear that the viability of punishment and/or reward strategies is linked to the size of populations, and the balance of cooperators and noncooperators. In larger populations where cooperation is likely to be relatively frequent, for instance, rewards are simply untenable because the cost of those rewards is likely to be very high. In these contexts, punishment is just much more affordable.

The connection between the size of a community and the mechanisms available to most effectively produce cooperation – or at least not shirking – has been a central theme in work on common-pool resources (and on collective action more generally). Hardin (1968) provides a seminal account of the common-pool resource problem. He describes a pasture, available to anyone, in which each herder's personal gains from increasing the size of their herd far outweigh the personal costs of damaging the shared pasture. Each herder has a strong incentive to overuse the pasture immediately rather than cautiously preserve it so that all herders can benefit over the long term. The end result is a "tragedy of the commons" – herders pursue their own best interests, and the pasture is destroyed.

Building on this work, Elinor Ostrom's (1990) *Governing the Commons* provides what is likely the most influential discussion of "how best to govern natural resources used by many individuals in common" (1; but see also the related body of work on the difficulties in sustaining collective action, starting with Olson 1965). There certainly has been a considerable body of work since (see, e.g., Anthony and Campbell 2011), and that work has contributed greatly not just to how we understand the management of environmental resources, but to how we understand and build institutions for collective action more generally. What is critical here, however, is the effectiveness of various incentives to produce cooperation in the use of common-pool resources. Ostrom has emphasized the importance of face-to-face communication in producing more efficient outcomes (e.g., Ostrom 2002; Ahn et al. 2010); her findings are echoed in work that shows that the relative effectiveness of punishments over rewards disappears in public-goods experiments in which, after each round, players are able to reward or punish the person who has just cooperated (or not) with them (Rand et at. 2009). In short, "targeted" interactions may allow rewards to matter as much, if not more, than penalties. But targeted (person-to-person) interactions are possible only when community size is small.

One implication is that the relative effectiveness of punishment may be conditional on the size of the community in which cooperation is required. Altruistic punishment may only be an effective strategy once community size exceeds some limit, then. But that limit may be relatively small – once we are interacting with others we do not know well, which is nearly always the case in national politics for instance, then using face-to-face communication (a) instead of penalties and rewards or (b) to affect the relative effectiveness of penalties and rewards is either impractical or impossible. So too, as Oliver has suggested earlier, is our ability to pay out rewards, rather than inflict penalties, on a large scale. For most of the kinds of political environments on which we have focused previously, sanctions for noncompliance appear to be the dominant, most effective, and most affordable strategy.

What is the importance of this literature to an argument about negativity in politics? There is, first, evidence in work on altruistic punishment that negative emotions can be particularly powerful, and evidence in research on common-pool resources finds that penalties will often be more effective than rewards are. That said, the latter literature also points to other ways of governing the commons, in particular ways that focus more on positive than on negative feedback. This will be important in the final chapter, when I consider changes in the design of political institutions.

Negativity versus Reason? (and Defining Negativity)

There is a growing body of work on the role of emotion in political psychology. That literature is not concerned with negativity per se. But this work does speak to the importance of "affect" in politics; indeed, it suggests that affect and emotion may not be contrary to, but are rather a central part of, political reasoning. This literature also helps identify two different types of negativity relevant here. A short review is in order.

Work on emotion and reason has a long lineage, starting with ancient Greek philosophers concerned with the role of emotion in political life. One central question, reflected in this early work but revisited over and over again, is this: Are reason and emotion opposed, in the sense that we rely on one or the other, or are there ways in which the two can be complementary, or at least used simultaneously? Some early thinking supported the former proposition. One can, in this view, rely on reason or emotion; or, rather, the ideal is to rely on reason, and relying on emotion tends to get in the way of sensible decision making. This line of thinking is evident in the ancient philosophical movement referred to as Stoicism (see, e.g., Brennan 2005), but also in work by seventeenth-century thinkers including Descartes. It is also apparent in early (though, in comparison with Descartes, relatively recent) work in psychology and neurology.

That said, modern political philosophers have for the most part abandoned the idea that reason and emotion are in opposition. Indeed, even at the time of the Stoics there was considerable debate on the matter; questions on the interrelatedness of emotion and reason are evident in the writings of Cicero (writing in the first century BC, around the time of Stoicism), as well as in the work of Aristotle and Plato before him. Aristotle's work suggests that practical reasoning in many cases relies on the emotions (Abizadeh 2002; Elster 1999); Plato suggests a similarly nuanced relationship between emotion and reason – a relationship in which the former can most certainly accompany, and even enhance, the latter (Tarnopolsky 2004, 2010).

This symbiotic relationship proposed in political philosophy is supported by work in psychology and neurology. Damasio's (1994) writing on the issue is particularly well known. Damasio's work builds on accounts of the famous case of Phineas Gage, a nineteenth-century railway worker who suffered a brain injury, and a modern-day equivalent, Elliot, who suffered similar frontal-lobe injuries as a consequence of a sizable tumor. The behaviors that both Phineas and Elliot exhibited after their injuries suggested to Damasio that reason and emotion are linked, both physiologically and functionally speaking. That is, Damasio argues, reason and emotion do not emerge from entirely exclusive parts of the brain, and the effective use of reason depends in part on emotion.

Damasio's hypothesis is supported by a considerable body of work in psychology suggesting, for instance, that the ability to monitor and react to emotions is important to life success (Goleman 1995; Mayer and Salovey 1993), and that emotions can be important to attention and perception (Niedenthal and Kitayama 1994; Zajonc 1998), memory (Bradley et al. 1995; Cahill 1996; Phelps and Anderson 1997), and reasoning and decision making (Forgas 1995; Schwarz and Clore 1996). Indeed, neurological work suggests that the brain is organized partly as an affect system, where stimuli have more than just purely objective features – where something hot can be pleasant, or not, depending on prevailing conditions, for instance (Shizgal 1998). Indeed, the importance of affective responses is evidenced by the fact that organisms, including but not exclusive to humans, have developed reflexes – affective rather than cognitive reactions – for dealing quickly with stimuli (Berntson et al. 1993; Zajonc 1980).

We should not at this stage get pulled too far from politics, however, and we indeed need not do so. Work on political information processing suggests a similarly important role for emotion. There is, on the one hand, a body of work suggesting that emotions can be important determinants of political attitudes. Abelson et al. (1982) use survey questions on candidate qualities and find that various affective responses (afraid, angry, happy, etc.) were systematically related to candidate ratings. (I return to their findings in some detail in Chapter 3.) Conover and Feldman (1986) explore the political effect of emotional responses to economic information; these authors suggest that taking into account emotional reactions, rather than just cognitive ones, makes a real difference to how we understand and measure information effects. People may well forget the details in a given media story, for instance, but their emotional reaction to that story may be more enduring. And these authors find that affective judgments, above and beyond cognitive ones, are systematically related to presidential assessments. (See also Kinder 1978.)

Marcus and colleagues suggest a similarly important role for emotion in their "affective intelligence" theory of political information processing (Marcus 2002; Marcus and MacKuen 1993; Marcus et al. 1995, 2006). The crux of the argument is similar to what I have reviewed in the psychology and neurology literatures earlier: "[T]he human mind uses emotional evaluations of threat and novelty to engage action and rational calculation" (Marcus et al. 2006: 3). Individuals process information more thoroughly when they are anxious; it follows that emotion and rationality can be fundamentally intertwined. (For other work on the importance of affect in political information processing, see Just, Crigler, and Neuman 1996b; Ottati et al. 1992; Rudolph et al. 2000; Way and Masters 1996.)

Emotions and reason are not diametrically opposed, then; in fact, they may be fundamentally interdependent, for political considerations as for other domains. This link between emotion and reason is important here because it suggests that negativity, as an affective characteristic of information/media content/people, may be important to politics. Note that this is different than saying that we react to information that has potentially negative consequences. Negative consequences can be purely objective – a given policy change might mean we pay more tax (and we don't want to do that), for instance. The work on emotion and reason suggests that we should perhaps consider two different versions of negativity: objectively negative assessments (less disposable income) and emotionally negative assessments (anger about the tax change brought about by the party we voted for).

We might alternatively make the following distinction: there are characteristics that are *qualitatively* negative, such as fear or anger, and there are characteristics that are *quantitatively* negative, such as a monetary value that is lower than we expected or a proposal that shifts policy away from our preferred level. Both types of negativity may matter. The existing literature on emotion clearly focuses on the former; the chapters that follow deal with both. For instance, changes in the unemployment rate, used in Chapter 4, are quantitatively defined as positive (decreases) or negative (increases), but the tone of media content, used in Chapter 5, reflects, some combination of the two forms of negativity – tone is captured using words that could be either (or both) qualitatively or quantitatively positive or negative. The same is true for the measures used in Chapter 3's analysis of impression formation: rating candidates for intelligence or honesty is a fundamentally quantitative venture in the context of a survey experiment, but in reality it likely is a more qualitative reaction. The survey instrument produces quantitative data from what is normally a qualitative, largely emotional sentiment.

The difficulty of separating out the qualitative/emotional and quantitative (/objective?) components of negativity may be why the vast literatures reviewed in preceding sections tend to either avoid defining negativity or remain agnostic about which forms of negativity matter most. Forthcoming chapters are guilty as well, insofar as they explore biases in responses to information that is defined as negative by both qualitative and quantitative means. At a minimum, the debate about emotions in politics makes clear that (a) the two forms of negativity are not easily separable, and (b) both matter to politics. Though ideal, then, a clear separation between quantitative and qualitative versions of negativity may not matter where assessing the role of negativity in politics is concerned. Either form of negativity is important.

Negative Political Institutions?

Work on blame avoidance highlights the role of negativity in policy making.[6] In that literature, the underlying assumption is that it is a focus on negative information by voters that drives biases, and incrementalism, in government. This is one potential outcome of negativity in politics.

There is a potentially more profound impact of the negativity bias where policy making and political institutions are concerned, however, one hinted at in some of the literatures reviewed earlier but not yet laid out explicitly. It is the political version of what I have discussed in regard to social and cultural institutions in Chapter 1, namely the possibility that many major political institutional arrangements are designed to process positive and negative information in roughly the same way as the human brain. That is, political institutions have been designed to highlight negative information and to largely ignore positive information. This may not just be a consequence of the fact that these institutions are populated with humans, whose brains are predisposed toward this asymmetry. It may be, as work on common-pool resources suggests, a fundamental aspect of the design of those institutions.

Consider, briefly, the fundamental importance in work on political institutional design accorded to checks and balances. These were central to early (and current) thinking about presidential systems; they were similarly core ideas in the evolution of parliamentary systems; and discussions of federalism, and of courts, focus in great detail on the importance of checks and balances. Representative democracy has been, to a large extent, about giving the power to

---

[6] The prominence of error detection and loss aversion is apparent in legal matters as well. For example, the act of committing a crime is treated more harshly than the failure to prevent that crime from happening; as Levy (2003) writes, "Similarly, social norms against hurting another are probably more compelling than norms to help another" (230).

govern to one group and then surrounding that group with as many checks and balances as are necessary to minimize error.

One consequence of focusing such a large proportion of our representative democratic systems on "checks" may be a predominance of negative information in everyday politics. We should not lose sight of the fact that we have made governments – this is no small feat, and requires a certain amount of optimism. But once a representative democratic system is established, the regular functioning of that system is predominantly negative in tone. To be clear: only sitting governments produce (they hope) predominantly positive information; all other institutions/individuals/parties/groups involved in governance produce predominantly negative information. This makes good sense: we cannot simply let elected representatives do what they wish, with only periodic elections to hold them at bay. Indeed, without the many checks in a system of government, the amount of information that citizens have to assess government performance would be greatly reduced. But the need for constant error monitoring means that everyday politics is rather negative.

There is much more to review where institutional negativity is concerned – consider these paragraphs a foreshadowing of a much more detailed discussion in Chapter 7. In the meantime, this chapter has revealed passing if not prolonged discussions of various forms of asymmetry across a wide range of political science subfields. Prospect theory has played an important role in work on comparative politics, and especially international relations. Work on political and voting behavior has intermittently drawn on theories from psychology, mainly to account for the tendency of politicians and government to be penalized for negative trends but not similarly rewarded for positive ones. Similar tendencies are apparent in work on blame avoidance in policy making and in the management of common-pool resources. These and other bodies of literature suggest that the notion that negative information has a greater impact than positive information might travel, beyond psychology, and economics, and physiology, to a wide variety of political domains.

3

(Political) Impression Formation

> The evil that men do lives after them; the good is oft interr'd with their bones
> – Shakespeare

A set of new investigations into negativity biases in public opinion begins here, with an analysis of U.S. presidential evaluations, building directly on models of impression formation in the psychological literature discussed in Chapter 1. As past work in psychology suggests, negative domain-specific evaluations matter more to overall U.S. presidential assessments than do positive domain-specific evaluations. Analyses demonstrating this fact, which follow in this chapter, are partly a replication of past work, albeit with considerably more data and a somewhat different approach to modeling the asymmetry. But subsequent analyses then extend considerably what we know about political impression formation. First, comparative results make clear that the same dynamic is evident in other countries, supporting the notion that the negativity bias is not just a U.S. phenomenon. Subsequent analyses reveal heterogeneity in negativity biases as well. In short, they make clear that some people rely more strongly on negative information than do others. A final section then considers the difficulties in distinguishing "neutral" in interval-level measures – difficulties that make capturing the negativity bias difficult in some circumstances, and that point to the possibility that some past work finding a lack of evidence of a negativity bias may have been mistaken.

Each of these issues is dealt with in turn throughout this chapter. Demonstrations rely on individual-level survey data drawn primarily from the American National Election Studies, but also from a series of Australian National Election Studies. In sum, results make clear the connection between work on impression formation in psychology and public attitudes toward political candidates. Moreover, they provide strong illustrations of a negativity bias in political behavior.

Evaluations of Presidents

The empirical demonstration of asymmetry begins here with an illustration of what is essentially the "impression formation" story in psychology, but applied in the political realm. Recall that the literature on impression formation suggests that our view of others will be more heavily affected by negative assessments than by positive assessments. This dynamic is easily captured in election surveys, which regularly ask for respondents' overall assessments of presidents and/or party leaders, alongside a host of other variables capturing a wide range of domain-specific assessments. This chapter relies on responses to these, using the American National Election Study (NES) to illustrate the ways in which political leaders are more affected by negative assessments than by positive ones.

There are several bodies of literature concerned with leader assessments in the United States and elsewhere. Generally speaking, existing work focuses on one or more of several related issues, for example: How do assessments on leader traits (e.g., intelligent, caring) relate to overall leader evaluations? How do assessments of leader traits relate to vote choice? How do overall leader evaluations relate to vote choice? In each case, as we shall see, there is the possibility of a negativity bias.

The clearest case – where both the basic symmetric relationship and the case for asymmetry are concerned – is the link between leader traits and overall leader evaluations. Overall leader evaluations are typically captured using a thermometer score, the NES version of which is as follows:

> I'd like to get your feelings toward some of our political leaders and other people who are in the news these days (1990: have been in the news). I'll read the name of a person and I'd like you to rate that person using (1986–LATER: something we call) the feeling thermometer. Ratings between 50 and 100 (1986–LATER: degrees) mean that you feel favorably and warm toward the person; ratings between 0 and 50 degrees mean that you don't feel favorably toward the person and that you don't care too much for that person. (1986–LATER: You would rate the person at the 50 degree mark if you don't feel particularly warm or cold toward the person.) If we come to a person whose name you don't recognize, you don't need to rate that person. Just tell me and we'll move on to the next one. (1978–1984: If you do recognize the name, but you don't feel particularly warm or cold toward the person, then you would rate the person at the 50 degree mark.)

Alongside these general attitude questions about candidates, there are in some surveys a series of leader traits questions. The NES versions are as follows:

> I am going to read a list of words and phrases people may use to describe political figures. Think about the President. In your opinion, does the phrase [*trait1*] describe the President extremely well, quite well, not too well, or not well at all? What about [*trait2*]? Does the phrase [*trait2*] . . .

Traits are presented in a list. The most commonly used in the NES over the past three decades are "intelligent," "knowledgeable," "moral," "provides strong leadership," and "cares." These trait questions were initially used to better understand structure of feelings toward candidates, the focus of work led by Kinder and colleagues (Kinder et al. 1979; Kinder 1983, 1986). Related research focused on the characteristics important to citizens' view of an "ideal president" (Kinder et al. 1980), for instance, and on the structure of trait "dimensions," and variation in the importance of traits across candidates (e.g., Funk 1999; Pancer et al. 1999). (A thorough account of the literature is available in Bittner 2011.)

Relationships between traits and other variables also have been investigated. That responses to traits questions are connected to overall thermometer scores has always been relatively clear. Asymmetric relationships between traits and thermometer scores – exactly as we would expect following the impression formation story in the Preface – have also seen some attention in the literature. Lau (1982) finds evidence that negative information matters more than positive information does in overall assessments, for instance. Klein (1991, 1996) finds that trait scores below the mean matter more to overall assessments of U.S. presidents – over several elections – than do trait scores above the mean. And building in part on the work by Kinder (1978), Goren (2002: 634) finds an asymmetric impact of traits on leader evaluations, mediated by partisanship: "[P]artisan bias strengthens the impact of character weakness on evaluations of opposition party incumbents." There is, in short, a good deal of evidence suggesting an asymmetric connection between leader traits and overall leader assessments.

The objective of analyses here is to further explore this asymmetric relationship between traits and general assessments, first by extending the sample to a greater number of U.S. elections and by looking more closely at the how the asymmetric relationship differs from the symmetric one. To do so, the analysis relies on the cumulative data file for the NES. The variables used here are not available for all years, but are available over a reasonable number of elections: analyses that follow rely on data from the six presidential elections over the twenty-year period from 1984 and 2004. (Estimations thus benefit from a sample size of a little more than 10,000.)

The models themselves are relatively simple. The dependent variable is an interval-level variable, capturing responses to the "thermometer" question, on a scale of 0 to 100, about the current president. (See question wording presented earlier.) The current president is in a larger list of political leaders, but the analysis that follows focuses on these presidential responses only. This variable is modeled as a function of a relatively simple set of demographic variables, party identification, election-year dummy variables, and leader traits. More specifically, the variables are as follows:

Female: a variable equal to one for female respondents

Age: a variable equal to the age of the respondent at the time of the survey

Education: A binary variable equal to 1 for respondents who have more than high school education (i.e., some college, or completed college or university)

Party Identification: A variable equal to 1 for respondents whose party ID matches the president's party. Party ID is based on the standard question, "Generally speaking, do you usually think of yourself as a Republican, a Democrat, an Independent, or what?"

Traits: Trait questions vary somewhat by year. Not all traits were used each year, nor were all traits presented to all respondents. In an effort to maximize the number of respondents, I rely just on those traits that are most commonly used: "intelligent," "knowledgeable," "moral," "provides strong leadership," and "cares." Each variable is rescaled so as to be centered on zero: "extremely well" is 1.5, "quite well" is .5, "not too well" is −.5, and "not well at all" is −1.5. Centering on zero in this way means that positive assessments have positive values and negative assessments have negative values. This is useful when we look for asymmetry, below.

The models thus control for some of the basic demographics known to affect vote choice, and examine the relative contribution of five different trait assessments to overall feelings about the current president.

Results are estimated using simple ordinary least squares (OLS), and presented in three stages in Appendix Table B.3.1: first with basic demographics alone, then with the symmetric traits variables, and finally with traits divided so that positive ratings can take on different values from negative ratings. The most important results – coefficients for the various traits variables – are summarized in Table 3.1.

The first columns show OLS coefficients for each of the standard (symmetric) traits variables. We can see here that all traits are positively and significantly related to the thermometer score. A one-point increase in the (−1.5 to +1.5) rating for intelligence is associated, for instance, with an average 1.73-point increase in the thermometer rating. As has been seen in past work, some traits seem to matter more than others: "intelligent" and "knowledgeable," for instance, have much smaller coefficients than "cares." This is the basic symmetric model.

The test for asymmetry is in the following columns that show results from models in which each of the five traits variables are allowed to have an asymmetric effects – specifically, these models allow negative assessments to take on different coefficients than positive assessment. They do so by splitting each trait variable in two: for instance, *Intelligent(pos)* is equal to *Intelligent* when *Intelligent* is greater than zero, and *Intelligent(pos)* is equal to zero otherwise; *Intelligent(neg)* is equal to *Intelligent* when *Intelligent* is less than zero, and *Intelligent(neg)* is equal to zero otherwise. *Intelligent(pos)* and *Intelligent(neg)* thus capture all of the variance in *Intelligent*, but allow for data on one side of neutral to have a different effect than data on the other side of neutral. Coefficients for both should still be positive: positive assessments (with values greater than zero) should pull the thermometer score up, while

TABLE 3.1. *Presidential Thermometer Scores and Traits, United States*

	DV: Incumbent Presidential Thermometer Scores					F-Test of Equivalence
	Symmetric			Asymmetric		
Intelligent	1.726*	(.321)	Positive	.528	(.473)	12.27*
			Negative	4.004*	(.716)	
Knowledgeable	2.366*	(.328)	Positive	1.313*	(.499)	10.70*
			Negative	4.597*	(.703)	
Moral	4.770*	(.275)	Positive	2.461*	(.459)	34.61*
			Negative	7.094*	(.498)	
Leadership	7.835*	(.283)	Positive	6.838*	(.477)	4.53*
			Negative	8.697*	(.561)	
Cares	9.362*	(.273)	Positive	5.465*	(.525)	78.23*
			Negative	12.821*	(.466)	
	Combined Positive			16.303*	(.618)	293.46*
	Combined Negative			37.214*	(.755)	

* $p < .05$. Cells contain OLS regression coefficients, with standard errors in parentheses. All estimates used the cumulative NES file, and all presidential elections from 1984 to 2004. Models include controls for gender, age, education, party ID, and election. Full models are listed in Table B.3.1.

negative assessments (with values less than zero) should pull thermometer scores down.

Models in Table 3.1 show evidence of asymmetry for all five traits; that is, for each of *Intelligent, Knowledgeable, Moral, Leadership,* and *Cares,* the coefficient for negative assessments is greater than the coefficient for positive assessments. Moving one unit on the positive side of the moral scale is associated with a 2.4-unit upward shift in the thermometer score, for instance, whereas moving one unit on the negative side of the moral scale is associated with a 7.1-unit shift. Moving one unit on the positive side of the intelligent scale has no statistically significant effect, whereas moving one unit on the negative side of that scale is associated with a 4-point shift. The gap between each of five asymmetric coefficients is statistically significant.

What are the implications of this asymmetry? In terms of model fit, the overall impact of allowing for this kind of asymmetry is relatively slight – the R-squared for the symmetric model is .61, while the R-squared for the fully asymmetric model is only marginally greater, .63 (see Table B.3.1). The asymmetric impact of each individual variable is critical theoretically, however – it demonstrates a fundamental issue in the way individuals process political (and nonpolitical) information.

Figure 3.1 illustrates the difference between the symmetric and asymmetric models – it shows the predicted values for the thermometer score, based on each of the models in Table 3.1. The dotted line in Figure 3.1 shows the symmetric effect – the steady upward shift in the thermometer rating associated with increasingly positive assessments of the president's intelligence. The solid line

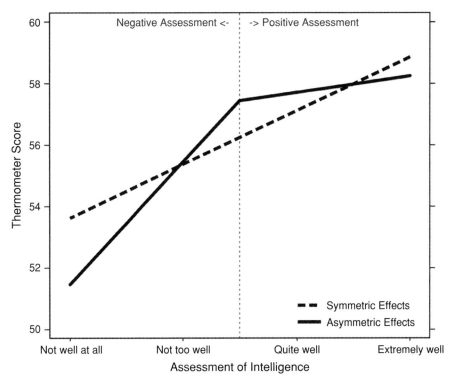

FIGURE 3.1. Impression Formation and U.S. Presidents: Intelligent.

shows the predicted effects allowing for asymmetry, that is, allowing for a slope on the negative side of neutral that is different from the slope on the positive side. The two slopes are noticeably different; more to the point, the asymmetric slope shows very little change on the positive side of *Intelligent*, but a striking drop on the negative side. The same is true in Figure 3.2, which shows similar results for *Moral*.

Results confirm the potential value of taking the negativity bias into account when thinking about the ways in which we judge political leaders. The overall impact of positive versus negative assessments shown in Table 3.1 serves to summarize things nicely: the linear combination of all positive coefficients is 16.303 (se = .618), while the linear combination of all negative coefficients is 37.214 (se = .755). Put differently, the effect of a one-unit shift on the negative side of neutral is associated with, on average, nearly twice the impact of a similar shift on the positive side of neutral.

Voting for Presidents

Is the same phenomenon evident when we look at votes rather than just thermometer scores? Thermometer scores are associated with voting decisions,

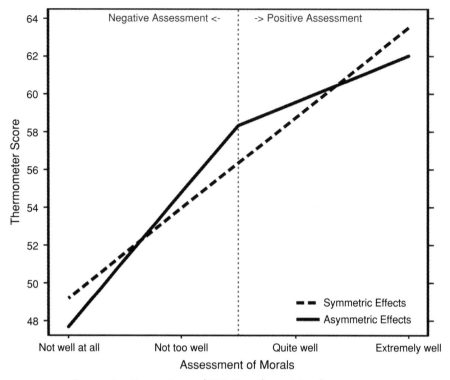

FIGURE 3.2. Impression Formation and U.S. Presidents: Morals.

to be sure. So we know already that the asymmetries discovered earlier are related to political outcomes, indirectly if not also directly. The connection between trait assessments and vote can be shown directly, however, by using the same model as earlier to estimate the likelihood of voting for the incumbent president.

There is already an existing body of work that attempts exactly this. That research finds evidence of the basic relationship, certainly: leader traits are connected to vote choice, both in the United States and elsewhere (e.g., Pierce 1993; Bean and Mughan 1989; Bittner 2011). There is evidence of asymmetry as well, as least where the connection between *traits* and voting is concerned, although it is more difficult to find similar levels of support for a negativity bias in the connection between general leader and/or party evaluations and vote choice, an issue discussed in more detail later. Indeed, there is some dis-agreement on how much, and even whether, these general assessments matter to parties' electoral success at all.

There are two arguments against the value of leader assessments in under-standing voting decisions. The first focuses on their limited substantive impact: King (2002) argues that while leader assessments may be in line with voting decisions, they rarely have a pronounced impact on the voting calculus. That is, the distribution of the vote tends to change only very marginally based on leader evaluations. (Note, however, that this conclusion is not at all clear; see Bittner 2011.) The other argument focuses on issues of endogeneity: Bartels (2002) suggests, for instance, that we cannot easily tell whether candidate traits and assessments drive the vote or simply reflect respondents' rationalization of their vote choice.[1] Thermometer scores covary with voting decisions, but the direction of causality is unclear.

These issues may be of only tangential importance here. I am not looking to improve models of vote choice by using leader assessments; I do not require that trait assessments have an exogenous impact on voting. What matters most for the current purpose is just that the connection between negative ratings and vote choice are stronger than the connections between positive ratings and vote choice are. If one believes that there is a causal impact of ratings on vote, then this asymmetry reflects the fact that voters give negative ratings more weight in their overall assessment. If, alternatively, one believes that the rating-vote connection is endogenous, then this asymmetry reflects individuals' tendency to give strong negative ratings to a candidate they did not vote for, while only giving somewhat positive ratings to the candidate they did vote for. Either way, there is an interesting asymmetry between positive and negative ratings.

These connections between traits and voting decisions are explored in Appendix Table B.3.1, with the most critical results reported in Table 3.2. The model is identical in every way to the one used for incumbent presidential thermometer scores (above), although in this case the dependent variable is binary and equal to one for respondents saying they voted for the candidate from the incumbent presidential party. Estimates are produced using probit regression; coefficients are reported as marginal change coefficients, interpretable in roughly the same way as regular OLS coefficients. Table 3.2 shows just the traits coefficients from the symmetric and asymmetric models.

The connection between trait ratings and vote is weaker than the connection between trait ratings and thermometer scores, as we should expect. (Many other factors drive vote choice, of course.) Nevertheless, in the basic (symmetric) model, all traits except intelligence are significantly related to vote choice. Again, "cares" matters a great deal – a one-point shift in "cares" is associated with an increase in the likelihood of voting for the incumbent presidential party by 23 percent.

The asymmetric model for voting decisions is also less clearly asymmetric than for thermometer scores, but, again, there is evidence of asymmetry overall. Three of the negative coefficients are not statistically different from their positive equivalents. The exceptions are *Leadership*, where the impact of a shift on the negative side of the scale has an impact more than four times greater

---

[1] Note that Lau (1982) tries to address this issue by focusing on voters who had not yet made the decision who to vote for.

TABLE 3.2. *Presidential Vote and Traits, United States*

	DV: Incumbent Presidential Party Vote					F-Test of Equivalence
	Symmetric		Asymmetric			
Intelligent	.021	(.017)	Positive	.002	(.025)	1.50
			Negative	.076	(.046)	
Knowledgeable	.054*	(.017)	Positive	.065*	(.027)	.10
			Negative	.047	(.043)	
Moral	.109*	(.015)	Positive	.088*	(.024)	1.34
			Negative	.139*	(.029)	
Leadership	.108*	(.015)	Positive	.037	(.026)	10.41*
			Negative	.218*	(.038)	
Cares	.229*	(.014)	Positive	.175*	(.032)	3.59^a
			Negative	.272*	(.027)	
	Combined Positive			.352*	(.033)	21.01*
	Combined Negative			.649*	(.031)	

* $p < .05$; $^a p < .10$. Cells contain marginal change coefficients from a binary probit estimation, with standard errors in parentheses. All estimates used the cumulative NES file, and all presidential elections from 1984 to 2004. Models include controls for gender, age, education, party ID, and election. Full models are listed in Table B.3.1.

than does an equivalent shift on the positive side of the scale, and *Cares*, where the impact of a shift on the negative side of the scale has an impact roughly 60 percent greater than does an equivalent shift on the positive side of the scale. Two of the other variables point toward a negativity bias, but the results are not on their own statistically significant. Only one trait, *Knowledgeable*, points in the other direction, but here the coefficients are very close to equal – indeed, statistically speaking, they are.

Summing the positive and negative coefficients is revealing. Doing so more clearly illustrates the (statistically significant) negativity bias in the connection between traits and voting decisions. Here, the linear combination of all positive coefficients is .352 (se = .033), whereas the linear combination of all negative coefficients is just less than twice the size, .649 (se = .031). Where vote intentions are concerned, the connection with negative ratings outweighs the connection with positive ratings by a factor of roughly 1.8:1.

Evaluations of Australian Prime Ministers

Is this asymmetry just an American phenomenon? If the evolutionary/biological story is correct – if humans really are hardwired to react more strongly to negative information – then there should not be anything particularly American about asymmetric responsiveness. That said, most existing research on the topic has been done in the United States, and the United States has a reputation for having particularly negative political campaigns, and media more generally.

(Whether this reputation is justified is unclear, mind you, but that particular discussion is beyond the scope of the current chapter.) It is easy to believe that asymmetric responsiveness is a peculiarly American trait, perhaps. It is mostly likely not.

The possibility that a negativity bias is a more general phenomenon is examined here with a replication of the analysis of U.S. presidents but using data for Australian prime ministers. There is nothing particular about Australia per se for this analysis; however, the Australian National Election Study is one of the few outside the United States that has consistently asked a range of close-ended trait questions alongside thermometer scores. I am thus able to estimate a near-identical model to the U.S.-based model offered earlier in the chapter.

The full estimation includes pooled Australian elections from 1993 to 2004 and the same control variables as in the earlier U.S. example. Specification for those variables is identical here, albeit focused on the incumbent prime minister rather than the incumbent president. There are a few minor differences. The thermometer rating in the AES is a 0–10 scale, for instance, and question wording is as follows: "Again using a scale from 0 to 10, please show how much you like or dislike the party leaders. Again, if you don't know much about them, you should give them a rating of 5. How do you feel about [name]." Trait question wording is: "Here is a list of words and phrases people use to describe party leaders. Thinking first about [name], in your opinion how well does each of these describe him – extremely well, quite well, not too well or not well at all? Now thinking about [name]. . . . " The traits commonly used in the Australian case are also a little different: intelligent, compassionate, sensible, leadership, and inspiring. As for the United States, Australian traits are rescaled so that "extremely well" is 1.5, "quite well" is .5, "not too well" is −.5, and "not well at all" is −1.5. For the symmetric models, the entire scale is used in its regular form. For the asymmetric models, the scale is divided at 0.

A summary of results is presented in Table 3.3, with full results shown in Appendix Table B.3.2. As in the U.S. models, in the symmetric model all five traits are positively and significantly related to the incumbent prime ministers' thermometer score. (Also like the United States, it is compassion – "cares" in the U.S. study – that seems to matter most.) The asymmetric models produce results that are, overall, similar to the U.S. results as well. There are some differences in the details, however. In this case, there is no sign of asymmetry for "sensible"; results for "intelligent" actually point toward a positivity bias, but the coefficients are not quite statistically different (p = .17); results for leadership also point toward a positivity bias. The two traits that show the strongest link with thermometer scores are compassionate and inspiring, however, and both of these show powerful negativity biases. As a consequence, the combined impact of negative traits outweighs the combined impact of positive ones. Indeed, while the magnitude of coefficients here is different than in the preceding U.S. models (because of a different range for the traits and thermometer variables, now on a

TABLE 3.3. *Incumbent Leader Thermometer Scores and Traits, Australia*

	DV: Incumbent Presidential Thermometer Scores				F-Test of Equivalence
	Symmetric		Asymmetric		
Intelligent	.106*	(.039)	Positive	.173* (.055)	3.15^a
			Negative	−.047 (.093)	
Compassionate	.878*	(.035)	Positive	.324* (.072)	77.62*
			Negative	1.309* (.061)	
Sensible	.685*	(.040)	Positive	.665* (.066)	.07
			Negative	.697* (.079)	
Leadership	.295*	(.035)	Positive	.399* (.058)	6.66*
			Negative	.113 (.074)	
Inspiring	.784*	(.034)	Positive	.492* (.070)	22.64*
			Negative	1.003* (.057)	
	Combined Positive			2.053* (.087)	43.53*
	Combined Negative			3.075* (.091)	

* p < .05; ^{a}p < .10. Cells contain OLS regression coefficients, with standard errors in parentheses. All estimates used a combined AES file, using all elections from 1993 to 2004. Models include controls for gender, age, education, party ID, and election. Full models are listed in Table B.3.2.

scale from 0 to 10), the ratio of the combined negative impact to the combined positive impact is nearly as great as in the United States: the combined negative impact is roughly 50 percent greater than the combined positive impact is. Looking trait to trait, there is less evidence of a negativity bias in Australia than there is in the United States; taking traits together, however, negative assessments appear to be as damaging to Australian prime ministers as they are to U.S. presidents.

Heterogeneity in the Negativity Bias

Models have thus far assumed that the negativity bias works the same way for everyone; that is, they have assumed that negative ratings matter more than positive ones, for all respondents. There is likely to be heterogeneity in the nature and magnitude of the negativity bias, however.

One likely source of heterogeneity is partisan identification. We may be more inclined to dwell on the negative for the other parties' candidates, for instance; for our own, we may actually underweigh negative assessments. This is the crux of Goren's (2002) argument, in which he draws on theories of motivated reasoning to build a model in which partisan identification mediates the negativity bias. Motivated reasoning theory suggests that individuals will try to interpret information in a way that is consistent with their predispositions (see, e.g., Baumeister and Newman 1994; Fischle 2000; Klein and Kunda 1992; Kunda 1990; Lodge and Taber 2000; Pyszczynski and Greenberg 1987). It follows, for Goren, that voters are likely to seek out information about the flaws of the candidate they do not support, and they are likely to give those flaws greater weight in their overall assessment of that candidate.

Goren's analysis focuses on the tendency for co-partisans to focus on traits on which the candidate is known to excel, and for other partisans to focus on the candidates' known weaknesses (based on aggregate-level ratings for the candidates on a range of traits). Here, I test the possibility of a negativity bias, mediated by partisanship, by re-estimating models of the relationship between overall assessments and trait ratings, but breaking respondents apart by partisan identification. I use the U.S. election studies, because they provide the largest body of data.

One relatively simple way to capture differences across in- and out-partisans is to interact the trait variables with the party ID variable – where party ID, as mentioned earlier, is a binary variable equal to one for respondents with the same party ID as the candidate in question. With five traits variables – ten once divided into positive and negative – however, there are simply too many interactions, and collinearity is an issue. To facilitate this kind of interaction, then, I begin by combining the trait variables into two indices: one capturing all five positive trait indicators and the other capturing all five negative indicators. In both cases, results are summed and divided by five, so that the range in each of the two variables is the same as that for the independent traits variables. In this way, we can compare directly the results of this two-variable approach to the results of the preceding ten-variable approach. Obviously, there should be some minor loss of information – different traits matter to somewhat different degrees, as we have seen in an earlier discussion, and the working assumption in this two-variable model is that all positive trait ratings have the same impact and all negative trait ratings have the same impact.

That said, the results in Table 3.4 suggest that the loss of information in the two-variable model is relatively small. The first column shows the results from a replication of the asymmetric model in Table 3.1, except that this one uses just measures of (a) positive and (b) negative traits combined. The coefficients for the combined indices in this case are only marginally different from the summed coefficients in Table 3.1. And having just two variables makes interactions much more feasible, so the results in the second column of Table 3.4 show the consequences of interacting these two variables with party ID. (The full models are included in Appendix Table B.3.3; Table 3.4 includes just the coefficients for the summed positive and negative indices, alongside the interaction effects.) In this second column, the positive and negative coefficients represent the impact of each for respondents who do not declare the same party ID as the incumbent president. For those who *do* have the same party ID as the incumbent president, the impact of positive trait ratings is the coefficient for *Positive* plus the coefficient for *Positive * Party ID*; negative ratings work the same way.

TABLE 3.4. *Democratic and Republican Presidential Candidate Thermometer Scores and Traits, United States*

	DV: Candidate Thermometer Scores							
	No Interaction		Party ID		Gender		Education	
Positive	15.909*	(.618)	15.962*	(.955)	17.003*	(.799)	16.474*	(.839)
Negative	40.362*	(.748)	40.529*	(.881)	38.038*	(.982)	37.082*	(1.047)
Positive * Party ID			.081	(1.254)				
Negative * Party ID			-1.276	(1.924)				
Positive * Female					-2.438*	(1.193)		
Negative * Female					5.207*	(1.432)		
Positive * Education							-.907	(1.180)
Negative * Education							6.288*	(1.427)

* p < .05. Cells contain selected OLS regression coefficients, with standard errors in parentheses. All estimates used the cumulative NES file, and all presidential elections from 1984 to 2004. Models include controls for gender, age, education, party ID, and election. Full models are listed in Table B.3.3.

That said, the direct effect of positive and negative ratings – that is, the impact for out-partisans – is roughly the same as in the previous model. The interactions are not statistically significant, although *Negative * Party ID* does point toward the possibility that in-partisans give marginally less weight to negative ratings. Results are too weak to credit, however. Overall, these results suggest that a negativity bias exists, regardless of partisanship.[2]

NES data provide a good opportunity to explore other sources of heterogeneity in the negativity bias, and Table 3.4 includes two likely suspects: gender and education. There exists relatively little past work focused on heterogeneity in impression formation across subgroups; there is, however, a small body of work on differences in reactions to negative stimuli across genders. Grabe and Kamhawi (2006) find that women report higher arousal for positively framed media stories, whereas men report higher arousal for negatively framed media stories. (These authors suggest that this may account for part of the gender gap in political knowledge; because news is predominantly negatively framed, it produces more attentiveness among men than women.) This is in line with evidence in psychology that women have a stronger avoidance response to negative stimuli than do men (e.g., Canli et al. 2002). Work on impression formation has provided rather mixed results regarding gender differences (Huma 2010), although the one study focused most clearly on heterogeneity in reactions to positive and negative information suggests that women are more likely to have more positive initial assessments and to react more strongly to negative stimuli as well. (Ito and Cacioppo 2005; in fact, the authors find that the individuals who exhibit a strong positivity offset also tend to have a strong negativity bias, although this more common for women than for men.) In sum, it seems possible that women will show a greater negativity bias in their rating of presidential candidates.

This would be in line with work in economics on gender differences in risk aversion. In a meta-analysis of experimental studies, Croson and Gneezy (2009) find evidence that women are more risk averse than men are. They review three explanations for the difference. One account focuses on the tendency of women to experience emotions more strongly than men do (see, e.g., Harshman and Paivio 1987); those emotions may then affect the assessment of the potential utility of risk-taking. In short, nervousness may lead female participants to see less potential value in a risky choice. Another account focuses on overconfidence, drawing on work suggesting that men tend to exhibit more overconfidence than do women across a range of situations (e.g., Lichtenstein et al. 1982; Niederle and Vesterlund 2007). A final account focuses on different interpretations of risky situations by men and women, where the former see risk

---

[2] The same is true when I estimate models for Democratic presidential candidates and Republican presidential candidates, separately for respondents with each of Democratic, Republican, and independent party IDs. That is, there is evidence of asymmetry throughout, and no evidence that in-partisans weigh negative ratings any differently than do out-partisans.

as a challenge needing a response, whereas the latter see it as a threat needing avoidance (see, e.g., Arch 1993). Determining which of these accounts is most likely is beyond the scope of the analysis here, of course. But it is nevertheless possible to see whether a gender difference exists.

Alongside gender, Table 3.4 includes a test for differences in the negativity bias across education levels. This interaction is motivated not so much by the literature in psychology as by work in political behavior in which education, or political sophistication, is found to augment the connectedness between a range of separate attitudes about policy and/or politics. More sophisticated respondents are, in short, better able to connect one idea to the next, and thus more likely to have coherent, structured attitudes. It follows that education might either (a) enhance the asymmetry bias, insofar as it makes it more likely that individuals connect their negative trait ratings to their overall candidate assessments; or (b) decrease the negativity bias, by making individuals better able to connect their positive trait ratings to overall assessments. Past work on the matter suggests the latter: Gächter et al. (2007) suggest that education tends to enhance individuals' ability to correctly perceive trade-offs and thus reduces loss aversion.

Table 3.4 thus includes two more models, interacting the positive and negative assessments with both gender and education. In the case of gender, recall that the variable is equal to one for female respondents; for education, the variable is equal to one for those who went to school beyond their high school diploma. In both cases, the interactions are statistically significant, and both point toward a strengthening of the negativity bias. Results for gender suggest that, in comparison with the coefficients for male respondents, the positive coefficient is weaker for women, and the negative coefficient is greater. Indeed, for men the impact of negative versus positive is roughly 2.2:1, whereas for women it is 3:1. Results for education suggest a similar story: for the less educated, the impact of negative versus positive is 2.2:1, whereas for the more highly educated it is 2.8:1.

The gender differences found here are thus in line with existing work on gender differences in risk aversion. And it is interesting, if a little hypothetical (which is to say, completely unproven by the data presented here), that the various accounts for gender differences, outlined earlier, point toward some combination of cultural but perhaps also evolutionary causes. Women may be socialized in ways that make them more cautious, or nervous, about risk. Women may also be less risk-taking because it had evolutionary advantages. (Note that the two accounts are not in competition with each other – socialization and evolution can work simultaneously. See, e.g., Belsky et al. 1991.) Consider work on how testosterone affects levels of competitiveness, which links behavioral differences to biological differences (for a review, see Bateup et al. 2002; for a direct link to economic behavior, see Hoffman et al. 2008). Consider also work that links differences in risk aversion to evolutionary theories about sexual selection (for a review, see Dreber and Hoffman 2011). The gender difference observed in Table 3.4 likely supports some combination of cultural and evolutionary accounts.

The findings for education are, in contrast, at odds with existing work suggesting that education leads to more accurate/balanced assessments of gains and losses, and thus less risk aversion. The impact of education may be quite different in the context of presidential evaluations, perhaps. But it does seem clear in Table 3.4 that education enhances the connection between negative trait assessments and overall evaluations, while making no difference where positive trait assessments are concerned. Like the findings for gender, this evidence of heterogeneity in the negativity bias is new in political science and suggests a host of additional research possibilities. For the time being, however, what is perhaps most critical is the fact that although the negativity bias varies in magnitude across partisanship, genders and education groups, it is evident in all cases. That is, we are not talking about whether the negativity bias exists or not, but rather about the magnitude of the bias.

Where Exactly Is Neutral?

One major advantage of the analyses thus far is that they rely on trait questions for which there is a clear dividing line between negative and positive. There are two clearly positive responses and two clearly negative ones – "extremely well" and "quite well" versus "not so well" and "not well at all." Dividing variables into positive and negative is not always so simple, however. For a good number of variables, including thermometer scores, the neutral point is unclear. As a consequence, so too is the negativity bias.

Do negative ratings on thermometer scores matter more to vote intentions (among other variables) than positive ratings do? We cannot easily tell, because thermometer scores have an ambiguous neutral point. To be fair, the introduction to thermometer ratings used in surveys often flags 50 as a midpoint. (See NES wording earlier.) But it seems unlikely that respondents actually regard 50 as neutral; moreover, it is unlikely that they regard all scores above 50 as positive. Consider the following hypothetical: a survey respondent is asked about two candidates. They give a score of 80 to one and a score of 55 to the other. This is very likely – indeed, the distribution of responses in NES data suggest this is rather typical. Does a score of 55 suggest that the respondent is simply neutral about the candidate, or that they dislike him/her? Probably the latter.

The issue is highlighted in a recent paper by Aarts and Blais (2011), in which the authors look for signs of an asymmetric connection between thermometer scores for parties and leaders and vote intentions across eight countries (Australia, Canada, Germany, Netherlands, Norway, Spain, Sweden, and the United States). Results do not support the notion that assessments of parties and leaders are dominated by the negative; rather, they suggest that (a) average ratings for *all* parties and leaders, across *all* countries, are above 50; and

(b) below-50 thermometer scores matter no more to vote choice than do above-50 scores.[3]

If 50 is indeed the neutral point for thermometer scores, then it appears not just as though positive ratings matter as much as negative ones do, but that people are mostly pleased with all parties and leaders. Note that this includes parties and leaders receiving rather small proportions of the vote. This seems unlikely, not just given public disaffection for parties captured in other survey questions, but given that many of the smaller parties in multiparty systems will have very few partisans. These parties' high ratings will necessarily be the product of above-50 thermometer scores from the vast bulk of respondents who are not voting for them, then. At a minimum, it seems worth considering the possibility that scores of 50, and perhaps even some unknown range above 50, should be regarded as (at least mildly) negative.

This issue has been identified before. In a paper exploring Sears' (1969: 424) contention that there is a "predominance of positive evaluations" in Americans' views of political leaders and parties, Sniderman et al. (1982) consider the use of thermometer scores as indications of positivity and negativity. They note first that thermometer scores give the "impression of positivity" – the overwhelming majority of responses (more than 80 percent) give over-50 scores to each of the major parties. They write:

> This would seem too much of a good thing for the first post-Watergate presidential election. The feeling thermometers may accurately sort out those who feel very positively about the parties from those who feel less so. But even if it reliably preserves the rank-order of individuals, this technique probably overestimates how many are positive (120).

The authors go on to note other variables showing the large proportion of respondents who give the parties poor ratings on other (not-thermometer) questions. It looks, they suggest, as though a good number of respondents who appear positive using thermometer scores (where 50 is assumed to be the neutral point) are in fact mostly negative about parties.

Results from a 1979 NES Pilot Survey point in the same direction. In a study focused on the effects of moving to a different design for the thermometer scoring card used in face-to-face interviews, Weisberg and Miller (1979: 21) compare thermometer scores to vote intentions. They find that:

> few people would vote for candidates they rate below 50. The 50 category also turns out to be fairly negative, with few respondents being willing to vote for a candidate they rate 50.... There are too few cases in key categories to be sure exactly where the ratings really become positive. It appears that ratings of 60 with the old thermometer card are still negative while ratings of 55 and 60 with the new card are somewhat negative.

---

[3] Thermometer scales vary country to country, so strictly speaking all estimations do not rely on 50 as the neutral point, but its equivalent, depending on the scale.

The difference between cards is not critical here; the difficulty in determining a neutral point – somewhere above 50 – clearly is. It follows that the actual distribution of positive and negative thermometer ratings is not quite as it seems using 50 as the neutral point.

Just how far up the thermometer scale does "negative" go? Researchers have used a number of different cutoffs from as low as 51 to as high as 80 (in ascending order; see Miller et al. 1979; McEvoy 1971; Buell and Sigelman 1985). The answer seems to vary across interview modes – both across different pictures of thermometers and from cards to telephone interviews (Weisberg and Miller 1979). The answer also seems to vary across individuals. Wilcox et al. (1989) explore individual-level differences in thermometer scores and find that mean thermometer ratings across sixteen groups (not including parties and leaders) were systematically related to respondents' education, gender, and church attendance, for instance. Standard deviations in thermometer scores vary systematically as well, suggesting that certain groups (including the more highly educated) use a wider range of thermometer scores than do others.

How then can we distinguish the neutral point in thermometer scores – a neutral point that is on average something above 50, but that also likely varies from one individual to the next? Clearly it is hard, and as a consequence, we are as yet unable to easily test the possibility of a negativity bias in the application of thermometer ratings to other attitudes and behaviors (such as voting). We know that negative information on traits matters more than positive information does, both for thermometer scores and for voting. We know this in large part because trait assessments are captured using response categories for which the neutral point is clear. But thermometer scores, with an ambiguous neutral point, present a real problem where assessments of asymmetry are concerned.

Regardless, this much seems to be clear: not all evaluations are negative. There are good candidates and good parties, and there are large bodies of evidence suggesting that we are able to recognize them as such. But there is also a growing body of work, including the analyses presented in this chapter, suggesting that negative information – when we can identify it as negative, at least – can be particularly powerful in political behavior. This clearly is true where impression formation of political candidates is concerned. Other domains in which negative information may be particularly powerful are the subject of the chapters that follow.

Taking Stock

Work on the negativity bias in impression formation quite clearly translates relatively easily to the political context. Past research has already identified a negativity bias in presidential evaluations; earlier in this chapter, those analyses were extended to a much larger body of data in the United States, not just for presidential assessments but for voting decisions as well. They were also extended beyond the United States: a similar dynamic is also evident in assessments of Australian prime ministers. Results in this chapter thus suggest the possibility that the negativity bias is not an American phenomenon, a fact that will be tested much further – that is, across a far wider range of countries – in the chapter that follows.

The results introduced earlier also make clear that there is heterogeneity in the negativity bias, at least where presidential evaluations are concerned. Analyses support past work suggesting that women show a greater negativity bias then do men. It also appears as though education enhances, rather than reduces, the role of negative information in the assessment of political candidates. The fact that is most critical may not be the details of heterogeneity, however, but the fact that even accounting for that heterogeneity, a negativity bias is evident across all cohorts, by partisanship, gender, and education. To be clear: the magnitude of the negativity bias varies across individuals, but that bias always appears to be there. (Being a popular political leader must be a pretty tough job.)

Of course, not only political leaders suffer from the negativity bias. Chapters 1 and 2 make clear that the negativity bias should be widespread, readily evident across a wide range of domains, political and otherwise. The following chapter sticks to the political sphere, but widens the scope beyond leaders – to the economy, economic sentiment, and government approval.

4

Economic Sentiment and Government Approval

Bad news goes about in clogs, good news in stockinged feet.

– Welsh proverb

The preceding chapter focused on negativity biases in individual-level political behavior. Here I turn to aggregate-level data. Results are driven by the same underlying, individual-level tendencies, but a major advantage of aggregate-level survey data is that they are more readily available over extended periods of time and across many countries. Aggregate-level data also provide an opportunity to consider not just the immediate, asymmetric impact of negative versus positive information, but also the possibility that the impact of negative (or positive) information varies over time.

The chapter begins with time-series models of economic expectations using a combination of data from the Michigan Consumer Surveys and the European Economic Sentiment Index. Results suggest that economic expectations react asymmetrically to macroeconomic trends, not just in the United States but across the developed world. Then, the chapter connects both U.S. presidential evaluations and UK government approval with economic expectations – it examines asymmetries in the link between how voters feel about the economy and how they feel about their leaders/governments. These analyses are important in that they provide additional evidence of negativity biases in political behavior. But they are also partly just a precursor to the penultimate section, which explores the possibility that the negativity bias shifts in periods of predominantly positive or negative information. Overall, negative changes in the economy matter more to public preferences than do positive changes. *But do negative changes in the economy matter as much when the economy is already rather bad?* The answer to this question appears to be no, and that answer forms a critical part of my view of negativity in politics. The negativity bias is reduced when the information environment becomes predominantly negative.

This helps explain why we are not endlessly negative – at some point, when things are particularly bad, we start focusing on the positive. This finding opens up the possibility that negativity in politics is self-correcting.

There are two parts to the story that follows, then. On the one hand, there is evidence of compounding asymmetries: from macroeconomics to economic expectations, and then from economic expectations to assessments of governments. In each case, negative change matters more than positive change. On the other hand, analyses also make clear that there are limits to the negativity bias. Repeated findings of negativity in media content and in public attitudes can lead to the impression that things can only get more and more negative. But this is not the case. There are negativity biases throughout the political world, to be sure, but the very process that generates that negativity bias also appears to limit it.

Asymmetry in U.S. Economic Sentiment

Evaluations of presidents and prime ministers in Chapter 3 have offered a relatively clear case of asymmetric responsiveness to negative versus positive information. One other domain in which a negativity bias has been given some attention is economic sentiment – focused in some cases on the impact of economic shifts on sentiment itself, but in many cases on the connection between (a) the economy, and/or sentiment, and (b) government popularity and/or voting behavior.

The present section focuses on economic sentiment itself (while voting behavior is addressed in a subsequent section that follows). In so doing, this work has much in common with research in economics focusing on the aggregate-level implications of loss aversion. The literature is vast; for our purposes, note just that a negativity bias in both consumer sentiment and consumption, reacting to a range of economic measures, has been identified in the United States and elsewhere (e.g., Apergis and Miller 2006; Shea 1995; Shirvani and Wilbratte 2000; Kuo and Chung 2002; Patterson 1993; Karnizova and Khan 2010; Bidwell et al. 1995). Relatedly, there is a body of work exploring the asymmetric responsiveness of markets to news about economic sentiment (e.g., Akhtar et al. 2011; Busse and Green 2002; Chan 2003; Chen et al. 2003; Chuliá et al. 2010; Jain 1988; Kurov 2010; May 2010; McQueen et al. 1996.) In political science, and motivated in part by work suggesting the political significance of economic sentiment, my own past work (Soroka 2006) also finds strong evidence of a negativity bias in the relationship between economic changes and economic sentiment in the United Kingdom. The asymmetry is partly driven by media content (discussed in the forthcoming chapters), but also by the direct, asymmetric reaction of the public to upward and downward changes in the unemployment rate (or leading indicators).

With the same motivations in mind, this chapter explores aggregate-level, asymmetric responsiveness in economic sentiment. As in Chapter 3, I begin with

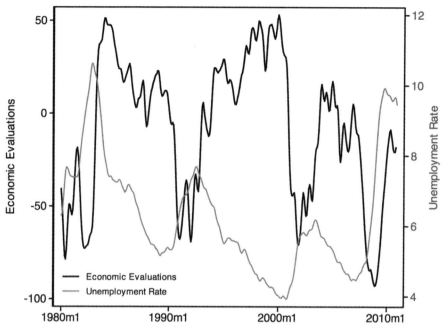

FIGURE 4.1. Economic Sentiment and Unemployment, United States

an exploratory analysis in the United States. I start with a simple time-series of economic sentiment, drawn from the Michigan Consumer Sentiment Index survey in which (retrospective egotropic) economic sentiment is captured using the following question: "We are interested in how people are getting along financially these days. Would you say that you (and your family living there) are better off or worse off financially than you were a year ago?" I use a simple measure, in which the percent saying "worse now" is subtracted from the percent saying "better now." Positive values indicate that more people feel the economy is "better now," whereas negative values indicate that more people feel the economy is "worse now." In principle, the measure ranges from −100 to +100. In practice, over the period investigated here, the measure runs from −94 (in November 2008) to +59 (in January 2001).

The resulting series is illustrated in Figure 4.1, alongside the unemployment rate. Clearly, the two are related – when unemployment is high, the public's view of business conditions tends to be low. Asymmetry is not easily identified in the figure, however, so we turn to a time-series analysis regressing economic sentiment on levels of and changes in economic conditions. Following recent work (e.g., De Boef and Kellstedt 2004), economic sentiment is modeled as an error-correction model (ECM) – that is, a model in which current changes in the dependent variable are regressed on lagged levels of the dependent variable alongside both lagged levels and current changes in the independent variables. In so doing, the model allows for an equilibrium relationship, captured in the long-term impact of lagged levels on current changes, as well as the impact of short-term factors in the impact of one-period-lagged changes. (For more information on EMCs, see Banerjee et al. 1993; in political science, see Clarke and Stewart 1994). The model used here is as follows:

$$\Delta \, \text{Sentiment}_t = \alpha_0 + \beta_1 \Delta \, \text{Economy}_t + \beta_2 (\text{Sentiment}_{t-1} + \beta_3 \, \text{Economy}_{t-1}) + \epsilon_t$$

$$(4.1)$$

where β_1 captures the short-term impact of the economy on economic sentiment and β_2 captures the long-term equilibrium relationship.

Note that an additional advantage of the ECM setup is that short-term changes are rather easily divided into positive and negative shifts. Increases in unemployment, for instance, are negative, whereas decreases in unemployment are positive. The same is true for inflation, also used later in the chapter. And so the ECM allows us to test, rather easily, the possibility of asymmetric reactions to positive and negative economic shifts, in the short term at least. (But note that whether no change in unemployment or inflation is actually the neutral point is up for discussion. This issue is discussed in more detail later.)

Full results for the models of symmetric and asymmetric effects are displayed in Table 4.1. The first columns show results from a basic symmetric model, where the economy is represented by both unemployment and inflation. Variables in levels are included in the first rows; variables in changes are included in subsequent rows. The coefficient for lagged economic sentiment is negative, as expected – higher levels of sentiment in the previous month tend to be associated with lower increases (or greater decreases) in the current month. Lagged levels of unemployment and inflation are also negative (although the coefficient for unemployment slips just below statistical significance). Again, this is as we should expect – higher unemployment and/or higher inflation lead to lower levels of economic sentiment. Concurrent changes in both unemployment and inflation are negatively signed, as they should be, but neither is statistically significant.

The impact of concurrent changes in economic indicators is more robust in the second set of columns in Table 4.1, which show results from a model allowing for asymmetric responsiveness. Here positive changes in unemployment and inflation are statistically insignificant, but negative changes are clearly significant. A one-point increase in unemployment is associated with an average decrease of 7.4 points in economic sentiment; a one-point increase in inflation is associated with an average decrease of 2.9 points. The impact of a decrease in unemployment or inflation is nil.

A final model in Table 4.1 repeats the process but replaces unemployment and inflation with the misery index – a sum of the current unemployment rate plus the rate of inflation. Model fit decreases somewhat, and though there are

TABLE 4.1. *Economic Sentiment, United States, Retrospective Egotropic*

	DV: Δ Economic Sentiment$_t$					
	Model 1		Model 2		Model 3	
Levels						
Sentiment$_{t-1}$	−.121*	(.028)	−.138*	(.029)	−.106*	(.023)
Unemployment$_{t-1}$	−.513	(.268)	−.513	(.269)		
Inflation$_{t-1}$	−.226*	(.112)	−.211	(.112)		
Misery Index$_{t-1}$					−.252*	(.107)
Changes						
Δ Unemp$_t$	−3.400	(1.987)				
Δ Inflation$_t$	−.829	(.761)				
Δ Unemployment$_t$ (Pos)			1.543	(3.617)		
Δ Unemployment$_t$ (Neg)			−7.390*	(3.145)		
Δ Inflation$_t$ (Pos)			.921	(1.282)		
Δ Inflation$_t$ (Neg)			−2.987*	(1.403)		
Δ Misery Index$_t$ (Pos)					.470	(1.311)
Δ Misery Index$_t$ (Neg)					−2.533	(1.354)
Constant	4.975*	(1.975)	6.163*	(2.036)	3.778*	(1.304)
N	394		394		394	
Rsq	.055		.069		.054	
Adj Rsq	.043		.053		.045	

* $p < .05$. Cells contain OLS regression coefficients, with standard errors in parentheses. Model includes monthly data from January 1978 to November 2010. Survey data are from the Michigan Consumer Sentiment Index survey, where the measure is % saying "better now" minus % saying "worse now" in response to the following question: "We are interested in how people are getting along financially these days. Would you say that you (and your family living there) are better off or worse off financially than you were a year ago?"

hints of an asymmetric relationship, negative shifts in the misery index fall just below statistical significance. Clearly there are benefits to including unemployment and inflation independently. That said, the misery index provides a nice summary of the basic relationship between positive and negative shifts in the economy and economic sentiment. It is useful in further analyses, which follow.

Indeed, the first of those analyses is included in Table 4.2. The results explore the possibility that a negativity bias is evident in responses not just to the retrospective egotropic question, but in other measures of economic sentiment as well. The existing literature distinguishes between four types of economic sentiment, based on two dimensions: (1) egotropic, relating to respondents' own income, versus sociotropic, focusing on the country generally; and (2) retrospective, related to past economic conditions, versus prospective, related to expectations of future conditions. (The literature is vast, but in political science see, e.g., Lewis-Beck and Stegmaier 2007; Kinder and Kiewiet

TABLE 4.2. *Effects of Changes in the Misery Index on Economic Sentiment, United States*

Dependent Variable	Independent Variables			F-Test of Equivalence
Retrospective Egotropic	Δ Misery Index$_t$ (Pos)	.470	(1.311)	1.81
	Δ Misery Index$_t$ (Neg)	−2.533	(1.354)	
Prospective Egotropic	Δ Misery Index$_t$ (Pos)	−.098	(1.015)	4.01*
	Δ Misery Index$_t$ (Neg)	−3.563*	(1.066)	
Retrospective Sociotropic	Δ Misery Index$_t$ (Pos)	−.497	(2.027)	1.38
	Δ Misery Index$_t$ (Neg)	−4.512*	(2.074)	
Prospective Sociotropic	Δ Misery Index$_t$ (Pos)	−.882	(1.365)	1.94
	Δ Misery Index$_t$ (Neg)	−4.079*	(1.420)	

* $p < .05$. Cells contain OLS regression coefficients, with standard errors in parentheses. Model includes monthly data from January 1978 to November 2010. Survey data are from the Michigan Consumer Sentiment Index survey, where the measure is % saying "better now" minus % saying "worse now" in response to the questions noted in the text. Full models are listed in Appendix Table B.4.1.

1981.) The archetypal questions drawn from the Michigan surveys are as follows:

Retrospective egotropic (as above): We are interested in how people are getting along financially these days. Would you say that you (and your family living there) are better off or worse off financially than you were a year ago?

Prospective egotropic: Now looking ahead – do you think that a year from now you (and your family living there) will be better off financially, or worse off, or just about the same as now?

Retrospective sociotropic: Would you say that at the present time business conditions are better or worse than they were a year ago?

Prospective sociotropic: And how about a year from now, do you expect that in the country as a whole business conditions will be better, or worse than they are at present, or just about the same?

These measures have been shown to have varying relationships with political variables, such as presidential or government approval. But no existing research considers the possibility that a negativity bias may be more or less evident in one or more of them. Table 4.2 includes results from the first such test, then. Only the coefficients for positive and negative changes in the misery index are shown in Table 4.2; full results are listed in Appendix Table B.4.1. Retrospective egotropic evaluations actually show weaker evidence of asymmetry than do prospective egotropic evaluations. Indeed, while coefficients point toward asymmetry in all four cases, prospective egotropic evaluations are the only ones for which the coefficient for negative changes is significantly different from the one for positive changes. However, for both sociotropic measures, the negative coefficient is statistically significant whereas the positive coefficient is not; indeed, in no case are positive changes in the misery index systematically related to economic sentiment. Asymmetry is thus not a peculiar result for retrospective egotropic evaluations – it is evident across a range of measures of economic sentiment, and perhaps most strongly where prospective egotropic evaluations are concerned, a possibility that we will test again later. In the meantime, it is clear that a one-unit negative shift in economic conditions has a strong negative impact on economic sentiment; a one-unit positive shift in economic conditions appears to have no impact at all.

Asymmetry in European Economic Sentiment

Is asymmetric responsiveness to the economy a U.S. phenomenon? Recall that we expect asymmetric responsiveness to be pervasive – in the United States, certainly, but also around the world. In the preceding chapter, we saw a simple extension of work on leader traits from the United States to Australia. In the case of economic sentiment, the net can be cast much wider.

Economic sentiment outside the United States is captured here using questions from the Joint Harmonized EU Programme of Business and Consumer Surveys, as follows:

Retrospective egotropic: How has the financial situation of your household changed over the last 12 months?

Prospective egotropic: How do you expect the financial position of your household to change over the next 12 months?

Retrospective sociotropic: How do you think the general economic situation in the country has changed over the past 12 months?

Prospective sociotropic: How do you expect the general economic situation in this country to develop over the next 12 months?

In each case, analyses rely on net measures (% positive –% negative). Monthly data are available from February 1985 to February 2011, although there is some variation across countries. Table 4.3 shows the seventeen countries for which data are available, alongside the first and last months included in the estimations that follow. (Data availability here is based not just on the ESI data but on the availability of economic measures as well.)

The model itself is identical to the model used for the United States in the preceding section, although in this case the analysis is based on a time-series cross-sectional dataset. Economic indicators are from the OECD.Stat database. Estimates are produced using GLS with fixed effects.[1] Full results are listed in

---

[1] Note that results are robust and change little using other estimators, e.g., OLS with panel-corrected standard errors.

TABLE 4.3. *Countries and Sample Sizes in TSCS Estimation*

Country	Sample Size	First Month	Last Month
Austria	184	1995m11	2011m2
Belgium	313	1985m2	2011m2
Czech Republic	193	1995m2	2011m2
Denmark	313	1985m2	2011m2
Finland	279	1987m12	2011m2
France	313	1985m2	2011m2
Germany	230	1992m1	2011m2
Greece	178	1985m5	2010m12
Hungary	228	1992m3	2011m2
Ireland	300	1985m2	2011m2
Italy	313	1985m2	2011m2
Netherlands	313	1985m2	2011m2
Poland	117	2001m6	2011m2
Portugal	296	1986m7	2011m2
Spain	296	1986m7	2011m2
Sweden	184	1995m11	2011m2
United Kingdom	313	1985m2	2011m2

Appendix Table B.4.2; Table 4.4 shows just the coefficients for positive and negative shifts in the misery index.

The relative impact of negative over positive shifts in the misery index is, in sum, roughly similar in European countries to what we found in the United States. In each case in Table 4.4, there is a stronger impact of negative shifts

TABLE 4.4. *Effects of Changes in the Misery Index on Economic Sentiment, EU*

Dependent Variable	Independent Variables		F-Test of Equivalence
Retrospective Egotropic	Δ Misery Index$_t$ (Pos)	$-.385$ (.232)	7.60*
	Δ Misery Index$_t$ (Neg)	-1.431^* (.233)	
Prospective Egotropic	Δ Misery Index$_t$ (Pos)	$-.317$ (.284)	6.49*
	Δ Misery Index$_t$ (Neg)	1.501^* (.286)	
Retrospective Sociotropic	Δ Misery Index$_t$ (Pos)	-1.098^* (.432)	.54
	Δ Misery Index$_t$ (Neg)	-1.616^* (.435)	
Prospective Sociotropic	Δ Misery Index$_t$ (Pos)	-1.126^* (.516)	.17
	Δ Misery Index$_t$ (Neg)	-1.476^* (.518)	

* $p < .05$. Cells contain GLS regression coefficients, with standard errors in parentheses, from a fixed-effects TSCS estimation. Model includes monthly data from January 1985 to February 2011. Survey data are from the Joint Harmonized EU Programme of Business and Consumer Surveys, relies on % saying "got a lot better" or "got a little better" minus % saying "got a little worse" or "got a lot worse" in response to questions noted in the text. Full models are listed in Appendix Table B.4.2.

TABLE 4.5. *Effects of Changes in the Misery Index on Economic Sentiment, EU, by Country*

	Δ Misery Index$_t$ (Pos)	Δ Misery Index$_t$ (Neg)
Austria	−.423	−1.544
Belgium	.302	−1.338
Czech Republic	−.784	−1.305
Denmark	.024	−3.564*
Finland	.364	−1.579*
France	−.767	−1.093
Germany	−.463	−.813
Greece	.025	−.442
Hungary	−.073	−1.510*
Ireland	−2.116	−2.525
Italy	.199	−3.092*
Netherlands	−3.189*	−.225
Poland	−1.413	−5.734*
Portugal	.008	−1.386
Spain	.425	−2.324*
Sweden	.218	−.875
United Kingdom	−.205	−2.084
Average	−.463	−1.849

* $p < .05$. Cells contain OLS regression coefficients, with standard errors in parentheses. Model includes all available monthly data from January 1985 to February 2011. Survey data are from the Joint Harmonized EU Programme of Business and Consumer Surveys, relies on % saying "got a lot better" or "got a little better" minus % saying "got a little worse" or "got a lot worse" in response to questions noted in the text. Full models are listed in Appendix Table B.4.3.

than of positive shifts, although while the difference between the positive and negative coefficients is statistically significant for both egotropic measures, it is not for the two sociotropic measures. Again, it is egotropic prospective evaluations for which we find the greatest asymmetry. Here, the impact of positive shifts in the misery index are negligible, while a one-point negative shift in the misery index is associated with an average 3.6-point decrease in economic sentiment.

TSCS estimates may mask differences across countries; moreover, it is difficult to distinguish the extent to which coefficients are driven by over-time variance within countries as opposed to cross-sectional variable across countries. Table 4.5 accordingly presents results on a country by country bases. Results are estimated using OLS, for each country independently. The full models are shown in Appendix Table B.4.3. Table 4.5 shows just the critical coefficients – those for positive and negative concurrent changes in the misery index. And because results do not change dramatically from one measure of economic sentiment to the other, Table 4.5 shows results from the measure that we started with, above – retrospective egotropic evaluations.

By-country estimates are much less robust than the TSCS estimates, to be sure. But sample sizes are also considerably smaller here, not just in comparison to the full TSCS estimation, but in comparison to the preceding U.S. estimates as well. (U.S. estimates rely on nearly 400 months' worth of data, whereas European countries range from 313 cases down to just 117, in Poland.) Even so, there is evidence of asymmetric responsiveness across most countries. In all countries, the coefficient for negative changes in the misery index is correctly negatively signed; coefficients for positive change are variously signed. In six countries, the negative coefficient is statistically significant, whereas the coefficient for positive changes is not. And in all but one country, the magnitude of the negative coefficient is greater than the magnitude of the positive coefficient (albeit to varying degrees – there are clear differences between the coefficients in Denmark, for instance, but less clearly in Ireland).

The Netherlands is the only real outlier here. In this case, it is positive changes that are systematically connected to economic sentiment. I cannot account for the difference in this country – it may be that there is no negativity bias; it may be that macroeconomic indicators do not adequately (or at least differently) capture the state of the national economy, or the parts of the national economy that matter most to economic sentiment. I suspect, given the pervasiveness of the negativity in other countries, that the latter options are more likely, but I do not investigate the issue further here.

With that one exception, however, there is relatively strong evidence here that economic sentiment responds asymmetrically to changes in the economy. This is true in the United States and across all but one EU country (including the EU countries for which data are available, that is). This has clear implications for macroeconomics, of course; the fact that there is a vast body of work connecting economic sentiment to voting behavior means that this has important implications in politics as well. This political link is investigated below.

Economic Sentiment and Government Approval

Trends in economic sentiment have political implications. This proposition requires little justification – it is as clear in daily newspapers as it is in the academic literature on political economy. There is a vast literature connecting economic attitudes to government popularity and voting (e.g., Happy 1989; Lewis-Beck 1988; MacKuen et al. 1992; Price and Sanders 1993; Nadeau et al. 1994, 1996; Clarke and Stewart 1995; Sanders 1996, 1999) and to public preferences for policy as well (e.g., Durr 1993; Stevenson 2001).

There is also a small literature exploring asymmetries in these relationships. The political science literature has been motivated in large part by the observation in the *American Voter* that "changes in the party balance are induced primarily by negative rather than positive attitudes toward the party controlling the executive branch" (Campbell et al. 1960: 554). Following this observation,

Bloom and Price (1975) were among the first to explore the possibility that negative economic circumstances mattered to congressional election outcomes more than did positive economic circumstances – their results suggested that economic expansions had no impact on the vote, but economic contractions did – and Claggett's (1986) "re-examination" confirms their findings with a larger body of data. Similar asymmetries have been found in work on presidential elections. Tufte's (1978) analysis of macroeconomics and vote shares points to a negativity bias (in plots at least; he did not model the asymmetry): Mueller (1973) finds that rising unemployment (negatively) affects presidential popularity, whereas falling unemployment has no effect.[2] (Also see Lanoue 1987; Nannestad and Paldam 1997.)[3]

Discussions of asymmetry in the impact of positive and negative shifts in the economy on presidents have tended to focus on relatively short periods of time and often on specific elections. It is possible to examine asymmetries using much more comprehensive bodies of data, however; this section thus provides new and much more comprehensive analyses of asymmetries in the relationship between the economy and government approval. The first analyses rely on monthly time-series of both economic sentiment and U.S. presidential approval. Approval ratings are drawn from Gallup polls, based on the following question, "Do you approve or disapprove of the way [first & last name] is handling his job as President?," where a net approval measure is the percent of respondents approving minus the percent of respondents disapproving.[4] Approval is graphed alongside (prospective sociotropic) economic sentiment (with both series lowess-smoothed using bandwidth .02) in Figure 4.2. There is clearly a relationship between the two, although it is far from perfect. The figure illustrates what we already know about presidential approval, then: the economy matters, but not exclusively. Consider the drop in economic sentiment and the concurrent rise in presidential approval following 9-11, for instance, or the rises in approval that regularly follow an election, regardless of economic sentiment (following 2008 in particular).

It is of course possible to examine the relationship between these two series in a more detailed way, and test for an asymmetric relationship, using a slightly

---

[2] Note that there are some contrary findings as well. Headrick and Lanoue (1991; following in part on Norpoth 1987) do not find strong evidence of an asymmetric relationship in the United Kingdom, although they suggest that this may be the function of the period under study (which included mainly negative economic trends). This is discussed in more detail later in the chapter.

[3] It is notable that, using individual-level data from a number of European countries, Lewis-Beck (1988) finds no evidence of a greater effect of negative economic views than positive economic views. The analysis relies on two questions dealing with retrospective and prospective views of the government's economic policies, however, and may thus confuse judgments of government with economic assessments.

[4] Data are drawn from the compilation of Gallup results available at http://www.presidency.ucsb.edu.

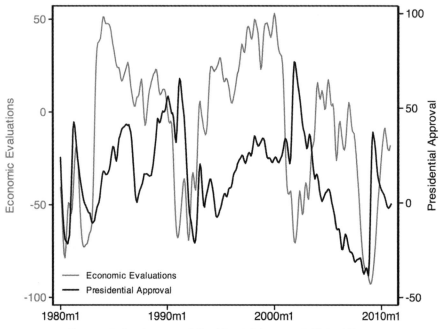

FIGURE 4.2. Economic Sentiment and Presidential Approval, United States

adjusted version of the model of economic sentiment used earlier, in which sentiment is moved to the right-hand side of the model and the dependent variable is now presidential approval:

$$\Delta \text{Approval}_t = \alpha_0 + \beta_1 \Delta \text{Sentiment}_t + \beta_2 (\text{Approval}_{t-1} + \beta_3 \text{Sentiment}_{t-1})$$
$$+ \delta_1 \text{Cycle}_t + \varepsilon_t \qquad (4.2)$$

Note that the model also includes measures that capture the electoral cycle ($\delta_1 \text{Cycle}_t$). Work on presidential approval has sometimes included variables capturing a "presidential honeymoon" (e.g., Clarke and Stewart 1996; Brody 1991; Keech 1982); work on other countries has identified cyclical trends in government popularity as well (e.g., Johnston 1999). Where the current case is concerned, it may be an individual's time in the presidency that matters to the gradual decay in approval; alternatively it may be the length of a political party's tenure in the presidency. (That is, it may be that George H. W. Bush has lower approval to start because he is following Ronald Reagan, another Republican, or it may be that Bush starts with the same new-president advantage as Reagan did.) One need not choose one or the other here – instead, the model includes count variables capturing the number of months that a president has been in office and the number of months that his party has held the presidency. Each starts at zero and counts upward monthly. In both cases, variables are included

TABLE 4.6. *Economic Sentiment and Presidential Approval, United States*

	DV: Δ US Presidential Approval$_t$			
	Retrospective Egotropic	Prospective Egotropic	Retrospective Sociotropic	Prospective Sociotropic
Δ Sentiment$_t$ (Pos)	.178 (.100)	.157 (.129)	.056 (.085)	−.000 (.095)
Δ Sentiment$_t$ (Neg)	.324* (.108)	.247* (.124)	.075 (.080)	.279* (.103)

* $p < .05$. Cells contain OLS regression coefficients, with standard errors in parentheses.

in their linear and quadratic forms to allow for the possibility of a nonlinear trend.

Full results are included in Appendix Table B.4.4. Where time is concerned, it appears to be an individual's time in the presidency that matters most – those time variables are negatively signed and statistically significant, as expected. Where current changes in approval are concerned, results point to the significance of negative rather than positive shifts in economic sentiment. These most critical results are summarized in Table 4.6.

The table shows the coefficients for positive and negative changes in economic sentiment, testing each of the four possibilities where measures of sentiment are concerned. In each case, the impact of negative changes is greater than the impact of positive changes, although for retrospective sociotropic sentiment neither is statistically significant. In each of the other cases, however, only the negative shifts are statistically significant. Asymmetries in reactions to macroeconomic trends have real-world political implications.

Do the same results obtain outside the United Stastes? Figure 4.3 shows equivalent time series data for the United Kingdom (another country for which government approval measures are available over an extended period of time). The measure of economic expectations is the sociotropic prospective question from the ESI data used earlier; Government Approval is based on responses to the MORI question, "Are you satisfied or dissatisfied with the way the Government is running the country?" The measure shown here takes the percent of respondents saying "satisfied" minus the percent of respondents saying "dissatisfied." There is a clear relationship between economic sentiment and government approval. Whether that relationship is asymmetric is the focus of analyses in Table 4.7.

Results here are based on a replication of the model of U.S. presidential approval, although in this case the focus is the UK government. Variables capturing the impact of the electoral cycle are the same, although in this case it appears to be the length of each Government that matters rather than the length of the party's control of the Government. (Full results are included in Appendix Table B.4.4). In Table 4.7, we see the impact of each of the four different types of economic sentiment on Government approval. For three of the four evaluations, negative shifts in sentiment seem to matter

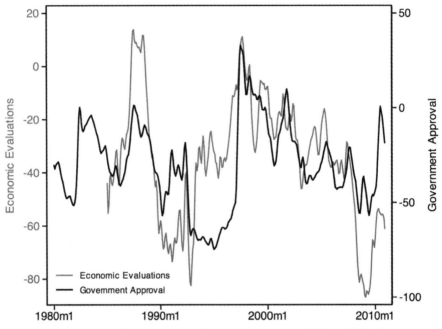

FIGURE 4.3. Economic Sentiment and Government Approval, United Kingdom

more to government approval. The case is clearest for prospective egotropic evaluations, where negative shifts are significantly different from positive ones; the other two cases point in the expected direction, but results are less robust.

As in the United States, retrospective sociotropic evaluations are an outlier in the United Kingdom; indeed, there appears to be a positivity rather than a negativity bias in this case. The difference may well be a product of the well-recognized endogeneity in retrospective economic evaluations (see, e.g., Duch et al. 2000; Wlezien et al. 1997; Evans and Andersen 2006). Respondents who favor the current government are more likely to view recent economic trends through rose-colored glasses. Economic evaluations are in this

TABLE 4.7. *Economic Sentiment and Government Approval, United Kingdom*

	DV: Δ UK Government Approval$_t$			
	Retrospective Egotropic	Prospective Egotropic	Retrospective Sociotropic	Prospective Sociotropic
Δ Sentiment$_t$ (Pos)	.181 (.202)	.180 (.175)	.400* (.113)	.156 (.095)
Δ Sentiment$_t$ (Neg)	.273 (.166)	.323* (.158)	.117 (.118)	.199* (.097)

* $p < .05$. Cells contain OLS regression coefficients, with standard errors in parentheses.

case not a driver of government approval, then, but a partial reflection of it. One consequence here appears to be the disappearance of a negativity bias. The situation is different for other economic evaluations, however. Egotropic evaluations, and perhaps prospective sociotropic evaluations as well, point toward the same kind of negativity bias in government approval as we have already seen for evaluations themselves.

Note that the asymmetries revealed in Tables 4.6 and 4.7 serve to compound the consequences of a negativity bias in economic perceptions. Negative changes in the economy have a greater impact on evaluations of the economy than do positive changes, so economic evaluations are themselves already more responsive to negative change. Negative changes in those evaluations (excluding retrospecitve sociotropic evaluations, that is) then appear to be more systematically connected to changes in presidential/government approval.

Asymmetric Reactions to Change, across Levels

Preceding analyses have revealed asymmetric reactions to short-term negative versus positive change in both economic indicators and economic sentiment. One of the underlying assumptions of those models has been that the magnitude of the asymmetry is constant across varying levels of the independent variables. Put more specifically, estimates of asymmetric reactions to changes in unemployment, for instance, have assumed that reactions to negative or positive changes in the unemployment rate are the same regardless of the current level of unemployment.

This assumption seems questionable. Consider the following two possibilities. In the first, the unemployment rate shifts upward from 4.0 percent to 4.3 percent; in the second, the unemployment rate shifts upward from 12.0 percent to 12.3 percent. The increase in both cases is .3 percent. Preceding analyses suggest that the .3 percent increase has a greater impact on attitudes than would a .3 percent decrease, to be sure. But does a .3 percent increase (or decrease) have the same impact regardless of where unemployment currently stands? Are public attitudes differently affected by an upward shift from 4.0 percent to 4.3 percent, as opposed to 12.0 percent to 12.3 percent?

It seems likely that reactions to short-term changes in economic indicators are conditional on the current levels of those indicators. When unemployment is high, increases may affect attitudes less – unemployment is already high, after all, and people are already concerned. When unemployment is comparatively low, in contrast, short-term increases may matter a great deal. It is possible to examine this possibility empirically, through an adjustment of the ECMs estimated earlier. To do so, I return to models of economic sentiment, with the following adjustment:

$$\Delta \, \text{Sentiment}_t = \alpha_0 + \beta_1 \Delta \, \text{Economy}_t + \beta_2 (\text{Sentiment}_{t-1} + \beta_3 \text{Economy}_{t-1})$$
$$+ \beta_4 \Delta \, \text{Economy}_t \, {}^* \text{Economy}_{t-1} + \varepsilon_t, \qquad (4.3)$$

where β_4 captures the possibility that the impact of the current month's changes in economic indicators are mediated by the last month's levels in those indicators.

I repeat this model for each of the four economic sentiment variables (egotropic/sociotropic, retrospective/prospective). The U.S. and EU data are for these estimations combined – that is, the sentiment variable is drawn from the Michigan Consumer Surveys for the United States and the Joint Harmonized EU Programme of Business and Consumer Surveys for all other countries. While the two measures have quite different levels, the over-time variance in each is very similar (and the difference in levels is accounted for in the fixed-effects GLS estimation).[5] And the economy is captured here not through the misery index, but by returning to unemployment and inflation separately. This is because whereas unemployment provides an ideal test of this hypothesis, inflation does not. For the former, the story is relatively clear: the impact of positive and negative changes in unemployment should vary systematically alongside unemployment rates; when unemployment is low, negative shifts should matter a great deal; when unemployment is high, negative shifts may matter less. Whereas the unemployment rate captures the level of unemployment at a given time, however, inflation is by definition expressed as a percentage point change. With inflation, we are never really talking about levels, but rather always about degrees of change (alongside increases or decreases in those degrees of change). The tests that follow accordingly focus on unemployment, although they do so while controlling for both lagged levels of inflation and current changes – positive and negative separately, allowing for the asymmetric effects of inflation demonstrated earlier.

Where unemployment is concerned, the potentially moderating effect of levels of unemployment is tested using four different specifications:

1. A first model simply interacts the standard interval-level unemployment measure with current changes in unemployment.
2. A second model then tests for the possibility that it is not the absolute unemployment rate that matters so much as whether that rate is higher or lower than is typical in a given country; 10 percent unemployment may matter less (that is, moderate the negativity impact less) in Greece than in Sweden, for instance. In this case, the unemployment rate for each country is both mean-centered and divided by its standard error.
3. A third model then allows for (one type of) a nonlinear moderating impact of unemployment levels. In this case, the unemployment rate is transformed into three categories: (-1) the lowest quartile for unemployment levels in a given country, (0) the interquartile range in unemployment levels for that country, and $(+1)$ the highest quartile for unemployment in that country. This model thus allows for the possibility

---

[5] For the U.S. measure, the variance is 33; for the EU measure, it is 38.

that there are significant differences in the negativity bias when levels of unemployment are especially low or especially high, relative to the average levels of unemployment in each country. Note that this model includes the threefold specification of unemployment as a linear variable; in so doing, it constrains the difference between the low-quartile and interquartile range to be the same as the difference between the interquartile and high-quartile. That is, there is an assumed linear effect of moving from low-quartile, to interquartile, to high-tercile categories.

4. A fourth model relaxes this linear assumption by interacting positive and negative changes with two binary variables each, one for low-quartile levels of unemployment and the other for high-quartile levels of unemployment.

Results for all models are included in Appendix Table B.4.5. *All* results point in the same direction, namely to a shifting importance of positive and/or negative changes across varying levels of unemployment. This is the case across all four measures of economic sentiment as well. In each case, when the economy is doing badly, negative changes in unemployment appear to matter less and positive changes in unemployment appear to matter more.

Results for the models using standardized levels of unemployment (Model 2) are stronger than models using absolute levels (Model 1), insofar as they produce somewhat more robust estimates of the direct and interacted effects of concurrent changes in unemployment. In both Models 1 and 2, however, the interactions tend to be insignificant. (This is partly a consequence of collinearity, of course.) The models relying on a threefold specification of unemployment levels produce much more significant effects. Allowing for nonlinearity in Model 4 makes no real difference to results – indeed, most coefficients suggest that the moderating effect of moving from low-quartile, to interquartile, to high-quartile unemployment levels is linear.[6]

Table 4.8 accordingly focuses just on the results from Model 3. The table shows four coefficients from each model. The first column of coefficients shows the estimated the direct effects of positive and negative changes in unemployment. Because the three-category unemployment variables used in interactions is coded -1, 0, $+1$, the coefficients for direct effects capture the impact of changes in unemployment when levels are in the interquartile range. As we have seen earlier, the impact of negative changes is higher than the impact of positive changes, although here there is once exception: prospective sociotropic expectations show slightly stronger effects for positive changes than for negative ones. The difference between the coefficients is not statistically significant,

---

[6] Consider results for both sociotropic evaluations, for instance, where coefficients for low-quartile and high-quartile interactions are nearly mirror images of each other. Results for egotropic measures are noisier, admittedly, but the impact of economic conditions on these measures is consistently less robust in any case.

TABLE 4.8. *Asymmetric Responsiveness across Varying Levels of Unemployment, United States and EU*

Dependent Variable	Independent Variables	Direct Effect		Interaction with Levels of Un$_{t-1}$	
Retrospective Egotropic	Δ Un$_t$ (Pos)	.022	(.713)	−1.578	(.912)
	Δ Un$_t$ (Neg)	−3.752*	(.567)	1.434*	(.679)
Prospective Egotropic	Δ Un$_t$ (Pos)	−.134	(.822)	−.774	(1.051)
	Δ Un$_t$ (Neg)	−2.895*	(.651)	2.119*	(.783)
Retrospective Sociotropic	Δ Un$_t$ (Pos)	−2.900*	(1.301)	−4.587*	(1.637)
	Δ Un$_t$ (Neg)	−6.418*	(1.028)	5.272*	(1.219)
Prospective Sociotropic	Δ Un$_t$ (Pos)	−3.511*	(1.476)	−3.876*	(1.867)
	Δ Un$_t$ (Neg)	−1.835	(1.148)	2.908*	(1.392)

* $p < .05$. Cells contain GLS regression coefficients with standard errors in parentheses. Full models are listed in Appendix Table B.4.5 (where these results are drawn from Model 3).

however, and the interactions suggest that at low levels of unemployment, the negativity bias is readily apparent in this measure as well.

To understand how the negativity bias shifts across levels of unemployment, we need to take into account the coefficients in the final column of Table 4.8. For the egotropic measures of economic sentiment, only the coefficients for negative changes are significant. Each is positive, suggesting that the (negative) impact of negative changes in unemployment is reduced as unemployment levels worsen. Consider the results for retrospective egotropic assessments, for instance: when unemployment is low, the impact of negative changes in unemployment is $-3.752 - 1.434 = -5.186$; when unemployment is high, the impact is just $-3.752 + 1.434 = -2.318$. When the economic climate is negative, negative changes matter less.

Similar shifts are evident across all measures in Table 4.8, and for both sociotropic measures there are statistically significant shifts in the impact of positive changes as well. (Note that the interactions for positive changes are correctly signed in the egotropic models, just not statistically significant.) Figure 4.4 makes clearer the differential impact of negative versus positive changes in unemployment, across low to high unemployment levels. The figure is based on results for retrospective sociotropic economic sentiment – the measure that is most affected by unemployment rates. The figure shows the estimated impact of a one-unit shift in unemployment rates, positive or negative, across lagged levels of unemployment. The dark bars show the overall trend in the estimated effects for positive and negative changes; the estimated standard error is shown with capped bars at each of the low-quartile, interquartile, and high-quartile unemployment levels. Although models produce negative coefficients for unemployment change (where increases in unemployment lead to decreases in economic sentiment), for the sake of this figure the sign

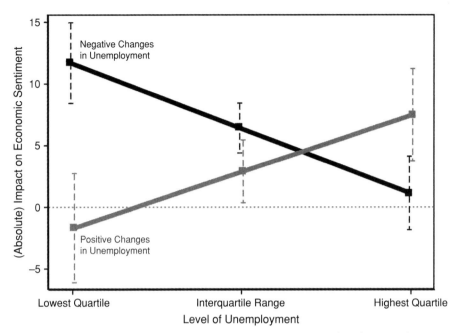

FIGURE 4.4. Asymmetric Responsiveness across Varying Levels of Unemployment, United States and EU

of the coefficients is reversed – this way, larger impacts are higher on the y-axis.

Results point to the possibility that the negativity bias readily evident in many of the preceding results is an average of what actually are different degrees of asymmetry, across varying levels of positive or negative information environments (in this case, lower or higher levels of unemployment). When unemployment is low, the gap between the impact of negative versus positive information is at its highest. It is at this point that negative changes have quite a marked impact on attitudes, whereas positive changes have no impact at all. As unemployment increases, however, the gap between the impact of negative and positive changes narrows. At high levels of unemployment, monthly increases in unemployment matter less than they do at low levels of unemployment. Indeed, when unemployment is high, negative changes matter very little. Positive changes in unemployment matter much more, however.

It is interesting that the gap between positive and negative changes when unemployment levels are high is not as great as the gap between them when unemployment levels are low.[7] The positivity bias during bad periods does not appear to be as great as the negativity bias during good periods, at least

---

[7] Note that this is not a consequence of the assumption of a linear interactive effect, that is, of reliance on results in Model 3 rather than Model 4. See Appendix Table A.4.5.

in the data investigated here. I do not want to put too much emphasis on these point estimates; there may be improvements to be made in the way the moderating effect of unemployment is specified, and in the inclusion of other measures of economic change (varying across levels of economic success). For the time being, however, models in Table 4.8 point to a fact that is critical to understanding negativity in modern politics (and indeed elsewhere as well). The narrower, more cautious interpretation is as follows: changes in economic indicators matter differently across levels of those indicators; that is, changes in unemployment are reacted to based in part on current levels. The end result here is that the gap in the impact of negative versus positive change in unemployment is greatest when unemployment is comparatively low. But there is a broader, more ambitious interpretation as well: a significant negativity bias is in all likelihood at least partly dependent on an information environment that is *not* predominantly negative.

Endlessly Negative?

Chapter 3 demonstrated a negativity bias in the way individuals connect traits to overall assessments of candidates. Results illustrated the tendency for negative information to weigh more heavily than positive information does in our assessments of political candidates. The current chapter has shown essentially the same dynamic, on a different topic, and using a very different body of data. In short, the chapter has shown that aggregate-level public opinion data on the state of the economy is affected more by short-term negative changes in the economy than by similar positive changes. This is not just true in the United States – it is true across sixteen of seventeen European countries (both western and eastern). These cross-national results lend support to the idea that a negativity bias is not (just) cultural – it may be (partly) biological. From the United States to Finland, Poland, and Spain, there is evidence that negative information has a greater impact on public opinion than does positive information.

Results presented earlier also suggest that these asymmetries may be magnified as they move from the economy to politics. An asymmetry is apparent not just in the connection between economic indicators and economic sentiment, but between economic sentiment and government approval. In both the United States and the United Kingdom, we have seen both that economic sentiment is affected more by downward than by upward change in the economy, and we have seen that government approval is more affected by downward than by upward change in economic sentiment. These compounding asymmetries mean that negative changes in the economy may have quite profound political consequences, even as equivalent positive changes matter very little. And compounding asymmetries are likely not exclusive to the economic domain. For instance, given the mass media's focus on negative information (see the following chapter), our tendency to react more strongly to negative information in the real world is enhanced by the propensity for media to provide information that is already biased toward the negative.

That said, the magnitude of the negativity bias changes over time. When the economy is doing comparatively well, the impact of negative change seems to be particularly strong. When the economy is doing poorly, however, the gap in the impact of negative versus positive change narrows. In this more negative environment, we react somewhat less to negative change and somewhat more to positive change. Existing levels mediate the impact of changes in the economy.

Note that these findings fit well with "frequency-weight" theories of impression formation (Skowronski and Carlston 1989), as well as theories of loss aversion in economics. In both cases, expectations play a critical role in conditioning the relative impact of positive and negative information. In short, these theories suggest that we give greater weight to information further from our expectations, and it is the tendency to expect mildly positive information that produces stronger reactions to negative information. Results in this chapter have shown that existing levels of information clearly condition responses to change. They also have illustrated the potential for the negativity bias to disappear entirely under certain conditions, namely when the balance of information is already predominantly negative. A negativity bias may be dependent on an information environment, which is, on balance, slightly positive.

These results are absolutely critical. We are not in an endless negative spiral in part because a negative bias depends on a mildly positive information environment, and when the information environment becomes more negative, the negativity bias decreases (or even disappears). This idea is discussed further in the concluding chapter. For now, the analysis turns to media content, both for further evidence of the negativity bias and for additional information on the mildly positive balance of information that produces it.

5

Media Content

The real news is bad news.

– Marshall McLuhan

Mass media content is written by people and for people, and should thus exhibit the same kinds of biases as have been seen in Chapters 3 and 4. Just as people show asymmetric responsiveness to negative versus positive information, so too should mass media.

Making the case for asymmetries in media content is, admittedly, relatively easy. Indeed, it is not clear that a case needs to be made at all. Mass media have a widespread and well-earned reputation for focusing on the negative. A literature review that follows makes clear just how widespread this view is. There is near-universal agreement that media content leans toward the negative.

There is however relatively little work that provides a good sense, empirically speaking, of just how biased toward the negative media are. What exactly is the difference between the distribution of positive versus negative information in media and the distribution of positive versus negative information in the real world? That is the central question addressed in this chapter. That media exhibit a negativity bias is relatively clear; exploring and documenting the extent of that bias is the aim here.

The fact that we do not already have a good sense for the magnitude of the negativity bias is most likely a product of a few impediments, namely, inadequate measures of both the real-world and media content. Adequate measures tend to be hard to come by. This chapter nevertheless presents some efforts to capture both the distribution of information in the real world and in media content. The analytical portion of the chapter begins with an analysis of the relationship between news and trends in crime, using a unique case study: crime news content and actual crime rates in Bloomington, Illinois, one of the few police jurisdictions to keep (and make available) all crime reports over an extended period (1991 to the present). Access to crime reports from the Bloomington PD, and a database of all crime stories in the Bloomington *Pantagraph*, allows for a relatively rare, direct comparison of actual crime and crime reporting. The chapter then turns to a somewhat broader approach. Taking advantage of automated coding techniques, the chapter explores the relationship between economic news and macroeconomic indicators, drawing on 74,000 content-analyzed economic news stories in the United States, United Kingdom, and Canada. Both economic and crime news exhibit the same basic dynamic: a much greater reaction to negative shifts than to positive shifts. Media content, in short, reacts to information in roughly the same way as do humans.

Negativity in Media Content

Clearly, mass media news content is largely negative. There are many accounts and discussions of this fact; one of the best known is Patterson's *Out of Order*. The book focuses on the mass media's increasing power in the U.S. political process, but in describing that role it provides a particularly cogent account of the tendency for mass media to be both sensationalist and negative in their orientation toward politics. Patterson portrays the biases in media reports not just as a consequence of heightened attention to negative information, but rather as a product of an increasingly hostile relationship between journalists and politicians. Post-Watergate journalism, Patterson suggests, is imbued with the sense that most politicians lie most of the time – even though there are good reasons to believe that this is not the case. Journalists' attitudes, and the resulting biases in story selection and framing, obstruct rather than enhance the relationship between politicians and publics. The public is accordingly less informed, and less interested, than they might otherwise be. Problems with political engagement in the United States are partly due to the fact that "[t]he press sends the wrong message" (14).

Farnsworth and Lichter's accumulated work on U.S. election campaigns (e.g., 2007) points toward similar issues. The authors find a "general pattern of negativism," and indeed increasing levels of negativity, in the tone of election-period U.S. television news content from 1988 to 2004. Importantly, those arenas over which candidates have more control such as interviews, speeches, and ads are more positive than are regular news stories. This suggests that the negativity bias is not a supply-side issue – it is not that candidates and parties release only negative information – but rather a demand-side issue: journalists seek out and publish critical/negative accounts. Like Patterson, Farnsworth and Lichter point toward public cynicism and disengagement as likely by-products of negativity in media content. The following captures the tone of the book quite nicely: "Journalists have descended into a mode of reporting that is notable for its negativity, for its near-silencing of the candidates themselves, and for its obsessive pursuit of the trivial.... America's elections, its central marketplace of ideas, is being filled by mainstream media with junk food that slowly rots our political discourse" (186).

Similar themes are evident in a wide range of work that focuses more closely on journalistic norms, or the sociology of journalism. Cappella and Hall-Jamieson's (1997) *Spiral of Cynicism* echoes many of the criticisms of journalists apparent in Patterson's work. Sabato's (1991) *Feeding Frenzy* similarly focuses on the post-Watergate tendency in American mass media to over-magnify certain events and to provide more cynical and contentious coverage of politics. Fallows's (1996) *Breaking the News* is one example of a number of books written by journalists lamenting both the increasing negativity in U.S. news content and the resulting damage to the quality of public debate on major political issues.

These are just a few examples of the considerable body of literature discussing negativity in news content, and empirical evidence of the trend abounds. Consider Miller, Goldberg, and Erbring's (1979) coding of 1974 newspaper content, for instance, suggesting that 31 percent of articles include criticism whereas just 6 percent include praise. Benoit et al. (2005) examine *New York Times'* coverage of presidential campaigns from 1952 to 2000 and find that 57 percent of coverage was negative whereas only 39 percent was positive – and this was true in spite of the fact that most candidate messages (e.g., television spots, debates) were positive. Similar results are evident in Just et al.'s (1996) analysis of 1992 election coverage. There exists, in short, a wide body of work showing the relatively high proportion of news content that is both sensationalistic (e.g., Davie and Lee 1995; Harmon 1989; Hofstetter and Dozier 1986; Ryu 1982) and negative (in addition to the work already cited, see, e.g., Diamond 1978; Kerbel 1995; Lichter and Noyes 1995; Niven 2000; Robinson and Levy 1985; Tidmarch 1985).

Much of this work echoes accounts of negativity evident in work by Patterson or Farnsworth and Lichter. There are other potential explanations as well, however. For instance, Altheide (1997; see also Altheide and Snow 1979, 1991) offers a quite different, but largely parallel, account of the importance of negativity and sensationalism in modern news content. He argues that mass media increasingly rely on "problem frames" and a discourse of fear, and that these emphases have led to a popular and political culture in the United States in which fear is pervasive. Drawing in part on work by Marshall McLuhan, Altheide argues that news media tend to rely on a limited number of "formats," which makes easier the production (and assimilation) of news; and that the formats used are defined in part by the nature of the communications medium through which information is transmitted. Where U.S. news content is concerned, commercial imperatives encourage television journalists to present news in a more entertainment-oriented format, and one way in which to achieve this is to focus on the "problem frame," and particularly on fear, which makes news content seem both more contentious and more interesting. (On the melding of news and entertainment, see also work by Neil Postman.) While many of the preceding authors view negativity in news content largely as a product of decisions made by journalists, Altheide emphasizes the importance of communications mediums (and commercialism).

Both perspectives are captured in Hallin's (1992) work on "sound bite news," in which he finds that the average length of a sound bite on network news declined, from 1968 through 1988, from forty-three to nine seconds. The shift is striking and serves for Hallin as an opportunity to examine changes in news formats over the twenty-year period. The words of politicians (and sources more generally) no longer dominate news stories; rather, their words are chopped up and reshuffled to produce a narrative determined not by the source, but by the journalist. This more journalist-determined account of daily affairs is a product of (a) advances in technical expertise and capacity, (b) a post-Watergate, more actively critical journalistic aesthetic, and (c) increasing commercialism and the resulting need to generate and keep audiences. Importantly, each factor does not just contribute to a reduction in the length of sound bites – it also encourages criticism and negativity (for roughly the same reasons as those outlined earlier). Hallin's account thus combines journalist-, medium- and economic-centered accounts of negativity in media content. It makes clear that technical and professional factors have been contributing to an increasing focus on negative information in news content.

Hallin's multisource account of the nature of new content is also echoed in the vast body of work on media gatekeeping, discussed in some detail in Chapter 2. There is, in sum, a considerable body of evidence suggesting that media tend to exhibit a negativity bias, and a correspondingly broad set of hypotheses about why this is the case. Rather little of this work suggests the possibility that is the focus here, however, namely the human behavioral tendency to prioritize negative over positive information. (There are two notable exceptions, however: Shoemaker 1996a and Ju 2008). But note that none of the aforementioned hypotheses precludes the possibility that media negativity is driven by this peculiarity in human behavior; indeed, some of those hypotheses may depend on it.

For instance, the underlying assumption in work emphasizing the role of competition in driving up media negativity is that media outlets attract audiences more easily with negative content. The same is true for work emphasizing the impact of media formats and entertainment. When there is a pressure to present news in a more entertaining, easily accessible, and more widely attractive way, media are well served by leaning more strongly toward negative themes. Work by Altheide and colleagues in particular thus seems to be heavily dependent on the notion that people, for one reason or another, are more easily interested in negative information.

Critiques of the post-Watergate state of American journalism by Patterson, Farnsworth and Lichter, and others are not very different in this regard. This work not only suggests that negativity seems to produce an audience; it points to a paradigmatic change in the nature of political journalism as a consequence of the Vietnam War and Watergate – that is, as a consequence of one or two negative events. Patterson's work is particularly valuable in making this argument. The thrust of his work is that, even as politicians are regularly honest and typically seek to fulfill campaign promises, journalists remain focused on cynical interpretations and negative information. Journalistic practices, Patterson (and many others) argues, seem to have shifted permanently following several scandals in the 1970s. In essence, the entire practice of journalism reacted asymmetrically to negative information. A few scandals have led to a deeply suspicious and pessimistic approach to political reporting, and no amount of positive information seems able to undo the damage.

The notion that institutions may react to information asymmetrically, just like the humans that create and populate those institutions, is taken up in later chapters. For now, what is most critical is that while there is a considerable body of work suggesting a negativity bias, we do not have an especially clear sense for just how large that negativity bias is. Exploring the magnitude of the negativity bias in media content is the focus of the remainder of this chapter.

Crime Reporting in Bloomington, IL

The phrase "if it bleeds, it leads" is both a well-known and accurate description of television news content, particularly where crime news is concerned. Much of the work discussed in the preceding section focuses mainly on news in the context of election campaigns. But the same tendencies are clearly evident in non-campaign periods as well, across a wide range of politically relevant issues.

Here I explore directly the relationship between crime rates and crime reporting. The existing body of work on the subject already suggests both (a) a weak link between crime rates and the frequency of crime stories, and (b) a tendency to give more coverage to crimes that are more violent. Garofalo's (1981) literature review provides a nice summary of work up to the late 1970s; Sacco's (1995) review provides a more recent account. Most of the existing findings are illustrated by Graber's (1980) study of crime rates and reporting in Chicago in 1976, however. Among the most interesting of Graber's findings is the fact that while murders accounted for .2 percent of all crimes in the 1976 police index, they received 26.2 percent of crime mentions in the *Chicago Tribune*; and while nonviolent crimes made up 47 percent of police statistics, they were just 4 percent of mentions in the *Tribune*. Sheley and Ashkins (1981) find a similar disjuncture in the proportions of violent and nonviolent crime, looking at New Orleans media at about the same time.

The disjuncture between crime rates and crime reporting is evident not just in the cross-sectional gaps between coverage of violent and nonviolent crimes, but in longitudinal trends in crime, media, and opinion. Lowry et al. (2003) find that American public concern about crime is linked with the volume of media coverage, and not necessarily the actual crime rate. Barlow et al. (1995) suggest that coverage of crime in the United States increases during periods of high unemployment, even when the crime rate does not; their analysis fits well with Fishman's (1978) argument that the reporting of crime waves may be more about politics and ideology than about actual crime rates. Where the current analyses are concerned, the important finding in this longitudinal work is simply that there are marked gaps between crime rates and crime reports.

What accounts for these gaps? The most common difference between real-world crime and media crime reports is the latter's emphasis on the more negative crimes. Crimes tend not to be positive, of course, but they do vary in their degree of negativity or sensationalism, and existing work suggests a selection mechanism for crime that is roughly similar to what we have discussed where politics is concerned – namely, that more negative material gets more coverage. This means not just that violent crime gets more coverage than nonviolent crime; the more *violent* the crime, and/or the more victims, the more coverage. (See, e.g., Chermak and Chapman 2007; Johnstone et al. 1994; Chermak 1994.)

These findings are clearly relevant to the current study, in that they both (a) demonstrate a negativity bias in story selection and (b) do so in a domain in which, unlike political news, cynical journalists are less likely to be the driving factor. The latter is particularly important to the argument that a negativity bias in media is linked to negativity biases in human behavior more generally, and we will return to it in more detail at the end of the chapter. In the meantime, this section focuses on a new and more comprehensive explication of the relationship between reality and media content on crime.

The focus is on Bloomington, Illinois, a city that is remarkable here because of the availability of both crime rates and newspaper content over an extended period. The following analyses of crime reporting in Bloomington are based on a combination of two databases. The first is kept by the Bloomington Police Department (BPD). The BPD was relatively early in its shift to an electronic database. The database I was provided includes all reported incidents from January 1, 2002 to April 30, 2010 – 104,332 incidents over that 3,042-day period, and all incidents in the dataset are labeled by offense codes and the accompanying offense descriptions. The second database includes all stories dealing with crime in the local newspaper, the *Bloomington Pantagraph*. Stories were downloaded from the Nexis full-text index, from January 2005 (the first year for which complete data from the *Pantagraph* is available) to April 2010. Stories were selected based on Nexis-assigned topic codes – any story with a crime-related topic code as a "major" theme was included.[1] The resulting database includes 2,077 crime stories.

---

[1] Information on Lexis-Nexis topic codes is available at lexisnexis.com.

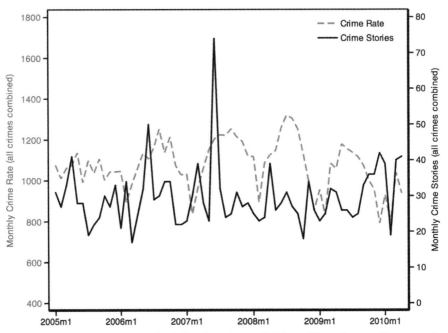

FIGURE 5.1. Crime Rates and Media Coverage of Crime, Bloomington *Pantagraph*, 2005–2009

Both incidents and stories were categorized into subtopics. For newspaper stories, subtopics were assigned using a combination of existing Nexis topic codes and full-text searches for specific keywords (e.g., murder). All full-text searches were conducted using Lexicoder, relatively simple Java-based, multi-platform software designed for the automated content analysis of text (www.lexicoder.com). Incidents from the BPD database were assigned based on the existing offense descriptions.

Analyses that follow rely on just two broad categories of offenses: (1) violent crime, including murder, assault, arson, weapons-related, sexual (excluding prostitution), kidnapping, and bomb threats; and (2) nonviolent crime, including all remaining offenses, such as robbery, civil, fraud, trespassing, substance, property, and so on. Figure 5.1 sets out the basic data – the total number of offenses and the total number of stories, monthly, from 2005 to 2010.[2] The figure shows that the crime rate in Bloomington was relatively steady over the five-year period, hovering at about 1,000 incidents per month. Crime reporting also remained relatively steady, at roughly thirty stories per month. There

---

[2] Note that Stories on Blagojevich are excluded from this and subsequent analyses. Those stories were categorized as crime-related by Nexis, but they are not relevant for what we are looking at here – they are related to political scandal more than crime per se. Including the stories makes little difference to the analysis reported later in the chapter, however.

TABLE 5.1. *Media Coverage of Crime, Bloomington* Pantagraph, *2005–2009*

	Crime Stories			Crime Incidents		
	% violent	% nonviolent	Monthly Average	% violent	% nonviolent	Monthly Average
2005	36.4	63.6	29	13.3	86.7	1,057
2006	32.2	67.8	30	12.3	87.7	1,094
2007	23.1	76.9	32	14.3	85.7	1,123
2008	36.0	63.6	27	13.4	86.6	1,124
2009	31.8	68.2	30	13.4	86.6	1,028

The major categories coded here as "violent" crime include murder, homicide, assault, sexual assault, and weapons-related crimes.

are fluctuations in the series, certainly. But note that the relationship between increases or decreases in one series and increases or decreases in the other is relatively weak. Indeed, the correlation between the two series using these monthly data is .01. Clearly, increases in media coverage of crime are not necessarily related to a concurrently increasing crime rate.

Of course, the existing literature does not suggest that crime rates are accurately reflected in the volume of coverage that media give to crime. Rather, it suggests that media content is systematically biased toward reporting certain types of crime, namely violent crime. The general balance of violent versus nonviolent crime, both in Bloomington and in the *Pantagraph*, is shown in Table 5.1. The table shows the average number of both crime stories and crime incidents, monthly, for each year from 2005 to 2009. (Note that 2010 data were available only until April, so that year is excluded from this table.) Again, we see a relatively steady attentiveness to crime in the *Pantagraph*; the steady crime rate is also apparent. So too is the steady gap between the proportion of stories focusing on violent crime and the proportion of incidents actually involving violent crime. Indeed, the *Pantagraph*'s balance of violent to nonviolent coverage gives roughly twice as much weight to violent crime as we might expect given the actual distribution of incidents (about 32 percent versus 15 percent). The complexion of crime, gleaned from the pages of the *Bloomington Pantagraph*, is rather different from reality. Basically, it is much more violent.

The gap between crime in the Bloomington *Pantagraph* and crime in reality is particularly clear in Figure 5.2. The figure shows two distributions. The top panel shows the proportion of incident reports, from January 2004 to April 2010, falling into the violent and nonviolent categories. Roughly 16 percent of those incidents were related to violent crimes, while the remaining 84 percent were nonviolent. The bottom panel shows the proportion of news stories on violent and nonviolent crimes. This bottom panel is, essentially, the picture of crime that *Pantagraph* readers would have (assuming they read all stories

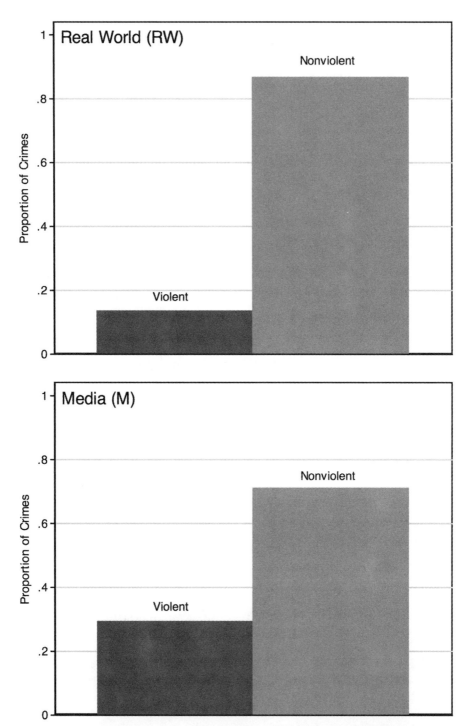

FIGURE 5.2. Occurrence of Violent versus Nonviolent Crime, Real World and Media Coverage

TABLE 5.2. *Media Coverage of Crime, Bloomington* Pantagraph, *2005–2009*

	DV: Crime Stories$_t$ (weekly)			
	Model 1		Model 2	
Crime$_t$	−.002	(.006)		
Violent Crime$_t$			.049*	(.030)
Nonviolent Crime$_t$			−.009	(.007)
Crime Stories$_{t-1}$	.246***	(.059)	.237***	(.059)
Change in Unemployment$_{t-1}$	−.397	(.383)	−.418	(.382)
Constant	5.727***	(1.484)	5.637***	(1.479)
N	265		265	
R-sq	.067		.078	
adj. R-sq	.056		.063	

* p < .10; ** p < .05; *** p < .01. Cells contain OLS regression coefficients, with standard errors in parentheses. All estimates are based on weekly data, from the beginning of 2005 to April 2010.

and remembered them all). In the news, crime is roughly twice as violent as in reality.

One real advantage to Figure 5.2 is its portrayal of news content and reality as distributions of information. One approach in studies of media selection is to look at individual pieces of information, or stories, and whether they find their way into news content. The expectation is often that trends in the selection (or not) of those individual stories are emblematic of a broader phenomenon – a system of biases that produces a picture in media that is fundamentally different from reality. This is the approach in, for instance, Meyrowitz's (1994) fascinating study of the exclusion of Larry Agran from the Democratic Party's 1991–1992 primaries, or in Herman and Chomsky's (1988) comparison of selected political deaths in Latin America versus Poland. In both cases, the authors reveal biases in the selection of individual stories and use those biases to make claims about the system in general.

Figure 5.2 is an effort to do the same, but drawing on a much larger body of data than past work has done, over a much longer period of time. Figure 5.2 captures the gap between the news on and the reality of crime across a nearly six-year period.

It is possible to explore the longitudinal relationship between crimes and crime news as well, of course. Table 5.2 presents results from weekly time-series models intended to explore further the relationship between violent versus nonviolent crimes and crime reporting. The table shows results from a simple autoregressive distributed lag model, as follows,

$$\#\text{Crime Stories}_t = \alpha_0 + \beta_1 \#\text{Crime Stories}_{t-1} + \beta_2 \, \text{Crime}_t$$
$$+ \, \beta_3 \Delta \text{Unemployment}_{t-1} + \varepsilon_t, \tag{5.1}$$

in which the current number of crime stories is regressed on the number of crime stories in the preceding week alongside current levels of crime incidents. Lagged changes in unemployment are included in the model as a control, allowing for the possibility that a worsening economy will lead the newspaper to allocate more space to economic news and less to crime. (Note, however, that the unemployment rate is positively correlated with crime rates, in line with findings by Barlow et al. 1995.)

The first columns of Table 5.2 show results from this simple model – results that show no significant relationship between the overall number of incidents and crime reporting. The second columns of Table 5.2 show a slightly revised model in which crime incidents are divided into violent and nonviolent incidents. Results are telling: there is no significant relationship between nonviolent crime and crime reporting, but violent crimes are systematically related to the number of weekly crime stories.

The Bloomington data thus illustrate what many have thus far believed about media reporting of crime. In short, the *Pantagraph* paid markedly more attention to violent crime than to nonviolent crime, and while this is just one newspaper, there is no reason to believe that these findings are unique to Bloomington.

Why is it that violent crimes find their way into newspapers more reliably than nonviolent crimes do? The answer, already noted earlier in the book, is that violent crimes are most often viewed as worse than nonviolent crimes; and even when nonviolent crimes seem especially bad (such as incidents of large-scale corporate malfeasance), we expect those to more reliably find their way into the news as well. The fact that we see "badness" as a critical driver of newsworthiness is worth noting, however. So too is the possibility that "goodness" matters for newsworthiness.

Unfortunately, the near-total absence of goodness from stories about crime (save perhaps for stories on the successful capture of criminals, or the release of the falsely accused) makes crime an imperfect topic with which to explore the impacts of both negativity and positivity in media content. With crime, then, we are able only to look at variations in degrees of negativity. Results do indeed suggest that more negative stories get more coverage. But work on impression formation reviewed in previous chapters points to the importance of comparing not just negative and less negative information, but negative and positive information. To accomplish this we need to turn to another topic, one that generates both bad *and* good news.

Economic News Content in the United States, United Kingdom, and Canada

Unlike crime news, economic news can be good or bad. Unemployment, inflation, and leading indices can all increase or decrease. And in most cases an increase in one or the other is not only readily captured numerically, but also pretty clearly either positive or negative. Economic news thus provides a relatively unique opportunity to examine directly the relationship between the "real world" and media content. Put differently, it allows us to continue to explore the difference between the distribution of information in reality and the distribution of information in news content.

As in the preceding section, the difference between the two *distributions* of information is critical to the analysis here. Unlike results for crime, however, I am now able to look at interval-level measures of both the economy and media tone. I am thus able to get a much more nuanced picture of the gatekeeping process and the negativity bias.

The basic thrust of the distributional approach used here is captured in Figure 5.3.[3] The top panel shows a hypothetical probability density function of some real-world phenomenon, which is distributed across a range of tone. For the sake of simplicity – though perhaps also realistically given what we know about many real-world phenomena – the distribution of the real-world phenomenon across the range of x is Gaussian (with a mean of 0 and a standard deviation of 1).

If we were to receive all of this information directly, our experience would look exactly like the top panel of Figure 5.3, labeled RW (for "real world"). But if we receive it at least partly indirectly, through mass media, there is necessarily some kind of filter applied to the information before we receive it. That filter, or gatekeeping, can be depicted as a distribution as well – a distribution of the likelihood with which a given piece of information is selected for mediation. In the example depicted in the second panel of Figure 5.3, labeled G (for "gatekeeping"), this likelihood of selection varies systematically with dimension x.

Note that the illustration of G in Figure 5.3 owes much to Groeling and Kernell's (1998) analysis of networks' decisions to both commission and report on in-house polling on presidential approval. The authors examine whether networks are more likely to report on in-house polls that are favorable or unfavorable, or that show stasis versus change. Doing so allows them to plot the probability of reporting across varying degrees and directions of change in presidential approval. One strength of Groeling and Kernell's work – and an advantage of the current line of analysis as well – is that it shows likelihoods of reporting across the entire range of possibilities in x (in their case, all polling results). Results provide a very clear picture of the outcomes that are regarded as newsworthy, and those results do not depend on any a priori decisions about thresholds on dimension x.

The second panel of Figure 5.3 shows the likelihood with which editors or journalists will select and publish a given piece of information, across the range of tone. The likelihood of selection for a negative piece of information is

---

[3] Note that the description of a distributional approach to gatekeeping in this section draws considerably on Soroka (2012).

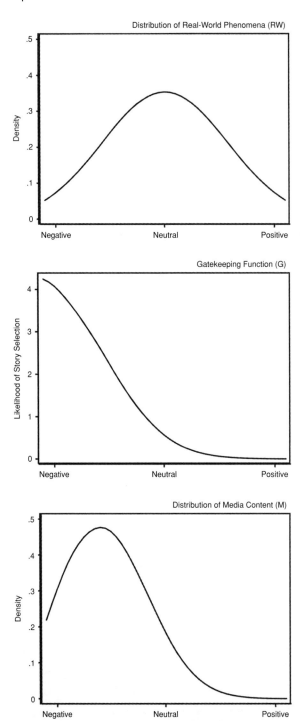

FIGURE 5.3. A Distributional Approach to Gatekeeping

about 2:1; put differently, a single negative event is likely to produce about two media stories. Conversely, the likelihood of story selection for a positive piece of information is about 1:4; put differently, only one in four positive events produce a story. This is a purely hypothetical example, of course, but one that fits with everything we have reviewed above.

The consequences of gatekeeping (G) are depicted in the bottom panel of Figure 5.3, showing media content (M). This distribution is produced by multiplying the distribution in the top panel by the selection mechanism in the second. That is,

$$M = RW * G. \qquad (5.2)$$

Note that media content in the bottom panel of Figure 5.3 is not dominated by very negative stories, because there are actually relatively few very negative stories to begin with. But moderately negative stories are more plentiful, and the multiplication of RW and G produces an M in which moderately negative stories clearly dominate.

This perspective on gatekeeping is not new in either process or outcome, but it is more formalized in its theoretical explication than much past work is. This has advantages and disadvantages where both theory and empirical analysis are concerned. Empirically speaking, the advantage of this distributional account is that it provides a model that can in principle be applied to real data, in a roughly comparable way across media outlets and countries and policy domains. The gatekeeping function (G) is of course not often directly observable, but we can in certain circumstances measure both real-world indicators (RW) and media content (M). By doing so, we can (following from Equation 5.2) solve for G as follows:

$$G = M \div RW. \qquad (5.3)$$

To be clear: given sufficient measures of both the real world and media content, we can directly measure the selection mechanism that turns the former into the latter. We can thus directly observe the gatekeeping function.

There are several difficulties. We must find an issue for which the "real world" is readily observable and clearly varies across a dimension that is reliably measurable. There must also be a corresponding, and measurable, dimension in media content. These are by no means insignificant problems, and there may as a consequence be a range of issues for which this distributional perspective is theoretically interesting but empirically useless.

There are nevertheless a good number of issues (and related dimensions) that are readily and reliably measured in both the real world and in media content – and macroeconomic trends are one example. These are regularly reported in media and readily available in the real world, already in the form of interval-level data series. The unit of measurement is different in media than in macroeconomic variables, of course: we cannot measure media content in

TABLE 5.3. *Sample Sizes, Economic News Database*

United States (1980–)	
New York Times	12,780
Washington Post	8,407
United Kingdom (1986–)	
Times (London)	11,281
Guardian	11,239
Canada (1986–)	
Globe and Mail	17,143
Toronto Star	13,113
TOTAL	73,963

percentage points of unemployment. But we can look at the distribution of macroeconomic indicators in standard units, the distribution of media tone in standard units, the differences between these two distributions, and – most importantly – the selection function that is required to convert one into the other.

That is the goal here, relying on simple summary measures of the economy, namely leading indicators series. Monthly leading indicators are based on the OECD Composite Leading Indicators (CLI, amplitude adjusted). The media measure is based on a database of economic news stories from two major papers in each of the three countries: in the United States, the *New York Times* and the *Washington Post*; in the United Kingdom, the *Times* (London) and the *Guardian*; and in Canada, the *Globe and Mail* and the *Toronto Star*. In each case data end in late 2011 and start as early as reliable data are available in Nexis. For the United States, that means that series begin in 1979; for the United Kingdom and Canada, 1985.

Previous work performs similar analysis using unemployment articles only (Soroka 2012). Here I rely on a general economic indicator, and so the media measure is similarly broad – I rely on all 74,000 news stories. Sample sizes across countries and newspapers are provided in Table 5.3.

All news stories are coded for topic and tone using Lexicoder, automated content analytic software that implements a relatively simply bag-of-words approach – that is, it counts the number of specific words, using a preestablished dictionary, in each article. Extracting employment articles is relatively simple – the dictionary includes a battery of words dealing with employment and jobs. The measure of tone is similarly simple, at least in principle: it relies on just two categories of words, positive and negative.

The reliability of this automated measure relies entirely on the quality of the dictionary of positive and negative words. Since the 1960s scholars have been developing lexicons in which words are classified as positive or negative. There are numerous machine-readable dictionaries available for research (e.g., Mergenthaler 1996, 2008; Pennebaker et al. 2001; Whissell 1989; Bradley and Lang 1999; Hart 1984). There is also a vast literature by computational linguists interested in developing sentiment lexicons (e.g., Subasic and Huettner 2001; Strapparava and Valitutti 2004; Turney and Littman 2002; Hatzivassiloglou and McKeown 1997). The one used here, the Lexicoder Sentiment Dictionary, was built on some of this existing work. In particular, it seeks to expand the scope of coverage without compromising accuracy. The LSD is the product of manually sorting and merging hundreds of affect-and-emotion categories from three of the largest and most widely used lexical resources for automated content analyses: Roget's Thesaurus (Roget 1911), the General Inquirer (GI, Stone et al. 1966), and the Regression and Imagery Dictionary (RID, Martindale 1975, 1990). A full description, and testing, of the dictionary is available in Young and Soroka (2012).

For the current purposes, suffice it to say that the final dictionary includes 6,016 words scored for positive or negative tone alongside the preprocessing of over 1,500 words. "Tone" for each article is then the percent of positive words minus the percent of negative words. The measure can in principle range from −100 (where every single word in the article is negative) to +100 (where every single word in the article is positive). Practically speaking, in these data the measure ranges from roughly −10 to +10.

I cannot completely avoid human coding, however, first because it is important to test the strength of the dictionary for the kind of economic news content used here, but also because I need human coding to determine the neutral point. In short, an equal number of positive and negative words may not be seen as neutral to humans. (The neutral point will be affected by, for instance, the structure and use of the English language, the style in which newspaper stories are written, and the effectiveness with which the dictionary captures positive or negative tone.) To properly estimate the gatekeeping function, I need first to establish the neutral point for the automated tone measure.

To do so, I compare the tone of articles as it is determined by the LSD to codes from 3 human coders, across 600 stories. The sample was selected so as to produce human codes, to a certain extent at least, distributed across the range of automated tone. The selection process was thus as follows. Based on the automated tone measure, the entire body of data was divided into three: one body of articles with tone one standard deviation below the mean, one body of articles with tone one standard deviation above the mean, and the remaining articles, all within one standard deviation of the mean. Then, for each newspaper, 150 stories were drawn entirely at random from each of these three subsamples.

The use of human coders in this case was closer to what is typical in computational linguistics than to what is found in political science and communications. In the latter, researchers typically train coders to assign identical codes. This is clearly important when one is assigning topics, or frames, but may not be effective where tone is concerned. For some computational linguists, differences

TABLE 5.4. *Mean Automated Tone, by Human Coding and Country*

	Human-Assigned Tone				
	Negative	Mildly Negative	Neutral	Mildly Positive	Positive
Combined					
Tone	−0.749	0.237	0.584	0.966	1.253
N	226	77	175	44	48
United States					
Tone	−0.783	0.262	0.743	1.071	1.572
N	71	31	58	18	12
United Kingdom					
Tone	−0.780	0.088	0.592	1.376	1.269
N	98	20	56	9	13
Canada					
Tone	−0.655	0.321	0.425	0.639	1.076
N	57	26	61	17	23

across human coders are regarded as capturing real variation, or ambiguity, given the natural and structural ambiguity in categories of sentiment (Subasic and Huettner 2001; Andreevskaia and Bergler 2006). Following this approach, codes from the three human coders are arranged here into a five-point scale: Negative, where all three coders selected negative; Mildly Negative, where two coders selected negative; Neutral, where two or more coders selected neutral; Mildly Positive, where two coders selected positive; and Positive, where all three coders selected positive.

Note that the approach used here is similar to those in Young and Soroka (2012) and Soroka (2012), although the current analysis takes two steps forward. First, there is no overlap between the stories used here and those used earlier. This analysis thus provides a useful replication, and second test, of earlier results. Second, this analysis includes far more economic news stories, across three different countries. Because it is the first cross-national comparison of the performance of the LSD vis-á-vis human coders, Table 5.4 shows combined results alongside results separated for each country.

Results are nicely summarized by the first rows, showing the distribution of stories and LSD-assigned mean tone scores for all stories combined. First, note that the LSD-assigned tone increases steadily as we move from negative to positive stories. (The differences between mean values are, at each step, statistically significant.) Second, note that the average mean score for stories regarded as neutral by human coders is not zero, but .58 (with an estimated standard error of .11). Third, note that even the mildly negative stories are scored above zero.

Differences across countries are minor, but it is worth noting that the estimated mean for neutral articles appears to be highest in the United States and lowest in Canada. This may have to do with the nature of writing across the newspapers sampled here, although I cannot tell from these data alone. What is most important for the current purposes is that, across all three countries, automated tone rises systematically across categories of human-coded tone, and that, across all three countries, neutral stories have an average estimated tone that is above zero, ranging from .43 and .74.

With this preliminary analysis in hand, I can proceed to an analysis of the distribution of positive and negative tone in economy measures and in media reporting on those measures. First, both the real-world (RW) and media (M) measures have to be converted into more directly comparable units, by dividing each by its standard deviation (and thus converting them both into standard units). The resulting distributions for the United States are illustrated in the top and bottom panels of Figure 5.4. In each case, the illustrations show smoothed (Epanechnikov) kernel density estimates, where the half-width is relatively low – just enough to produce a smoothed plot without obfuscating the underlying distribution.

The distribution for the CLI series is shown in the first panel. Recall that these are monthly changes in the CLI, which have several advantages over levels: they are, roughly speaking, normally distributed, and – most importantly – they have a natural neutral point, zero. There is also good reason to believe that media respond to change in, rather than levels of, economic indicators (see the discussion in Nadeau et al. 1999: 118).

The measured distribution of tone in media content is shown in the bottom panel of Figure 5.4. This panel shows not just a single distribution but a range of distributions – note that the dark line is surrounded by a number of lighter dotted lines showing proximate distributions, to account for margins of error around the estimated mean value for neutral stories. Recall that the mean for neutral stories was .58. The standard error of that mean, based on the relatively small sample of human-coded stories, is .11. So the distribution of tone is shown in Figure 5.4 adjusting for a range in tone – .58 plus or minus two standard errors.

Overall, the differences between RW and M are not as stark as we might expect, but we should not underestimate what even small differences between RW and M can mean for G; or, put differently, how powerful (nonuniform) G must be to have even a small effect on the distribution of information in media versus reality. That gatekeeping function is shown in the middle panel of Figure 5.4. To be clear: this is the selection mechanism that likely exists given differences between RW and M. As for M, G is shown here as a range of possibilities, based on the range of possibilities for M.

The selection mechanism is much as we would expect given the existing literature. The likelihood of story selection is almost always greater than one on the negative side of the range, and almost always less than one on the

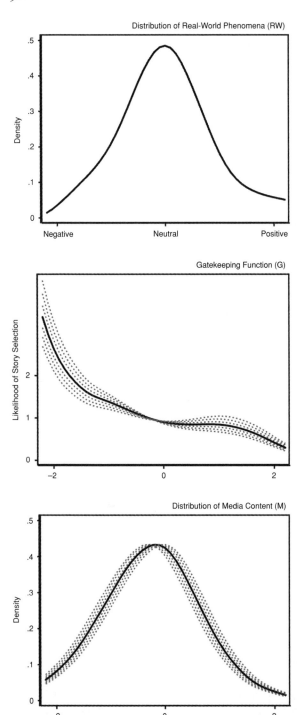

FIGURE 5.4. Gatekeeping for Economic News, U.S. Newspapers

positive side of the range. Somewhat more stylized accounts are as follows: (a) a modestly negative piece of information is roughly twice as likely to receive coverage as a similarly modestly positive piece of information, or (b) a single piece of negative information produces between one and two newspaper stories, while it takes roughly two pieces of positive information to produce just one story. Both accounts draw links between individual pieces of information and individual stories, however – links that are not directly observed here, only implied. Even a more cautious account is noteworthy, however: the distribution of information in media is more negative than is the distribution of information in the real world.

Does the same gatekeeping mechanism apply outside the United States? The literature on media negativity certainly focuses on the U.S. case; a resulting impression is that media negativity may be a peculiarly American phenomenon. Accounts of a cynical American media following the Vietnam War and Watergate seem to lend support to this idea. At the same time, work linking the negativity bias to *human*, not just *American*, traits and tendencies suggests that we should see a bias toward negativity outside the United States as well. Testing outside the U.S. context is thus much more than simple, cross-national replication – it is a (partial) test of the relative merit of a number of different hypotheses about the sources of the negativity bias, some sociocultural, some biological.

Figure 5.5 thus reproduces analyses of the gatekeeping function for economic news for both the United Kingdom and Canada. It is worth noting that these countries are, culturally speaking, not particularly different from the United States. There are differences between them, to be sure, but in the grand scheme of world cultures, these three countries may be among the most similar. The analysis is constrained to countries with readily available English-language national newspapers, however, because the tone dictionary is in English only. Even with that important caveat in mind, Figures 5.4 and 5.5 provide the first directly comparable measures of media selection biases across countries. And the results are telling: in both the United Kingdom and Canada, as in the United States, there is a tendency for media to over-select negative stories and under-select positive ones. The bias in the United Kingdom is roughly similar to what we have seen in the United States – a roughly 2:1 selection ratio for negative stories and less than 1:1 ratio for positive ones. In Canada, the bias appears to be a little smaller; here, the likelihood of story selection increases to maximum of 1.5:1 at the most negative end. Even so, the end result is a distribution of information in Canadian newspapers that is more negative than the distribution of information in the actual economy.

Clearly, these cross-national results provide weak evidence that the negativity bias in media is driven by biological rather than cultural factors – there are just too many similarities between the cultures of the United States, United Kingdom, and Canada. But the results do raise some questions about the relative merits of the various accounts of media negativity surveyed at the

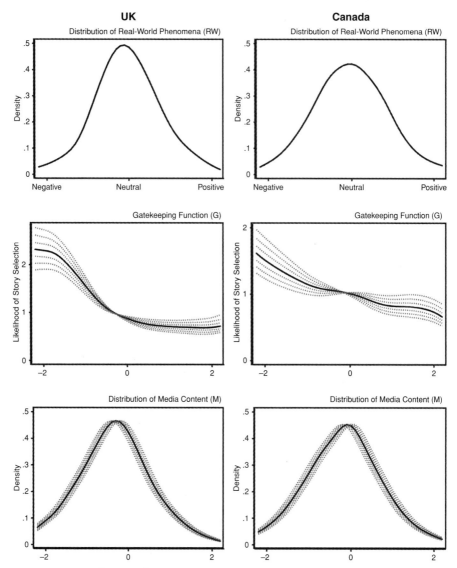

FIGURE 5.5. Gatekeeping for Economic News, UK and Canadian Newspapers

beginning of this chapter. I return to those theories in a final discussion later in
the book.

For now, it is worth noting simply that there is strong, cross-national evidence that media coverage of the economy is negatively biased. Put in the same
terms as the preceding analysis of crime, if we were to experience the economy
only through news content, we would have a somewhat more negative view
of the economy than if we were to experience it directly. (This is true most of

the time, at least. Note that the preceding analysis focuses on media content generally, and there are reasons to expect that that media content may be cautiously optimistic at certain times, for instance, following the election of a new president/government.) Of course, for most people both real-world and media content matters – we all typically experience the domestic economic directly, and through media as well. The relative balance of one or the other likely governs how realistic our view of the economy is. And past work suggests that in the case of the economy at least, much of our experience is direct – that is, not through media.

That is the crux of the distinction in the agenda-setting literature on obtrusive versus unobtrusive issues, at least, made famous by Zucker (1978) but discussed elsewhere too (e.g., Behr and Iyengar 1985; Soroka 2002). Related to work on "media dependency theory" (Ball-Rokeach and DeFleur 1976), this literature argues that the potential for the media to affect issue salience for the public increases for issues about which the public has little direct experience and decreases for issues the public tends to experience directly. The economy is for many of us one of the latter issues – an issue in which media accounts play a comparatively small role. This is good news because it suggests that our views of the economy are not profoundly biased (at least not because of media, that is). But there is bias, in media, and likely to a certain degree in our views of the economy as well. (Indeed, even as the economy is a relatively obtrusive issue, there is a considerable body of work showing that the public's views of the economy are shaped in part by media content. See, e.g., Soroka 2006, 2012; Nadeau et al. 1999.) The important point here is that a bias exists, and is in fact readily apparent in a domain for which the necessary data are available. Other, less obtrusive domains may exhibit greater degrees of media influence – and those domains likely exhibit the same systematic negativity biases we have seen in crime and economic coverage as well.

Conclusions

While the fact that media are negative is not a new finding, estimates of the scope of that negativity, across domains and countries and over extended periods of time, are. The similarity in results for the analysis of crime stories in the Bloomington *Pantagraph* and of economic news across six newspapers in three countries is rather striking. In each case, there is roughly twice as much negative information in news content as there is in reality.

Where does all this negativity come from? There are various accounts, as we have seen. In light of the evidence assembled here, some of those accounts seem likelier than others. More specifically, the argument that negativity in political news is a consequence of a particularly vicious relationship between journalists and politicians in the post-Watergate American context seems somewhat overstated. First, we know that this negativity extends well beyond the coverage of political campaigns, and indeed of politics more generally. There is certainly politics in reports on economics, and politics in reports of crime as well. But the role of politics in these is relatively low overall, and the negativity seems to remain, pretty powerfully. And other, even less political domains also exhibit negativity biases. Bartlett et al.'s (2002) study of medical reporting, for instance, suggests that negative medical findings are more likely to be reported in British newspapers. And work by Altheide and others linking the tone of modern mass media news to entertainment formats makes even clearer the fact that negative political coverage cannot be driven only, or perhaps even for the most part, by a peculiar relationship between journalists and politicians in the United States.

Cross-national evidence of a negativity bias, first shown in public responses to the economy across eighteen countries in Chapter 4, and now revealed in the coverage of American, British, and Canadian newspapers, also raises questions about the cynical-journalist hypothesis. It might be the case that there were instance of lying politicians in other countries as well, and as a consequence many countries' journalists now harbor a certain degree of animosity toward politicians. Alternatively it might be true that American journalism invariably affects journalists in other countries too, particularly the culturally similar countries investigated here. That said, we cannot easily investigate either of these hypotheses, and it seems just as plausible, if not more so, that evidence of negativity across countries is a consequence of a certain universality in the negativity bias, for humans, and for journalists as well.

Whether media negativity is actually global in scope, or even equally evident across the Western world, clearly requires more work. For the time being, there is ample evidence here that media exhibit the same tendencies that we have seen in individual's rankings of political candidates, and in aggregate-level trends in public opinion regarding the economy and government approval. It is worth noting that these asymmetries – in public opinion and in media – may interact. The human tendency to react more strongly to negative information may not just be reflected in media content; it may be enhanced by it. This is one of a number of topics dealt with in Chapter 7. First, however, Chapter 6 explores the physiology of the negativity bias; and in so doing, it illustrates one likely account for why the media explored in this chapter are inclined toward the negative.

6

Reactions to News Content

Sakit nang kalingkingan nararamdaman ng buong katawan. [Illness or pain in a small part (finger) is felt by the whole body.]

– Tagalog Proverb

The previous chapter demonstrated a negativity bias in media content. It also argued that the negativity bias is a product of our tendency to be more attracted to negative news – or, put more forcefully, it is a product of humans being hardwired to react more to negative than to positive information. This chapter explores this possibility further through two tests of our reactions to news content.

The tests take two (quite different) forms. First, I analyze data on newsstand magazine sales, weekly, over the past two decades, using sales data made available by *Maclean's* magazine in Canada. These data are matched to human-coded covers for every issue. Controlling for seasonal variation in magazine sales, as well as the subject matter of cover stories, the tone of cover stories/pictures appears to matter to newsstand sales: predictably, negative covers sell more than positive ones. This is taken as a first, aggregate-level indication that humans (or at least the media-consuming public) are indeed more interested in negative news content than in positive one.

The second test of a negativity bias in our reactions to news content occurs at a much lower level of analysis: it is based on results from psychophysiological experiments in which participants watch television news stories while we monitor heart rate, skin conductance, and subtle changes in the facial musculature. (These experiments were done in conjunction with, in the first case, Stephen McAdams in the Department of Music at McGill University, and in the second case, Penelope Daignault and Thierry Giasson in Communications at Laval University.) Psychophysiological techniques are well known in psychology but are used infrequently in political science. That said, results make clear the fact that we respond more strongly (physiologically speaking) to negative information than to positive information. Negative stories get and keep our attention; positive stories have a much more limited impact. These experiments thus point toward one account for the asymmetries found in preceding chapters. They make clearer still the possibility that negativity biases in politics and political communications are a product of biases in the ways in which humans react to positive and negative information.

Selecting the News We Read

Results in the preceding chapter suggest that there is a systematic bias in news content, and that the systematic bias may well be a product of media consumers' interest in negative rather than positive information. The data in that chapter only *suggest* the latter possibility, however – we have not yet actually seen evidence of biases in consumers' news selection.

Some past work nevertheless points to this possibility. There exists a small body of work observing individuals' selection of news stories, for instance, either in a lab setting or through monitoring selection from a CD or the Web at home. Meffert et al.'s (2006) findings in this regard are based on lab experiments in which participants select from a constantly changing list of stories about a fictitious election campaign. (The design is based on Lau and Redlawsk's [1997] "dynamic information board" technique.) In essence, the list of stories is intended to mimic the kinds of information that readers would be able to select from in a regular campaign, and, as in a regular campaign, experimental participants are asked simply to select whatever interests them – though in this case software then tracks participants' choices. Results suggest that participants are inclined to select negative over positive information. (There are a number of other studies that track news consumer behavior, but in which the focus is not on a negativity bias. See, e.g., Donsbach 1991; Iyengar et al. 2004; Tewksbury 2005; Coe et al. 2008.)

There are some difficulties with lab experiments where examining news selection is concerned, the most notable of which is that they really cannot easily produce a setting that is close to the way in which most consumers get their news. That said, it is also not easy to capture news consumption at home, at least not without having participants turn on some kind of tracker on their computers, at which point the "natural" news-consuming environment changes slightly as well. One way around some of these difficulties is to look at news consumption not at the individual level, but in the aggregate. Data exist on newspaper and magazine sales, after all, or on the number of times people click on news displayed on newspaper Web pages. The aim here is to use this kind of data to explore media consumers' tendencies in news selection, focusing on our proclivity to select negative information over positive one.

News magazine covers may be an ideal resource for this kind of investigation. Covers tend to focus on just one major story, and there are good reasons to

TABLE 6.1. Maclean's *Covers, by Topic, 2001–2008*

Topic	No. of Covers
Business	35
National Affairs	
Crime	13
Education	5
Environment	10
Health	43
Other	72
International Affairs	55
Culture	36
Entertainment	20
Human Interest	1
Other	2
Religion	15
Science/Technology	11
Sports	21
Survey/Year	16
University	13

Note: Data include all *Maclean's* covers from January 2001 to December 2008.

believe that newsstand sales are affected by what is on that cover. The central question here, then, is whether newsstand sales of news magazines are linked to the tone of the cover story, and this possibility is tested in the analysis that follows, using a database of all the covers of *Maclean's* magazine (the main national news magazine in Canada), matched to data on newsstand sales (where newsstand sales do not include subscriptions).

Sales will be driven by factors other than tone, of course, and so properly identifying the impact of tone requires a multivariate approach. First, all *Maclean's* covers were rated by human coders for tone using a simple three-point scale – positive, negative, neutral. At the same time, coders assigned a topic category. Topics were selected inductively – coders started with set of basic codes, but as coding continued, the topics were expanded to better capture the content of *Maclean's* covers. (And when the coding scheme changed, previously coded covers were recoded.) In the end, coders used seventeen different topics, listed in Table 6.1 alongside the frequency with which those topics appeared over the eight-year period for which data are available.

Note that national affairs articles are divided into five different subcategories. The same is not the case for international affairs articles, as most dealt with foreign affairs broadly defined. And there is, of course, some overlap – where a cover is about religion, for instance, it may be directed at national affairs, or international affairs, or both. The decision rules used for topic coding were thus as follows: if a cover clearly fits within one of the listed topics, it is assigned there, and the National Affairs: Other and International Affairs categories are used only when an article does not clearly fit into one of the other categories.

Of course, we are not directly interested in the distribution of covers across topics so much as in the distribution across tones. Where topics are concerned, however, it is worth noting first that the analyses that follow ignore covers in two categories: University, and Survey/Year. The former are the *Maclean's* version of university rankings, similar to what would be released in the United States in the *US News and World Report*. The latter are mainly year-in-review issues, released at the end of December. Issues in both cases are very popular, but they are also a different type of publication than the typical, weekly issue. They are accordingly ignored in the following analysis.

The distribution of tone for the remaining 339 issues is as follows: 15.9 percent positive, 38.4 percent neutral, and 45.7 percent negative. (Examples of covers are as follows: *Positive*: "Canada's Best MP," or "Eureka! A Cure for Mental Decline," or "Heroes of the Cross"; *Neutral*: "The Joy of Frugality," or "Measuring Health Care," or "How Will It End?" with a picture of Harry Potter; *Negative*: "Is God Poison?" or "Your Grocery Bill Is About to Hurt," or "The Scariest Man on Earth" with a photo of Mahmoud Ahmadinejad.) The fact that only 15.9 percent of covers are positive is perhaps a first indication of the relative weakness of positive covers where newsstand sales are concerned. There are relationships between tone and topic, of course – there are no crime or international affairs covers that are positive, only negative and neutral. For all other topics, however, there are examples of covers in each of the three tone categories.

With codes for both topic and tone in hand, I am able to model the impact that tone has on magazine sales. Table 6.2 presents results of a simple time-series model, as follows:

$$\text{Newsstand Sales}_t = \alpha_o + \beta_1 \, \text{Newsstand Sales}_{t-1} + \beta_2 \text{Tone}_t + \beta_3 \text{Topic}_t + \varepsilon_t,$$

$$(6.1)$$

Including lagged newsstand sales accounts for a combination of (a) variations in sales over the course of the year and (b) trends in sales that are a consequence of particularly newsworthy periods, such as elections. Tone is then captured in the first model using a three-category variable where -1 is negative, 0 is neutral, and $+1$ is positive. The possibility of an asymmetry in the impact of tone is tested in a second model, where there are dummy variables for positive and negative, with neutral as the residual category. This approach allows for the gap in sales between negative and neutral to be greater than the gap in sales between positive and neutral. Topic is then controlled for in each model with just two dummy variables, one for National Affairs

TABLE 6.2. Maclean's *Newsstand Sales*

| | DV: Newsstand Sales$_t$, Monthly, 2000–2008 | |
	Symmetric Model	Asymmetric Model
Tone	−862.893* (360.004)	
Tone: Negative		846.950 (559.100)
Tone: Positive		−888.417 (773.303)
Sales$_{t-1}$	.051 (.039)	.051 (.039)
Topic: Business	1496.643 (872.482)	1496.434 (873.815)
Topic: Domestic	−1069.054* (541.507)	−1071.232 (545.456)
Constant	6698.893* (465.300)	6711.138* (569.976)
N	337	337
R-sq	.047	.047
adj. R-sq	.035	.032

* $p < .05$. Cells contain OLS regression coefficients, with standard errors in parentheses. Based on weekly newsstand sales, 2000–2008, excluding Survey/Year and University issues.

covers (five categories combined) and the other for Business covers. The use of these two categories was based on a series of preliminary models using various combinations of topic variables. These were the only two categories for which there were systematically different sales levels – as Table 6.2 shows, generally lower sales for domestic covers and generally higher sales for business covers. These are only controls for our purposes here, however; including different combinations of topic variables makes very little difference to the coefficients, and allowing for interactions between topics and tone does not reveal any systematic differences in the impact of tone on sales from one topic to the next.

What then do the results in Table 6.2 suggest? The negative coefficient for tone in the first (symmetric) model shows that as tone becomes positive, newsstand sales drop. On average, a cover that is positive sells 863 fewer copies than a cover that is neutral and 1,726 fewer copies than a cover that is negative. This is no small shift, given that weekly newsstand sales during this period (excluding University and Survey/Year issues) average around 7,000. The asymmetric model does not reveal a nonlinear effect of tone; the coefficient for negative stories is roughly the same as the coefficient for positive stories (though they obviously have different signs), indicating that the gap in sales from neutral to negative is no greater than the gap in sales moving from neutral to positive. Even so, the impact of tone in these models is relatively clear: more positive covers lead to lower newsstand sales. This impact of tone on sales is illustrated in Figure 6.1, which plots expected sales across tone based on the symmetric model in Table 6.2.

These findings clearly buttress the argument that negativity in news content is a function, at least in part, of media consumers' interests. That consumer

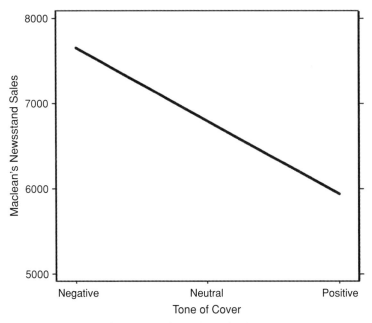

FIGURE 6.1. Tone of Covers and Newsstand Sales

interests matter does not preclude the possibility that other things matter as well, however. In particular, we should not assume that consumer interests are completely exogenous – what people want may partly be a function of what they get. This argument has been part of a recent literature on what publics expect of welfare states, for instance, where research suggests that even as redistributive policies are affected by public preferences, the publics' beliefs about what the state should do are conditioned by the nature/extent of the existing welfare state (i.e., Rothstein 1998). In short, preferences and policies can be endogenous – each affects the other over time. The same can be true for media content. We may be more attracted to negative news content partly because we have been socialized in systems where newsworthiness is associated with negativity.

The endogeneity of preferences for news content is, of course, rather difficult to show with these data. That said, even as we do not want to dismiss the possibility that socialization affects preferences for news content, there are also good reasons to believe that much of what drives our preferences for news is exogenous to the nature of news content. After all, preceding chapters have shown repeated instances in which humans tend to prioritize negative information. The following section provides further evidence that there may be something special about negative news.

Physiological Reactions to News Content

Chapter 1 has already outlined work in psychology, physiology, and neurology suggesting that humans may be hardwired to prioritize negative information over positive one. The subsequent chapters have also pointed to work suggesting that a negativity bias may be at least in part biological, and a product of evolutionary processes. The idea that we can explore the root causes of negativity biases in politics through physiological experiments does not come as any surprise, then. Alongside evidence of aggregate-level consumer behavior in news magazine sales, the experiments reported here are intended to demonstrate the possibility that the kinds of asymmetries discussed earlier may well have bases not just in consumer behavior, but in physiology as well. In so doing, the idea is to draw a clearer link between the way humans react (psychophysiologically) to information and the way journalists (and other political actors) select or create news stories.

The expectation in the following analysis is that participants will react quite strongly to negative information and rather little to positive information. The "reaction" we are interested in here is an emotional one – emotional, that is, as captured by physiological measures. The use of psychophysiological methods is motivated in part by recent work in political science that uses these methods to explore the possibility that there are physiological and perhaps also genetic sources of political preferences (e.g., Oxley et al. 2008), as well as work by Annie Lang and colleagues exploring psychophysiological reactions to media messages (e.g., Lang 1995). The experimental design draws on existing work in psychology, but also on recent work in communication.

Experiment #1: News Content

The first experiment, conducted with Stephen McAdams at McGill University, proceeded as follows.[1] There were forty-two participants – twenty-five male and seventeen female – ranging from eighteen to thirty-five years of age, reporting varying degrees of media attentiveness. Participants knew only that this was an experiment about the news, and that we would be monitoring their physiological responses as they watched. They watched a news program on their own, on a large computer monitor in a quiet room, wearing noise-canceling headphones. They were connected to a number of biosensors on one hand, on their face, and around their torso. The experiment lasted roughly 25 minutes, during which participants viewed 7 news stories. Stories were separated by 1 minute of grey screen; there was a countdown indicated with a large white number on the grey screen for the last 5 seconds, so respondents were not startled by the start of a new story. The experiment also began with a full 2 minutes of grey

---

[1] Both the study description and results in this section are drawn in large part from Soroka and McAdams (N.d.). Full details on participants and on news stories are available there.

screen, to establish a baseline for the various physiological readings and also to allow respondents to settle in and get used to the biosensors.

Stories were drawn from two months (mid-September to mid-November, 2009) of national evening newscasts on Global Television, one of the three major English-language broadcasters in Canada. Stories were selected on a variety of topics, political as well as general news, and covered a range of tone, from very positive to very negative. The stories were viewed and coded for tone and topic by two coders. In the end, this precoding led to the selection of nine stories: one clearly neutral, about the Toronto Film Festival, four that showed varying degrees of positivity, and four that showed varying degrees of negativity.[2] Topics varied from health care policy, to employment benefits, to vaccine shortages, to murder.

All respondents saw the Toronto Film Festival story first – a neutral and relatively boring story. They were then presented with six of the eight remaining stories. Those six were randomly drawn and randomly ordered. Not all respondents saw the same batch of stories: each viewed a somewhat different selection of stories, in a different order. When the experiment ended, participants filled out a short survey capturing demographics, media use preference, and past federal vote. Physiological responses were captured using a ProComp Infiniti encoder from Thought Technology Ltd. and purpose-built software designed at the Centre for Interdisciplinary Research in Music Media and Technology (CIRMMT) at McGill University. The analysis here focuses on two physiological responses in particular: skin conductance and heart rate.

Skin conductance (SC), reflecting the level of moisture exuded by the ecrine sweat glands, is captured by passing an infinitesimally small electrical current through a pair of electrodes on the surface of the skin – in this case, electrodes attached to the tips of the distal phalanx (outer segment) of the index and ring fingers, captured using Thought Technology's SC-Flex/Pro sensor. The current is held constant, and the electrodes monitor variations in current flow. More moisture (sweat) leads to less resistance, or, conversely, more conductance. The resulting conductance data can be used to look at both skin conductance levels (SCL) and skin conductance responses (SCR). The former is simply the level of conductance, measured in microSiemens; the latter is focused on the number of peaks in the SCL signal. In the analysis that follows, we focus on the former.

Variations in SC are useful as an indicator of physiological arousal (Simons et al. 1999; Lang et al. 1999; Bolls et al. 2001; see review in Ravaja 2004). Note

---

[2] The tone of the news stories was confirmed in two different ways. First, seven of the forty-two experiment participants had worked as coders in past content-analytic projects. They knew no more about the current project than the other participants did, but they were asked to perform one additional task: as they viewed stories, there were asked to code each for tone, using a seven-point negative-to-positive scale. These are what we might call "expert" coders. Stories were also rated on the same seven-point scale by fifty-two undergraduate students, during a lecture in a fourth-year political science class. Results from both experienced coders and students confirmed the initial coding of tone; full results are included in Soroka and McAdams (N.d.).

that arousal is not the same thing as valence – arousal refers only to the degree of activation, not the direction (positive or negative, pleasant or unpleasant) of the reaction (Larsen and Diener 1992; Russell 1980). But the degree of arousal is what is most critical in this experiment. We have stories, coded as positive and negative, and are interested in which ones generate the strongest reactions. The expectation is that negative stories will elicit a stronger reaction.

Heart rate was measured using a blood volume pulse (BVP) sensor, captured using Thought Technology's BVP-Flex/Pro sensor. The sensor uses photoplethysmography (measuring the amount of light transmitted through the finger tissue) to detect variations in the volume of blood in the distal phalanx of the middle finger. Because the volume of blood in vessels varies with heartbeats, the resulting waveform can be used to determine heart rate. In the following analysis, heart rate is examined at 5-second intervals.

Heart rate is often used as a measure of attentiveness, where decreasing heart rate indicates increasing attentiveness (Lang 1990; Mulder and Mulder 1981). Note that existing work suggests that heart rate is not exclusively about attentiveness, but can be linked to emotional arousal as well; indeed, the literature suggests that heart rate likely reflects a combination of arousal and attentiveness. My interpretation of heart rate relies in particular on work by Lang (1994), and hinges on the assumption that any acceleration in heart rate comes from arousal will be overwhelmed by the deceleration that comes with attentiveness. I thus expect heart rate to be lower for negative stories, showing greater levels of attentiveness.

For SC analyses, data are originally sampled 256 times per second, but downsampled for analysis by taking averages over 125-ms intervals. The SC signal is smoothed slightly for analysis, using Lowess smoothing with a bandwidth of .02. SC measures tend to decrease over the experiment (a consequence of measurement issues with the electrodes), so the SCLs are de-trended for analysis by regressing the entire time-series on a count variable, capturing time at 125-ms intervals. The count variable was included in both its linear and quadratic form, allowing for the possibility of nonlinear effects; predicted values were then subtracted from the original variable to produce the final de-trended series. Analyses of SCLs rely on these downsampled, smoothed, and de-trended SC series; for analyses of covariance (ANCOVAs), values are also averaged over 5-s intervals. Analyses of heart rate rely on a similarly lowess-smoothed trend, based on signals downsampled to 125-ms intervals, and averaged over 5-s periods.

Differences in psychophysiological reactions to negative versus positive news content are examined using within-respondent ANCOVAs. In each case, the physiological measure is modeled as a function of the following: (1) respondent IDs, to account for level differences in physiological symptoms across respondents; (2) an ordinal variable representing order of presentation of the stories, to capture the possibility that respondents' reactions change based on the number of stories they have seen thus far; (3) time (in 5-second intervals)

TABLE 6.3. *Physiological Reactions to Network News*

Physiological Measure	Tone of Story	
	Positive	Negative
Skin Conductance Levels (SCL)		
Mean, per story	17.871 (.016)	17.924 (.014)
Mean, at 10 seconds into story	17.897 (.019)	18.098 (.017)
Heart Rate		
Mean, per story	76.123 (.121)	75.285 (.103)
Mean, at 30 seconds into story	76.723 (.344)	75.099 (.150)

Note: Cells contain estimated values for SCL and Heart Rate, with standard errors in parentheses, based on ANCOVA models in Appendix Tables B.6.1 and B.6.2. N = 42 participants, across seven stories each, where physiological data are measured in 5-second intervals.

and time squared, to capture the (potentially nonlinear) tendency for both SCL and heart rate to decline slightly over the course of the experiment; and (4) a binary variable contrasting negative with positive and neutral stories, included directly and in interaction with the time variables. The direct effect captures the possibility that negative stories produce an initial impact that is greater or lesser in magnitude than positive stories; the interaction with time allows for the possibility that the effect of negative stories is more (or less) long-lasting.

Full results from the ANCOVAs are included in Appendix Tables B.6.1 and B.6.2. Here, Table 6.3 presents just some simple summary effects: it shows the predicted skin conductance levels and heart rate for positive versus negative stories (where the predictions are based on the models in Appendix tables). Because physiological measures vary with time, two results for each measure are shown. In the case of SCL, the table shows the estimated mean SCL over the entire story, as well as the estimated SCL at exactly 10 seconds into each story – based on variations in physiological measures, the point at which it becomes clear that the story is either positive or negative. For heart rate, the table shows estimated mean heart rate over the entire story, and because heart rate changes more slowly than SCL does, the estimated heart rate 30 seconds into the story.

Results in each case confirm our expectations. Negative stories show higher SCL and lower hear trate, suggesting both greater activation and greater attentiveness. In each case, results are statistically significant (see Appendix tables). This first experiment thus points to a physiological source for some (if not all) of the negativity biases outlined earlier.

Experiment #2: Political Advertising
The design of the first experiment is of course adaptable to other stimuli, and for those interested in political communication, one obvious extension is to replace television stories with campaign ads. As we have seen, there is a vast body of

literature on political advertising. And one argument for the proliferation of negative ads is no different from what we have just explored where news content is concerned, namely that political ads are common because viewers are more activated by negativity than by positivity.

This second experiment is a direct extension of the first, then, conducted with Penelope Daignault and Thierry Giasson of Laval University.[3] The experiment was conducted during the 2011 Canadian federal electoral campaign (in April and May of that year), and thus it has the advantage of using *current* ads being aired during the campaign. The selection of ads was based initially on the 145 electoral ads broadcast during both the 2011 and 2008 campaigns by the four main political parties, in both French and English. For the purposes of this preliminary analysis, all ads were coded for tone (positive, negative, or mixed; other variables are not analyzed here) by two research assistants. Final coding decisions were confirmed by the authors, and in the end the experiment focused on twenty-four ads: seven from the New Democratic Party (NDP), seven from the Conservative Party (CPC), seven from the Liberal Party (LPC), and three from the Bloc Quebecois (BQ), with the latter seen only by francophone participants. These ads were selected to be representative of the three tones: ten negative ones, four mixed ones, and ten positive ones. The two official languages were also represented, with twelve ads in English (four from each of three parties, excluding the BQ) and twelve in French (three from each of the four parties).

As in the preceding experiment, the thirty-one participants were mainly students, recruited through ads posted around the university campus. This experiment was similar to the preceding one in almost all other regards as well, although in this case participants were told they were going to watch ads rather than news – in each case, a participant would see twelve randomly drawn and ordered ads. The analysis of results is also very similar to the preceding experiment, with the following changes: (1) ANCOVAs include time as a linear trend only, not in its quadratic form, because the latter was insignificant in all models (this was likely a product of ads being just 30 seconds rather than several minutes long); (2) ANCOVAs include a categorical variable capturing the partisanship of the ad;[4] and (3) rather than just distinguishing between positive and negative, coding of ads (necessarily) included positive, negative, and mixed, where the latter included ads that alternated between positive information about one party and negative information about others.

Full results for SCL and heart rate are included in Appendix Tables B.6.3 and B.6.4. Table 6.4 shows the basic results – again, estimating SCL and heart

---

[3] The analysis in this section is drawn in part from Daignault et al. (2013). Full details on participants and on ads are available there.

[4] The objective where partisanship is concerned is to allow for the partisanship of the ad to interact with the partisanship of the respondent. These are just preliminary results with a relatively small sample, however, so this interaction is left for future analyses.

TABLE 6.4. *Physiological Reactions to Campaign Ads*

Physiological Measure	Tone of Story		
	Positive	Mixed	Negative
Skin Conductance Levels (SCL)			
Mean, per story	18.101 (.027)	18.115 (.029)	18.019 (.027)
Mean, at 10 seconds into story	17.956 (.041)	18.051 (.043)	18.097 (.042)
Heart Rate			
Mean, per story	86.990 (.538)	85.909 (.561)	85.139 (.531)
Mean, at 10 seconds into story	85.973 (.793)	84.892 (.841)	84.122 (.803)

Note: Cells contain estimated values for SCL and Heart Rate, with standard errors in parentheses, based on ANCOVA models in Appendix Tables B.6.3 and B.6.4.

rate based on full models. (The final line shows estimated heart rate at 10 rather than 30 seconds, even though the short interval is not ideal, because ads are only 30 seconds long.) Results are in line with what we have seen earlier. For ads, as for news, negative information leads to greater activation (higher SCL) and greater attentiveness (lower heart rate).

The inclusion of a mixed category in this case is telling. Where heart rate is concerned, mixed ads show a mean heart rate that is squarely between positive and negative ads – just as the ads are middling, so too is attentiveness. SCL presents a slightly different story, however. In this case, mixed ads are no different from negative ones. Negative information tends to lead to higher levels of activation, and this is equally true for ads that are entirely negative or just partly negative. In the end, a little negativity may go a long way.

The Market for News

Preceding analyses have explored what Iyengar et al. (2004) called the "market" explanation for news content: the possibility that negativity in news is partly a consequence of what people want to view. The explanation has been addressed in the earlier discussion in two quite different ways. First, aggregate-level sales data suggest that *Maclean's* newsstand sales increase when covers are negative. This finding (likely well known by those directly involved in news publishing) is rather powerful evidence that bad news sells. A second set of analyses then looks at the physiological sources of the strength of negative news. Using either network news stories or election campaign ads, it appears as though negative information leads to greater activation and attentiveness on the part of experimental participants.

The strength of the physiological experiments reported here is that they show the impact of negative information using actual news content and actual campaign ads. There is a body of work in psychology and communication with similar results regarding negativity, of course, but that work is one step removed from everyday politics. Even so, existing work buttresses the findings presented in this chapter (and vice versa). And the preceding experiments have the advantage of making very clear the influence that physiology may have on politics. In that way, the experiments are emblematic of the broader objectives of this book: to draw together work in disparate fields, and to build a more thorough account of the causes and impacts of negativity in the political sphere.

Whether these experiments are good evidence of the importance of evolutionary processes in political behavior is, admittedly, another matter. Recall the evolutionary account: evolution favors animals that exhibit a combination of mildly optimistic and loss-averse behavior; you have to be willing to try new food sources, but if your friend is poisoned in the process, you need to be the animal that does not try that food again. Evolution has produced animals with attentional systems that give preference to stimuli with adaptive significance, and foremost among those stimuli are signs of danger. In short, we are, as a cause of evolutionary processes, biased toward prioritizing negative information over positive one.

That said, even though these experiments suggest that there may be a physiological source for the negativity bias, they cannot demonstrate that this is because of evolution. As noted earlier, there is quite likely a circular process whereby our interests both define what news is about and are defined by it. Put differently, the production of predominantly negative information may well be one cause of our ongoing interest in it.

Even so, we do not quite have a chicken-and-egg problem here – media were at some point designed by humans, and though an iterative process may have increased our interest in negativity over time, the negativity bias quite likely started with us. Recall that early thinking – well before the development of modern mass media – saw error monitoring as the central function of mass media in representative democracy. Where political reporting is concerned, at least, mass media were for the most part designed to focus on negative information. The same may be true of other political institutions as well. This is one topic addressed in the following, concluding chapter.

7

Negativity in Political Institutions

> To kill an error is as good a service as, and sometimes even better than, the establishing of a new truth or fact.
>
> – Charles Darwin

Preceding chapters have outlined and added to an accumulating body of evidence that negative information plays a particularly significant role in political behavior and political communication. It follows that everyday politics can seem overwhelmingly negative. This is a product not just of the nature of people, but of the nature of institutions designed by people.

We have already seen some evidence of this in the preceding discussion of mass media. Media content is biased toward the negative not just because media consumers (and producers) are more attentive to negative information, but because news media were designed, at least where their role as a political institution is concerned, to monitor error. Indeed, it seems reasonable to argue that monitoring error is *the* central function of media in a representative democracy. This is the crux of the conception of media as a Fourth Estate, after all – as an institution, independent of both business and government, able (and obliged) to hold each to account.

Media are not the only institution designed with this function in mind, however. Indeed, it may be that most political institutions, like most people, prioritize negative information over positive information. Exploring this possibility is one of two aims for this final, concluding chapter. First, the sections that follow discuss the possibility that institutions have been designed to have a negativity bias, drawing on some foundational (and some more recent) work on the design and functioning of self-monitoring political institutions. A final section then turns to a review of findings in previous chapters and a consideration of what we have learned about both individuals and institutions. It asks, in short: Is negativity bad?

From Individual Behavior to the Design of Political Institutions

From the perspective of a political scientist, one of the most interesting findings in the experimental economics literature on altruistic punishment comes from a study allowing participants to choose the institutional environment in which they play a public goods game. Gurerk, Irlenbusch, and Rockenbach's (2006) experiment involves a relatively rare first step: at the beginning of each round, participants are able to select whether they play the game with rules that sanction noncooperation or without those rules. About a third of the participants choose sanctioning institutions in the first round of the game, but after several rounds of playing, more than 90 percent of participants select into sanctioning institutions, and cooperate accordingly.

These findings should be fascinating to those interested in the design of political institutions, not least because they seem to echo classic political philosophy about why we design and enter into social contracts. Consider in particular Hobbes's argument in *Leviathan* (here is a very poor rendition): rather than subject ourselves to the vagaries of the state of nature, we are willing to give up some freedom to a sovereign authority for the sake of protection. Gurerk and colleagues' experiment is very nearly a test of Hobbes's hypothesis.

There is one element critical to work on political institutions that is *not* a factor in Gurerk and colleagues' experiment, however. Political scientists tend to be interested not just in whether institutions can sanction individuals, but whether individuals can sanction institutions, or at least whether individuals can sanction actors within those institutions. It is this interaction that is at the heart of much of the vast body of work on democracy and representation. And much of the ongoing debate about the merits of one or the other political institution, even before Hobbes, centers on the degree to which both governments and publics are able to monitor each other.

Indeed, a considerable body of work on political-institutional design focuses not just on whether publics can monitor and hold governments accountable, but whether governing institutions can be designed so that this function is, at least in part, performed internally. We are interested in delegating not just the power to govern, but the regular monitoring required to ensure that power is not abused. And the focus of that internal monitoring tends to be much as we might expect, given what preceding chapters have identified about human behavior: like us, the political institutions we design give priority to negative information.

We have already seen that this is true for mass media, of course. Media content tends to be more negative than reality, and we tend to pay more attention to that negative information. But mass media are by no means the only (extra)political institution designed in this way. Indeed, there is a strong argument to be made that many political institutions have been designed with monitoring error as their primary function. The importance of blame avoidance in policy making (discussed in Chapter 2) is thus not just a consequence of humans' frequent preference to penalize rather than reward – it is a product of the institutions that humans have designed to produce, and police, policy. I consider some of the thinking behind some of those institutions here.

Separations of Power

A focus on the identification and correction of error in the design of political institutions is perhaps clearest in the vast body of political theory on the separation of powers. That work is generally traced to Montesquieu, whose collected writings include early and very influential discussions of the value of separating power among a "tripartite system": an executive, a legislature, and a judiciary. Driven in large part by a study of England at the time, Montesquieu saw the separation of powers as a central means by which to avoid the abuse of power by government. This quote from *Considerations on the Causes of the Greatness of the Romans on their Decline* is illustrative of Montesquieu's argument: "The government of England is one of the wisest in Europe, because it has a body which examines it continually, and such are its mistakes that they never last long, and, consequently, by the spirit of attention which they give to the nation, its mistakes are often useful" (as quoted in Courtney 2001).

The more complete version of Montesquieu's theory on the separation of powers is generally drawn from chapter XI of *The Spirit of the Laws*. That chapter has been discussed in great detail elsewhere (not just in recent work, e.g., Lutz 2000; Krause 2000; Resnick 1987; Shklar 1987; Carrither, Mosher, and Rahl 2001, but in eighteenth-century political philosophy as well, e.g., Blackstone, Burke, and *The Federalist Papers*). The most important issue here is that Montesquieu believed that dividing powers helps prevent any single individual or group from monopolizing political power, and that a system of checks and balances reduces the likelihood of error more generally. Indeed, an advantage of the English system for Montesquieu was not just that the legislature was able to act as a check on the monarchy, but that the legislature – being divided into two houses, each able to veto legislation – had an additional, internal system of checks and balances as well.

The importance of monitoring error in Montesquieu's constitutional system is made especially clear in Mansfield's (1989) description of what he called a "self-executing" constitution. Mansfield argues that "Montesquieu's system is a mechanism"; it is a system that is self-constraining, in that no single individual or group is able to abuse its power; but also it is a system that, through the separation of powers, is intended to monitor and correct its own errors. (This view of representative democracy as a self-correcting system, driven in large part by monitoring and responding to error, is echoed in other work discussed later in this chapter.)

Similar ideas about the need for constant monitoring are evident in the work of Machiavelli. McCormick (2003) has argued, for instance, that while Machiavelli is best known for his discussion of how elites can control citizens,

The Discourses in particular includes an extended consideration of why, and how, elites must be monitored and controlled by the public. Like Montesquieu, Machiavelli argues for a separation of powers in order to constrain governments: "In fact, when there is combined under the same constitution a prince, a nobility, and the power of the people, then these three powers will watch and keep each other reciprocally in check" (Book I, chapter II). Note that Machiavelli's separation of powers is extra-governmental, however – it includes "the power of the people." Indeed, Machiavelli argues that the ongoing tension between the people and the senate were central to the success of Rome over the more noble-dominated Sparta and Venice, for instance. McCormick writes, "For Machiavelli, whatever longevity might be gained the noble-dominated and socially harmonious model is lost in the substance of political culture, the quality of public policy, and the extent of military expansion. These can only be achieved as a result of an antagonistic relationship between elites and populace" (301).

Whereas Montesquieu is mainly interested in a self-monitoring system, encouraged through both divisions of power and check and balances, Machiavelli focuses more on external checks to power – on the need for a populace that is constantly monitoring and reacting to the decisions of elites. Elites are monitored by the population in both cases – either through representatives in a legislature or through populist politics outside government. But Montesquieu's focus on the possibility of building the monitoring function directly into the structure of political institutions is what makes his work so clearly influential in the founding of American governing institutions. (Although note that Machiavelli influenced the Founding Fathers in many other ways; see, e.g., Danoff 2000; Thompson 1995) Consider how clearly Montesquieu is echoed in work by John Adams, for instance:

> When the three natural orders in society, the high, middle, and the low, are all represented in the government, and constitutionally placed to watch each other, and restrain each other mutually by the laws, it is then only, that an emulation takes place for the public good, and divisions turn to the advance of the nation. (John Adams, *Works*, 5:90; as quoted in Thompson 1995)

Montesquieu is quoted directly and repeatedly in the *Federalist Papers* (e.g., by Madison in *Federalist* #47), and his concern with the importance of a separation of powers is a dominant theme throughout. Indeed, we can see in the *Federalist Papers* the importance of monitoring error through the separation of powers, a la Montesquieu (e.g., *Federalist* #47, 48, 51), as well as the importance of regular appeals to the public as means of maintaining control and reducing errors as well, a la Machiavelli (e.g., *Federalist* #50).

Note that the notion of checks and balances was central not just to the design of the central government institutions, but to the use of federalism as well – the federal structure, too, was seen by Madison and others as having the advantage of providing an additional set of checks and balances, whereby state governments could check the federal government, and vice versa. There is more recent work that echoes similar objectives where federalism is concerned. Weingast's work on "market-preserving federalism" is a particularly valuable example. Weingast (1995) argues that economic development requires a system in which states are strong enough to enforce property rights but not so strong as to be able to confiscate wealth, and specific forms of federalism – where one level of government can act as an effective check on the other – can be useful in this regard. (Also see North and Weingast's [1989] argument that economic development depends on government being sufficiently limited more generally – that is, through checks provided by political institutions including by not limited to federalism.) An important strength of federalism, then, is that it too produces a separation of powers, and in so doing increases the potential for monitoring and correcting error.

Monitoring and avoiding/correcting error was thus fundamental to the design of the Madisonian presidential system. That said, monitoring error is not just the focus of the American system. Let us not forget that Montesquieu, a progenitor of the notion of checks and balances, was particularly motivated by the English parliamentary system. It too reflected an elaborate system of checks and balances, and though the system has changed since Montesquieu's time, the monitoring of error still plays a central role.

Similar concerns about monitoring error are evident in the design of institutions elsewhere as well. Resnick (1987) has argued that Canadian political institutions were, inadvertently if not consciously, Montesquieuan in design: they were modeled on the British constitution, and they took to heart the need to have a combination of checks and balances – though perhaps particularly the need for elites to be able to check, and thus limit, the power of the legislature, seen as important in part because of the unruly republican experiment south of the border. In Germany, the collapse of the Weimar Republic and the rise of the Third Reich were viewed in part as a consequence of a lack of checks and balances. The political system designed by the Basic Law in 1949 consequently and consciously included much more extensive error-monitoring mechanisms through a combination of bicameralism and federalism (Karpen 1988; Kommers 1989; on the additional constraints of post-unification Germany, see Brauninger and Konig 1999). The design of the French Fifth Republic in 1958 reflects similar concerns – in this case, the need for strong and independent presidencies and legislatures, and the checks and balances that are a consequence of these opposing powers (Debré 1959, 1978). In short, separations of power have been a central concern across a wide range of political-institutional designs. In each case, the goal was to produce a system one principle objective of which was to carefully monitor and correct error.

(In fact, there is an argument to be made that monitoring and correcting error was not *one* principle objective in the design of these systems, but *the* principle objective. First we set up a system that monitors error, and then we elect a – heavily constrained and carefully monitored – government. In the absence of the former, we are very reluctant to do the latter.)

Self-Correcting Mechanisms
The emphasis on error monitoring is thus not exclusive to the American case – it is evident in the design of governing institutions around the world. It is not difficult to find evidence of what Mansfield called "self-executing" constitutions. And it is worth noting, then, that systems like the one Montesquieu suggested are not very different from the kinds of systems suggested in the 1960s by social scientists motivated by work in engineering and mathematics on "cybernetics" and "feedback." Karl Deutsch and David Easton are among the most prominent in this field – each was interested in describing a political system as a self-maintaining mechanism, whereby outputs were constantly monitored and inputs adjusted accordingly. These were not the only authors to be drawn to a view of political systems as a kind of servomechanism, however. Richardson (1983) offers a particularly valuable review, tracing the importance of feedback through the work of Adam Smith, J. S. Mill, Myrdal, Keynes, and many others. Richardson's argument is that the notion of social and political systems operating as a looped process, whereby outputs are monitored and feedback is used to adjust inputs, has a long heritage.

Note that these systems depend on ongoing processes of negative feedback, where deviations from some preferred level of policy are identified and reacted to, so that the next round of policy making can move more closely to that preferred level. Easton and Deutsch were among the first to outline this cybernetics-informed models of political systems, but Wlezien's (1995, 1996, 2004) work on the thermostatic model of public opinion and policy is among the clearest statements, and tests, of this negative-feedback-driven relationship. In a representative democracy, Wlezien suggests, the public should act like a thermostat. If the public wants more policy on, for instance, health, they make this clear to policy makers. Provided policy makers then provide more health policy, the public should adjust their preferences for change downward – they wanted more, they got more, and so, ceteris paribus, they no longer want more. Put differently (that is, in a way that better highlights the negative aspect of negative feedback), the public is getting exactly what they want, but their preferences change, or government action changes; the public notices this gap between what they want and what they are getting, and accordingly sends a signal to government to reduce the error.

There is now an accumulating body of evidence of this thermostatic relationship between public opinion and policy in representative democracies (in addition to Wlezien's work, see, e.g., Eichenberg and Stoll 2003; Erikson et al. 2002; Johnson et al. 2005; Soroka and Wlezien 2004, 2005, 2010; Wlezien and Soroka 2011, 2012). In linking the thermostatic model to the current discussion of negativity biases, however, there are two core questions: (1) Is feedback really predominantly negative?, and (2) Does "negative" feedback actually imply negativity?

On the first issue, the answer is yes – feedback is predominantly negative. This is absolutely necessary if political systems function as cybernetics theory suggests; the growing empirical literature on thermostatic responsiveness also shows that it is true in practice. Note that the expectation of predominantly negative feedback fits uncomfortably with work on public policy in which positive feedback plays a leading role. (See a related discussion in Weaver 2010.) There are, after all, vast bodies of work on path dependency in economics and political science – work that shows that once a certain path, institution, or policy is chosen, it is very hard for policy makers to change it fundamentally (e.g., Pierson 2000; Page 2006; Garrouste and Ioannides 2001). Note, however, that the typical account of path dependence/positive feedback focuses not so much on year-to-year micro-adjustments to policy as on major paradigm shifts. A given country sets up a pension regime, for instance, and that regime then creates a variety of strong incentives to maintain it.

When the focus is not so much on the establishment of a new regime as on the dynamic functioning of an existing regime or political system, negative feedback seems to predominate. The distinction is useful here because it reminds us that the creation of representative democratic institutions does not need to be fundamentally negative. (Although there are arguments that it was primarily a product of reactions to negative stimuli, mostly fear of death in a hostile environment.) But the ongoing functioning of those institutions is dependent, by and large, on the regular monitoring of negative information.

Which brings us to the second question: Is "negative" feedback necessarily negative? "Negative" in the literature on thermostatic responsiveness is seen only as the direction of the effect of policy on public preferences, after all – it is the sign of a coefficient, not a qualitative assessment of emotion or impact. But the functioning of models of self-correcting or self-monitoring systems is premised on monitoring error (i.e., the gap between what we want and what we are getting). The same is true for representative democracy, as seen through the lens of cybernetic models, but also through interpretations of Montesquieu's self-monitoring constitution: its success depends in large part on the regular monitoring of negative information (or of bad news). It is very easy to imagine a political system that functions mainly through penalties for error; it is rather difficult to envision a political system that functions mainly through rewards for success. (This is true empirically speaking as well – consider the work on common-pool resources reviewed in Chapter 2.) There are thus quite direct links between the negativity bias evident in human behavior and the negativity that appears to be predominant in the regular functioning of representative democracy. Although negative feedback is not necessarily emotionally or evaluatively negative, its importance to the functioning of representative systems of government may nevertheless mean that those systems depend on, and/or produce, information environments that are predominantly error-, penalty-, and/or negatively oriented.

Teleology, Nondemocratic Institutions, and History

One difficulty with the argument that political-institutional design reflects the negativity biases inherent in the way humans process information is that it can sound rather teleological. That is, it can sound as though institutions are destined to become negative, because that is how the human brain functions, and so the end-point of all political institutions necessarily involves a focus on negative information. Fukuyama's (1992) argument that the fall of communism brought an end to the natural evolution of political institutions – in the natural dominance of Western liberal democracy – is perhaps the most famous illustration of this kind of argument. The problem is that a teleological argument of this sort precludes the possibility of change in the future. It also ignores the wide range of political institutions, democratic and nondemocratic, with varying degrees of negativity biases, currently (and seemingly very durably) in existence.

To be clear, then, the idea that representative democratic institutions tend to reflect the same kind of negativity biases that are apparent in many areas of human behavior is not intended to be teleological. It is not necessarily the case that all institutions will exhibit negativity biases, nor is it the case that once institutions do show a negativity bias, this bias can never be reversed. It is possible to design institutions that focus mainly on positive feedback, and those need not necessarily evolve into institutions that are more negatively inclined. (Consider again the work on common-pool resources reviewed in Chapter 2.) It is also possible for there to be long-lasting institutions that never exhibit the kinds of negativity biases described earlier.

My own inclination (that is, my argument informed but by no means supported by evidence in preceding chapters) is to suggest the following. It tends to be the case that, for modern large-scale societies in which some version of the common good is pursued through collective self-rule, political institutions that focus mainly on negative feedback are relatively common and potentially advantageous. These are societies in which there is a great deal of information of which to keep track, and a focus on negative feedback helps reduce the amount of information that voters (and governments) must deal with. This amount of information is partly driven by the wider variety of policies pursued in modern states; it is also a product of the number of people involved. Achieving multiple goals for many people requires that all parties involved find some way to focus their attention. Negativity offers one possibility. (We cannot keep track of all the – mostly marginally positive – feedback, so we focus on the most deviant cases.) Where societies are smaller and/or the objectives of governments simpler, a focus on negativity may be less advantageous. The same is true for societies in which the common good, pursued through collective self-rule, is not a priority.

So nondemocratic institutions may not exhibit the same negativity biases as democratic ones. The goals of those political institutions are, after all, fundamentally different: either the common good is not a priority, or there is a belief that the common good can be determined by a small group of individuals, or even just one individual. (This latter view is especially central to totalitarian regimes. See, e.g., Sondrol 1991, or Weber's discussion of charismatic leadership in Gerth and Mills 1991: 245–250.) In either case, the task of monitoring information across many domains and many individuals is reduced. In short, the public in an authoritarian regime is not in the business of monitoring government (or they are at least being prevented from doing so). So authoritarian regimes need not include the institutional mechanisms for error monitoring that are common in democratic ones.

There is an alternative account of the role of negativity and error-monitoring feedback in authoritarian regimes, namely that authoritarian political institutions, like democratic ones, are focused on negativity, and particularly on checks and balances, but while democratic institutions focus mainly on controlling *governments*, authoritarian institutions focus mainly on controlling *publics*. Again, Hobbes's *Leviathan* is the critical resource: the purpose of a commonwealth is to escape the state of nature, in which the risk of death is very high. For Hobbes (and for many authoritarian leaders), we require government as a check on human impulses.

The difference between authoritarian and democratic regimes may thus have less to do with their focus on negative information and more with their focus on the ends toward which that information is used. Both systems involve error monitoring and predominantly negative feedback. But the object of control in democratic regimes is governments, and in authoritarian regimes it is publics. And note that the differences discussed in preceding paragraphs relate to the role of negativity in the design of political institutions. Democratic institutions tend to include checks and balances on governments; authoritarian institutions do not. This is not the same thing as saying that people (or leaders) in democratic regimes are more attentive to negative information than are people (or leaders) in authoritarian regimes. They are, mostly likely, not.[1] Most humans will tend to prioritize negative information over positive information, but their tendency to do so may be reflected differently, or may not be reflected at all, in the design of the political institutions under which they live.

(That said, citizens' negativity biases can both help structure and be affected by the design of political institutions. This may raise issues in democratic

---

[1] But note that insofar as authoritarian regimes produce worse outcomes for most individuals than democratic ones, we might expect negative information to be less outlying, and thus less powerful, to the attitudes of those living under authoritarianism. In short, citizens' expectations in authoritarian regimes may be worse, and, as we have seen in Chapter 4, the negativity bias may consequently be reduced. Losing your job in a system in which unemployment is relatively low is more shocking than is losing your job in a system in which unemployment is high, for instance.

regimes in which institutions enhance citizens' emphasis on negative information. This is discussed further in the section that follows.)

What accounts for variance in the ways in which error monitoring, or negativity, is institutionalized? There are some facts about human nature (like a negativity bias) that matter to the design of political institutions, but a host of other factors matter as well. In particular, history matters. There is a great deal of variance in political institutions, in part because institutions evolve, usually slowly, over time, and they are greatly conditioned by widely varying political, economic, and sociological histories of different parts of the world. History quite clearly matters to the design of political institutions, not in the sense that institutions gradually evolve toward a given end-point, but rather because history can set political institutions off on very different paths. (There is, of course, a vast literature on the role of history in institutional design. For recent reviews, see Pierson and Skocpol 2002; Sanders 2006.) It is uncontentious to suggest that different distributions of money, land, and power, over time, alongside the history of political institutions themselves, have led to quite different institutional regimes. But accounts of institutional design may well benefit from a consideration of the human tendency to prioritize negative information as well.

In sum, it is neither teleological nor antihistorical to suggest that many representative democratic institutions process information in ways that are similar to humans – in many domains, at least, prioritizing negative information over positive information. But as work on "new institutionalism" (see, e.g., March and Olsen 1984; 2006) makes clear, institutions both *reflect* and *affect* human behavior.

Institutions Are Not Just Negative

There is a second danger in making the argument that institutions are more focused on negative information: it can start to sound as though institutions themselves are fundamentally negative. That is not my argument here, however. The creation of political institutions – new governments, or even new policies (such as state-run health care) – can be viewed as fundamentally optimistic, and positive. We choose to cooperate, after all, and to build something based on the expectation that we will be able to continue to cooperate for a common purpose. This does not need to be just about escaping Hobbes's state of nature; it can be about achieving, through cooperation, better outcomes.

The fact that humans have chosen to cooperate, repeatedly, at many different levels of aggregation, and trying many different institutional forms, can (and I suspect should) be seen as an indication of our optimism. To recall work reviewed in Chapter 1, it should be viewed as evidence of our "positivity offset," that is, "the tendency for there to be a weak positive (approach) motivational output at zero input" (Cacioppo and Gardner 1999). It is this optimism, at least in part, that leads us to design political institutions in the first place; and that same optimism may be what produces predominantly positive feedback in new policy domains. Governments start producing something (education, health care), and our desire for more is driven in part by the optimistic belief that governments will be able to provide it, and will do it reasonably well.

Even the establishment of rules that enforce cooperation through penalties, then, is a reflection of the optimism that humans seem to have about the future. But it also reflects realities about human behavior in the present. Cooperation can lead to better aggregate-level outcomes, but that cooperation must be ensured, and encouraged – and given our tendency to react strongly to negative information, penalties are often the most efficient means of achieving this.

Is Negativity Bad?

The predominance of negative information in politics and political communication is, at this stage, relatively clear. Whether that negativity has deleterious consequences is not, however. In this final section, I review findings from preceding chapters and consider the implications and possibilities for political science and for everyday politics.

First, the findings in Chapters 3 through 7 can be summarized as follows:

1. The dynamics found in psychological studies of impression formation are evident in analyses of candidate approval and voting behavior; in both, negative information has a greater effect on overall assessments than positive information does.

2. These individual-level dynamics are evident at the aggregate level as well, including public reactions to economic trends, where negative changes in the economy matter more than (equivalent) positive changes in the economy.

3. Aggregate-level analyses, more readily available across a range of countries and cultures, also make clear that the negativity bias – at least where economic sentiment is concerned – is not culturally bound, but evident across a wide range of cultures.

4. Aggregate-level analyses also point to the importance of "frequency-weight" accounts of the negativity bias in which the relative strength of negative information is dependent on a predominantly positive environment.

5. The human tendency to focus on negative information is clear in news content as well, including in analysis of crime reporting and economic reporting, where the distribution of information in mass media is more negative than the distribution of information in reality.

6. This trend in media content fits with what we see in political behavior, but the link is made clearer still in analyses of reactions to news, which show both that negative covers sell more magazines and that individuals are more activated by and more attentive to negative than to positive TV news.

7. A negativity bias is also evident in the design and functioning of political institutions (including mass media), many of which are focused almost exclusively on monitoring error.

The first two of these findings are, given the existing literature in this and other fields, not surprising. There clearly are domains of political behavior in which negative information can matter a great deal. This is not necessarily a bad thing, both because negative information may be particularly valuable and because a focus on the limited body of negative information may be a quite reasonable and rational way to deal with what is almost certainly a vast and complex information environment. If the negativity bias is indeed premised on a generally positive environment, then focusing on negative information has the advantage of reducing the amount of material to deal with. Of course, there are other ways to select the information to which we pay attention. But negativity may be one reasonable option, even independent of the (quite likely evolution-inspired) possibility that our focus on negative information is at least in part attributable to the fact that negative consequences tend to be much more detrimental to survival than positive consequences are beneficial to it.

The findings from Chapter 4 that are critical to this account of negativity-as-information-reduction are also central in responding to concerns that we are invariably destined to fall into a pit of negativity. We are not, because the strength of negative information is most likely premised in part on its rarity. When the political environment is desperately negative, then, we should see a shift in attentiveness to positive information. Put differently, we can only get so negative, at which point the same system that produces that negativity may help us recover from it. (We might call this "self-limiting negativity.") This is not to say that politics will become mostly positive – negative information may still be more valuable, and thus holding on to a certain degree of negative information may be important. But politics may become somewhat less negative, at least temporarily.

If negativity biases are reduced in particularly negative environments, however, we might ask another question: How can politics repeatedly reflect negativity biases if those biases are dependent on an information environment that is predominantly positive? Presumably repeated negativity would produce an increasingly negative environment. And preceding chapters do seem to paint a picture of an information environment that is overwhelmingly negative. So how can a negativity bias still exist?

The answer is relatively simple: most of the information we receive on a daily basis does not come from media or politics, but from our regular, daily interactions at home and at work. As has been noted earlier, we eat some breakfast, get some things done, watch some television, and so on. For most of us, days are peppered with these marginally positive events, and political news makes up a relatively small proportion of our information environment. This is not to say that negativity cannot come from other (nonpolitical) areas.

But these negative events are, on most days, outliers, surrounded by series of events, interactions, and experiences that are relatively positive.

(Recall also that just as we are hardwired to focus on negative information in the present, we are also hardwired to remember positive information better over the long term. Chapter 1 reviewed the psychology literature on event recall, for instance, illustrating a tendency for humans to remember positive events more easily than negative events. A negativity bias in the present may well be sustained in part by a positivity bias over the long term.)

That said, the extent to which the negativity bias in politics waxes and wanes, and indeed the overall magnitude of the negativity bias to begin with, is partly dependent on the design and functioning of a range of political institutions. I have argued elsewhere that the negativity bias in media coverage of the economy serves to enhance the negativity bias already evident in citizens' reactions to the economy; we are reacting asymmetrically to information that already is asymmetrically biased (Soroka 2006). We have in this instance an institution that does not solve the negativity bias, but rather augments it, and findings in Chapters 4 suggest that this dynamic may be pervasive – that is, it may exist across a wide range of countries. The same might be true for political institutions, designed to focus on error monitoring and thus contributing to the preponderance of negative information in politics. Our own biases may be enhanced by the institutions we design.

This is, somewhat ironically, an instance of positive feedback. We are interested in negative information, and thus make institutions that focus on negative information, and thus get more negative information, and so on. But this is *not* path dependency. There is a limit to the negativity bias. And there are instances in which our biases change.

One central and as-yet-unresolved issue is whether there are, in fact, long-term detrimental effects of the focus on negativity in politics. There certainly is in an increasing number of analysts and commentators expressing concern about negativity in politics, and most developed democracies are now in a period of long-term declines in many forms of political participation and confidence in political institutions. These may be telltale signs of the need to seriously rethink political institutions, not just in terms of increasing the number of checks and balances (which is a common refrain), but in terms of shifting the balance of information away from the negative, using institutions to (partly) correct rather than enhance biases in human behavior.

Perhaps State Duma Deputy Oleg Mikheyev was (sort of) right: perhaps we do need media to be more positive. Journalists themselves actively debate this possibility: consider work on "civic journalism" that argues for a press that is more community based, more balanced and informative in its reporting, and more encouraging of dialogue and participation (e.g., Rosen 1999; Perry 2003). It may be time to rethink our view of the main functions of mass media in democracy. That said, as preceding sections have argued, media are not the only institution exhibiting a bias toward negativity and error monitoring.

Perhaps we need to rethink the design of political institutions as well. Work on altruistic punishment and common-pool resources may point us in one possible direction: perhaps the size of political institutions is just too big, and we need to rethink ways of making politics more local, and accordingly (potentially) more reward- rather than penalty-based.

I do not believe that this is true. My own inclination is to regard the negativity bias as a necessary, and largely effective, characteristic of political behavior and political institutions. It is a fascinating characteristic, to be sure, in large part because it helps demonstrate the link between what we do in politics and what we do in so many other aspects of our daily lives. But it may also be a relatively efficient way to deal with a very rich information environment. And, importantly, it likely comes with a built-in mechanism that prevents us from becoming unlimitedly negative. Admittedly, whether that mechanism is effective, even alongside institutions that seem to augment the negativity bias, is not clear. This is in, my view, an important goal for future work, and the Appendix that follows includes a start to that work – a more formal explication of the way in which negativity biases will vary based on the interaction between humans' built-in negativity biases alongside some weighted combination of negativity in the current and past information environments. To date, there is not enough information on each of these factors to know whether negativity is really a problem, however. We *do* have a relatively good sense for the wide range of domains in which there is a negativity bias. The issue now is to better understand, in these political contexts, if there are advantages to reducing (or augmenting) that bias, and how we might do so.

Appendix A

Preceding chapters have argued that there is a negativity bias in political behavior, and in politics more generally. The preponderance of negativity in politics, and particularly the steady rise in negative campaign advertising, makes it seem as though politics will only ever get more and more negative. This is unlikely to be the case, however. As has been argued earlier, the same dynamic that generates the negativity bias also limits it. Negative information matters more because it is relatively rare. As the information environment becomes more negative, the impact of negative information relative to positive information likely decreases.

The purpose of this appendix is to provide a somewhat more formal explication of this possibility. Let us begin by defining the negativity bias at time t for individual i as N_{it}, where

$$N_{it} = \frac{v_{it}}{\pi_{it}} \tag{A.1}$$

N_{it}, then, is a ratio of two coefficients: v_{it}, which is the attentiveness paid to negative information, and π_{it}, which is the attentiveness paid to positive information (for individual i at time time t). A value of 2 for N, then, reflects a bias in which negative information produces twice as much attention as positive information; a value of .5 reflects a bias in which negative information produces half as much attention as positive information. Given that it is a ratio of positive quantities, N is always greater than zero, and 1 is the dividing line between a negativity bias ($N > 1$) and a positivity bias ($1 <N> 0$).[1]

---

[1] But note that while using a ratio to capture N is intuitively appealing, it has some disadvantages as well. If, for instance, the denominator approaches zero, then the measure can produce wild fluctuations. There are, of course, other ways to capture the balance of negative to positive information. Depending on the nature of the data (specifically the prevalence of positive information), something other than a ratio may be important in order to make this model empirically useful.

The main predictor of N at time t is N at time $t - 1$. Put differently, N is highly autocorrelated – we expect that the negativity bias changes only slightly over time. That said, the negativity bias *does* change. As we have seen in Chapter 4, and as is suggested by work in psychology, the weight that individuals give to a piece of negative (positive) information decreases as the distribution of information becomes more negative (positive). That distribution of information, D, is, like N, a ratio – although in this case it is a ratio of negative information (I^v) to positive information (I^π), as follows:

$$D_{it} = \frac{I_{it}^v}{I_{it}^\pi} \tag{A.2}$$

A model of N_{it} thus includes both (a) N_{it-1} and (b) D_{it}, moderated by the preexisting negativity bias (N_{it-1}) – the bias through which D_{it} is interpreted. I suggest the following relatively simple specification:

$$N_t = \alpha + \beta N_{t-1} + \gamma (D_t - 1) N_{t-1} \tag{A.3}$$

β captures the strength of the autoregressive relationship – values less than 1 suggest that the bias will, *ceteris paribus*, decay over time, while values above 1 suggest that the bias accumulates. α also helps define the equilibrium relationship – higher values of α suggest a systematic tendency toward a negativity bias, whereas smaller or even negative values suggest a tendency toward a positivity bias.

The moderated impact of the current distribution of information (D) is captured in the last element in Equation A.3. The absolute magnitude of γ captures the weight, relative to β and α, by which the current distribution of information matters above and beyond (1) a general human tendency toward negativity and (2) individual i's negativity bias in the preceding period. Subtracting 1 from D means that its moderated impact switches direction depending on whether the information environment is biased toward negative (when $D - 1 > 0$) or positive information (when $D - 1 < 0$); and given that more negativity in the information environment should decrease the negativity bias, and more positivity should increase the negativity bias, the expectation is that $\gamma < 0$.

Equation A.3 is thus a relatively simple way of capturing the possibility that the negativity bias is partly dependent on the (non-)prevalence of negativity in the relevant information environment. Assigning values to the coefficients in Equation A.3 provides a useful illustration. Consider the following model:

$$N_t = 0.2 + 0.85 N_{t-1} + (-0.05)(D_t - 1) N_{t-1} \tag{A.4}$$

The equilibrium value of N in this model when the ratio of negative to positive information is a steady 4:5 – that is, when D is always 0.8 – is roughly 1.43. When the ratio is reversed, and D is always 1.25, the equilibrium value is roughly 1.23. Indeed, when negative information outnumbers positive information by more that 2:1 (when $D > 2$), the equilibrium value for N is less than 1. The negativity bias is lower when negativity is more prevalent.

The coefficients in Equation A.4 are entirely arbitrary, of course – there is no easy way of extracting what the coefficients might be in reality. That said, there is also one additional complication: there are reasons to believe that past values of v_{it} and π_{it} – the two components of N_{it} – do not decay at the same rate; rather, negativity (v_{it}) may decay more slowly. Consider a slight adjustment of Equation A.3, allowing for negativity and positivity in the previous period to decay (or accumulate) at different rates:

$$N_t = \alpha + \frac{\beta_1 v_{t-1}}{\beta_2 \pi_{t-1}} + \gamma(D_t - 1)N_{t-1} \qquad (A.5)$$

where the impact of D is still conditioned by N at $t - 1$, but where the current value of N can be affected differently by the two components of its past, v_{t-1} and π_{t-1}. If the impact of negative information does in fact decay more slowly, then we should expect that $\beta_1 > \beta_2$. And, as we have seen previously, there is work in psychology to suggest that this is the case, at least over the short to medium term. (Recall that it may not be the case over the long term, however.)

Note, then, that the negativity bias is a function of two static components: (1) the differential decay of negativity versus positivity (β_1 and β_2), and (2) humans' general tendency toward negativity (completely independent of information), α; and one dynamic component: (3) the relative impact of the current distribution of information moderated by the preexisting negativity bias (γ). If we could identify these coefficients, we would know whether the negativity bias is an efficient and harmless way to manage an information-rich environment (that is, a self-equilibrating process whereby increasingly negative environments will reduce, and even reverse, the negativity bias) or a systematic problem with humans, destined to lead us toward a slow decent into perpetual negativity. We cannot easily identify the coefficients in Equation A.5, however, so the long-term effect of the negativity bias in political behavior remains an open question.

Appendix B

This appendix includes a series of supporting tables for analyses in Chapters 3, 4, and 6. In all cases, portions of the estimations appear in the chapter text, and the full analyses are reported here. Tables are as follows:

Table B.3.1 Presidential Thermometer Scores and Traits, United States

Table B.3.2 Incumbent Leader Vote and Traits, Australia

Table B.3.3 Presidential Thermometer Scores and Traits, Interacted, United States

Table B.4.1 Economic Sentiment, United States

Table B.4.2 Economic Sentiment, EU

Table B.4.3 Economic Sentiment, EU, by Country

Table B.4.4 Economic Sentiment and Presidential/Government Approval, United States and United Kingdom

Table B.4.5 Economic Sentiment, United States and EU Combined

Table B.6.1 News Content, Within-Respondent ANCOVA: Skin Conductance Levels

Table B.6.2 News Content, Within-Respondent ANCOVA: Heart Rate

Table B.6.3 Campaign Ads, Within-Respondent ANCOVA: Skin Conductance Levels

Table B.6.4 Campaign Ads, Within-Respondent ANCOVA: Heart Rate

TABLE B.3.1. *Presidential Thermometer Scores and Traits, United States*

	DV: Incumbent Presidential Thermometer Scores, rescaled 0–9[a]		DV: Vote for Incumbent Presidential Party, binary[b]	
	Symmetric Model	Asymmetric Model	Symmetric Model	Asymmetric Model
Controls				
Female	.476 (.355)	.423 (.350)	.007 (.018)	.010 (.019)
Age (years)	−.019 (.010)	−.000 (.010)	−.001 (.001)	−.001 (.001)
Education (HS+)	−1.783*** (.362)	−1.715*** (.358)	.031 (.019)	.030 (.020)
Party ID (President)	13.178*** (.427)	13.141*** (.421)	.597** (.013)	.602** (.013)
Election – 1988	1.538* (.600)	.677 (.593)	−.114** (.030)	−.121** (.030)
Election – 1992	−3.167*** (.558)	−4.011*** (.554)	−.204** (.029)	−.211** (.029)
Election – 1996	1.385* (.664)	.706 (.656)	−.003 (.037)	−.007 (.038)
Election – 2000	−.253 (.734)	−.253 (.728)	−.018 (.040)	−.006 (.041)
Election – 2004	−1.786** (.680)	−1.229 (.671)	−.080* (.037)	−.070 (.037)
Traits (Symmetric)				
Intelligent	1.726*** (.321)		.021 (.017)	
Knowledgeable	2.366*** (.328)		.054** (.017)	
Moral	4.770*** (.275)		.109** (.015)	
Leadership	7.835*** (.283)		.108** (.015)	
Cares	9.362*** (.273)		.229** (.014)	
Traits (Asymmetric)				
Intelligent (Pos)		.528 (.473)		.002 (.025)
Intelligent (Neg)		4.004*** (.716)		.076 (.046)
Knowledgeable (Pos)		1.313** (.499)		.065* (.027)
Knowledgeable (Neg)		4.597*** (.703)		.047 (.043)
Moral (Pos)		2.461*** (.459)		.088** (.024)
Moral (Neg)		7.094*** (.498)		.139** (.029)

(continued)

127

TABLE B.3.1 *(continued)*

	DV: Incumbent Presidential Thermometer Scores, rescaled 0–9[a]		DV: Vote for Incumbent Presidential Party, binary[b]	
	Symmetric Model	Asymmetric Model	Symmetric Model	Asymmetric Model
Leadership (Pos)		6.838*** (.477)		.037 (.026)
Leadership (Neg)		8.697*** (.561)		.218** (.038)
Cares (Pos)		5.465*** (.525)		.175** (.032)
Cares (Neg)		12.821*** (.466)		.272** (.027)
Combined Positive		16.303*** (.618)		.352*** (.033)
Combined Negative		37.214*** (.755)		.649*** (.031)
Constant	49.375*** (.704)	56.951*** (.822)	−.627** (.116)	−.348* (.141)
N	10262	10262	6480	6480
R-sq	.632	.643		
adj. R-sq	.632	.643		
Pseudo R-sq			.594	.597

[a] Cells contain OLS regression coefficients, with standard errors in parentheses. All estimates used the cumulative NES file, and all presidential elections from 1984 to 2004.

[b] Cells contain binary probit regression coefficients, with standard errors in parentheses. All estimates used the cumulative NES file, and all presidential elections from 1984 to 2004.

* p < .05; ** p < .01; *** p < .001.

TABLE B.3.2. *Incumbent Leader Vote and Traits, Australia*

	DV: Incumbent Leader Thermometer Scores, rescaled 0–10			
	Symmetric Model		**Asymmetric Model**	
Controls				
Female	−.035	(.045)	−.047	(.045)
Age (years)	.001	(.001)	−.001	(.001)
Education (HS+)	.067	(.048)	.057	(.048)
Party ID (President)	2.060***	(.055)	2.037***	(.055)
Election – 1993	−.427***	(.074)	−.464***	(.073)
Election – 1996	−.693***	(.081)	−.748***	(.080)
Election – 1998	.333***	(.075)	.286***	(.074)
Election – 2001	.219**	(.070)	.206**	(.069)
Traits (Symmetric)				
Intelligent	.106**	(.039)		
Compassionate	.878***	(.035)		
Sensible	.685***	(.040)		
Leadership	.295***	(.035)		
Inspiring	.784***	(.034)		
Traits (Asymmetric)				
Intelligent (Pos)			.173**	(.055)
Intelligent (Neg)			−.047	(.093)
Compassionate (Pos)			.324***	(.072)
Compassionate (Neg)			1.309***	(.061)
Sensible (Pos)			.665***	(.066)
Sensible (Neg)			.697***	(.079)
Leadership (Pos)			.399***	(.058)
Leadership (Neg)			.113	(.074)
Inspiring (Pos)			.492***	(.070)
Inspiring (Neg)			1.003***	(.057)
Combined Positive			1.055***	(.124)
Combined Negative			2.016***	(.185)
Constant	4.258***	(.107)	4.820***	(.130)
N	7096		7096	
R-sq	.681		.687	
Adjusted R-sq	.681		.687	

Cells contain binary probit regression coefficients, with standard errors in parentheses. All estimates used the cumulative NES file, and all presidential elections from 1984 to 2004.
*p < .05; **p < .01; ***p < .001.

TABLE B.3.3. *Presidential Thermometer Scores and Traits, Interacted, United States*

	DV: Incumbent Presidential Thermometer Scores, rescaled 0–9			
	No Interaction	Party ID	Gender	Education
Controls				
Female	.400 (.358)	.402 (.358)	3.213** (1.039)	.403 (.358)
Age (years)	-.008 (.011)	-.008 (.011)	-.008 (.011)	-.008 (.011)
Education (HS+)	-1.709*** (.366)	-1.695*** (.366)	-1.705*** (.365)	.543 (1.031)
Election – 1988	15.278*** (.420)	15.008*** (1.062)	15.214*** (.420)	15.105*** (.421)
Election – 1992	1.872** (.604)	1.875** (.604)	1.853** (.603)	1.912** (.603)
Election – 1996	-5.518*** (.559)	-5.524*** (.560)	-5.576*** (.559)	-5.543*** (.559)
Election – 2000	.371 (.610)	.371 (.610)	.438 (.610)	.465 (.610)
Election – 2004	-.529 (.622)	-.583 (.626)	-.518 (.621)	-.401 (.621)
	.974 (.678)	.986 (.679)	.941 (.678)	1.094 (.678)
Traits (Asymmetric)				
Positive	15.909*** (.618)	15.962*** (.955)	17.003*** (.799)	16.474*** (.839)
Negative	40.362*** (.748)	40.529*** (.881)	38.038*** (.982)	37.082*** (1.047)
Positive * Party ID		.081 (1.254)		
Negative * Party ID		-1.276 (1.924)		
Positive * Female			-2.438* (1.193)	
Negative * Female			5.207*** (1.432)	
Positive * Education				-.907 (1.180)
Negative * Education				6.288*** (1.427)
Constant	54.804*** (.819)	54.842*** (.942)	53.560*** (.919)	53.637*** (.949)
N	10262	10262	10262	10262
R-sq	.625	.625	.625	.626
adj. R-sq	.624	.624	.625	.625

Cells contain OLS regression coefficients, with standard errors in parentheses. All estimates used the cumulative NES file, and all presidential elections from 1984 to 2004.

*p < .05; **p < .01; ***p < .001.

TABLE B.4.1. *Economic Sentiment, United States*

	DV: Δ Sentiment (Retropective Egotropic)$_t$					
	Model 1		**Model 2**		**Model 3**	
Levels						
Sentiment$_{t-1}$	−.121***	(.028)	−.138***	(.029)	−.106***	(.023)
Unemp$_{t-1}$	−.513	(.268)	−.513	(.269)		
Inflation$_{t-1}$	−.226*	(.112)	−.211	(.112)		
Misery Index$_{t-1}$					−.252*	(.107)
Changes						
Δ Unemp$_t$	−3.400	(1.987)				
Δ Inflation$_t$	−.829	(.761)				
Δ Unemp$_t$ (Pos)			1.543	(3.617)		
Δ Unemp$_t$ (Neg)			−7.390*	(3.145)		
Δ Inflation$_t$ (Pos)			.921	(1.282)		
Δ Inflation$_t$ (Neg)			−2.987*	(1.403)		
Δ Misery Index$_t$ (Pos)					.470	(1.311)
Δ Misery Index$_t$ (Neg)					−2.533	(1.354)
y	4.975*	(1.975)	6.163**	(2.036)	3.778**	(1.304)
N	394		394		394	
Rsq	.055		.069		.054	
Adj Rsq	.043		.053		.045	

	DV: Δ Sentiment (Prospective Egotropic)$_t$					
	Model 1		**Model 2**		**Model 3**	
Levels						
Sentiment$_{t-1}$	−.213***	(.034)	−.226***	(.034)	−.237***	(.033)
Unemp$_{t-1}$	−.449*	(.177)	−.434*	(.178)		
Inflation$_{t-1}$	−.447***	(.109)	−.455***	(.109)		
Misery Index$_{t-1}$					−.465***	(.101)
Changes						
Δ Unemp$_t$	−.007	(1.500)				
Δ Inflation$_t$	−1.961**	(.602)				
Δ Unemp$_t$ (Pos)			.281	(2.832)		
Δ Unemp$_t$ (Neg)			.096	(2.449)		
Δ Inflation$_t$ (Pos)			−.382	(.994)		
Δ Inflation$_t$ (Neg)			−3.812***	(1.102)		
Δ Misery Index$_t$ (Pos)					−.098	(1.015)
Δ Misery Index$_t$ (Neg)					−3.563***	(1.066)
y	9.381***	(1.863)	10.098***	(1.903)	10.657***	(1.719)
N	394		394		394	
Rsq	.121		.130		.126	
Adj Rsq	.109		.114		.117	

(continued)

TABLE B.4.1 (*continued*)

	DV: Δ Sentiment (Retrospective Sociotropic)$_t$					
	Model 1		Model 2		Model 3	
Levels						
Sentiment$_{t-1}$	−.042**	(.015)	−.047**	(.015)	−.042**	(.014)
Unemp$_{t-1}$	.835*	(.324)	.951**	(.327)		
Inflation$_{t-1}$	−.487**	(.167)	−.453**	(.167)		
Misery Index$_{t-1}$					−.182	(.152)
Changes						
Δ Unemp$_t$	−7.892**	(3.047)				
Δ Inflation$_t$	−1.349	(1.162)				
Δ Unemp$_t$ (Pos)			1.365	(5.542)		
Δ Unemp$_t$ (Neg)			−15.175**	(4.761)		
Δ Inflation$_t$ (Pos)			.055	(1.965)		
Δ Inflation$_t$ (Neg)			−3.170	(2.099)		
Δ Misery Index$_t$ (Pos)					−.497	(2.027)
Δ Misery Index$_t$ (Neg)					−4.512*	(2.074)
Constant	−3.644	(2.151)	−3.041	(2.173)	2.077	(1.649)
N	394		394		394	
Rsq	.078		.090		.035	
Adj Rsq	.066		.073		.025	

	DV: Δ Sentiment (Prospective Sociotropic)$_t$					
	Model 1		Model 2		Model 3	
Levels						
Sentiment$_{t-1}$	−.176***	(.029)	−.179***	(.029)	−.136***	(.025)
Unemp$_{t-1}$	.704**	(.228)	.732**	(.236)		
Inflation$_{t-1}$	−.314*	(.125)	−.312*	(.126)		
Misery Index$_{t-1}$					.006	(.099)
Changes						
Δ Unemp$_t$	.896	(1.963)				
Δ Inflation$_t$	−2.799***	(.797)				
Δ Unemp$_t$ (Pos)			.706	(3.764)		
Δ Unemp$_t$ (Neg)			1.266	(3.207)		
Δ Inflation$_t$ (Pos)			−1.969	(1.315)		
Δ Inflation$_t$ (Neg)			−3.757*	(1.455)		
Δ Misery Index$_t$ (Pos)					−.882	(1.365)
Δ Misery Index$_t$ (Neg)					−4.079**	(1.420)
Constant	−3.644	(2.151)	−1.699	(1.393)	1.535	(1.140)
N	394		394		394	
Rsq	.078		.122		.087	
Adj Rsq	.066		.106		.077	

Cells contain OLS regression coefficients, with standard errors in parentheses. Model includes monthly data from January 1978 to November 2010. Survey data are from the Michigan Consumer Sentiment Index survey, where the measure is % saying "better now" minus % saying "worse now" in response to the question listed in the text.
*p < .05; **p < .01; ***p < .001.

TABLE B.4.2. *Economic Sentiment, EU*

	DV: Δ Sentiment (Retropective Egotropic)$_t$					
	Model 1		**Model 2**		**Model 3**	
Levels						
Sentiment$_{t-1}$	−.050***	(.005)	−.051***	(.005)	−.046***	(.005)
Unemp$_{t-1}$	−.036	(.026)	−.037	(.026)		
Inflation$_{t-1}$	−.039	(.021)	−.029	(.021)		
Misery Index$_{t-1}$					−.026	(.017)
Changes						
Δ Unemp$_t$	−2.113***	(.362)				
Δ Inflation$_t$	−.759***	(.140)				
Δ Unemp$_t$ (Pos)			−.523	(.685)		
Δ Unemp$_t$ (Neg)			−3.090***	(.527)		
Δ Inflation$_t$ (Pos)			−.285	(.237)		
Δ Inflation$_t$ (Neg)			−1.285***	(.248)		
Δ Misery Index$_t$ (Pos)					−.385	(.232)
Δ Misery Index$_t$ (Neg)					−1.431***	(.233)
Constant	−.326	(.222)	−.096	(.229)	−.243	(.197)
N (cases/panels)	4363	/17	4363	/17	4363	/17
Rsq (within, between)	.034	.025	.037	.045	.033	.039
Rsq (overall)	.018		.020		.019	
sigma e	3.688		3.682		3.689	
sigma u	.681		.713		.632	
rho	.033		.036		.029	

	DV: Δ Sentiment (Propective Egotropic) $_t$					
	Model 1		**Model 2**		**Model 3**	
Levels						
Sentiment$_{t-1}$	−.086***	(.006)	−.087***	(.006)	−.082***	(.006)
Unemp$_{t-1}$	−.052	(.030)	−.053	(.030)		
Inflation$_{t-1}$	−.056*	(.025)	−.047	(.026)		
Misery Index$_{t-1}$					−.043*	(.021)
Changes						
Δ Unemp$_t$	−1.985***	(.443)				
Δ Inflation$_t$	−.779***	(.172)				
Δ Unemp$_t$ (Pos)			−.521	(.840)		
Δ Unemp$_t$ (Neg)			−2.881***	(.645)		
Δ Inflation$_t$ (Pos)			−.318	(.290)		
Δ Inflation$_t$ (Neg)			−1.291***	(.305)		
Δ Misery Index$_t$ (Pos)					−.317	(.284)
Δ Misery Index$_t$ (Neg)					−1.501***	(.286)
Constant	.434	(.280)	.658*	(.290)	.496*	(.249)
N (cases/panels)	4363	/17	4363	/17	4363	/17
Rsq (within, between)	.046	.073	.048	.090	.046	.088
Rsq (overall)	.025		.026		.026	
sigma e	4.519		4.516		4.519	
sigma u	.969		.992		.927	
rho	.044		.046		.040	

(continued)

	DV: Δ Sentiment (Retrospective Sociotropic)$_t$					
	Model 1		Model 2		Model 3	
Levels						
Sentiment$_{t-1}$	−.030***	(.004)	−.030***	(.004)	−.027***	(.004)
Unemp$_{t-1}$	.211***	(.044)	.211***	(.044)		
Inflation$_{t-1}$	−.069	(.038)	−.066	(.039)		
Misery Index$_{t-1}$					.059	(.030)
Changes						
Δ Unemp$_t$	−4.422***	(.700)				
Δ Inflation$_t$	−1.052***	(.260)				
Δ Unemp$_t$ (Pos)			−3.970**	(1.298)		
Δ Unemp$_t$ (Neg)			−4.697***	(.991)		
Δ Inflation$_t$ (Pos)			−.923*	(.441)		
Δ Inflation$_t$ (Neg)			−1.195**	(.461)		
Δ Misery Index$_t$ (Pos)					−1.098*	(.432)
Δ Misery Index$_t$ (Neg)					−1.616***	(.435)
Constant	−2.461***	(.405)	−2.400***	(.419)	−1.430***	(.371)
N (cases/panels)	4363	/17	4363	/17	4363	/17
Rsq (within, between)	.032	.004	.032	.003	.020	.008
Rsq (overall)	.023		.023		.015	
sigma e	6.846		6.847		6.886	
sigma u	.841		.841		.623	
rho	.015		.015		.008	

	DV: Δ Sentiment (Retrospective Sociotropic)$_t$					
	Model 1		Model 2		Model 3	
Levels						
Sentiment$_{t-1}$	−.088***	(.006)	−.089***	(.006)	−.083***	(.006)
Unemp$_{t-1}$	.156**	(.051)	.155**	(.051)		
Inflation$_{t-1}$	−.071	(.046)	−.063	(.047)		
Misery Index$_{t-1}$					.030	(.036)
Changes						
Δ Unemp$_t$	−3.057***	(.812)				
Δ Inflation$_t$	−1.151***	(.312)				
Δ Unemp$_t$ (Pos)			−4.626**	(1.546)		
Δ Unemp$_t$ (Neg)			−2.024	(1.165)		
Δ Inflation$_t$ (Pos)			−.881	(.528)		
Δ Inflation$_t$ (Neg)			−1.423*	(.552)		
Δ Misery Index$_t$ (Pos)					−1.126*	(.516)
Δ Misery Index$_t$ (Neg)					−1.476**	(.518)
Constant	−2.103***	(.489)	−2.177***	(.506)	−1.273**	(.442)
N (cases/panels)	4363	/17	4363	/17	4363	/17
Rsq (within, between)	.048	.106	.049	.104	.044	.132
Rsq (overall)	.036		.037		.034	
sigma e	8.205		8.205		8.220	
sigma u	1.128		1.126		1.014	
rho	.019		.018		.015	

Cells contain GLS regression coefficients, with standard errors in parentheses, from a fixed-effects TSCS estimation. Model includes monthly data from January 1985 to February 2011. Survey data are from the Joint Harmonized EU Programme of Business and Consumer Surveys, relies on % saying "got a lot better" or "got a little better" minus % saying "got a little worse" or "got a lot worse" in response to the questions listed in the text.

*p < .05;   **p < .01;   ***p < .001.

TABLE B.4.3. *Economic Sentiment, EU, by Country*

	Sentiment$_{t-1}$	Misery Index$_{t-1}$	Δ Misery Index$_t$ (Pos)	Δ Misery Index$_t$ (Neg)	Constant	N	Rsq	Adj Rsq
Austria	-.126*** (.034)	-.924** (.338)	-.423 (1.568)	-1.544 (1.368)	3.278 (1.911)	184	.089	.068
Belgium	-.132*** (.027)	-.411* (.183)	.302 (.869)	-1.338 (.997)	3.179 (1.791)	313	.076	.064
Czech Republic	-.117*** (.035)	-.115 (.135)	-.784 (.916)	-1.305 (.826)	-1.044 (1.385)	193	.074	.054
Denmark	-.165*** (.032)	-.498** (.161)	.024 (.984)	-3.564** (1.074)	5.716*** (1.550)	313	.099	.087
Finland	-.021 (.017)	.024 (.065)	.364 (.706)	-1.579* (.717)	.041 (.849)	279	.031	.017
France	-.076*** (.022)	-.051 (.110)	-.767 (.881)	-1.093 (.984)	-.615 (1.306)	313	.047	.035
Germany	-.054* (.023)	-.194 (.160)	-.463 (1.001)	-.813 (.949)	1.182 (1.565)	230	.028	.010
Greece	-.030 (.024)	-.010 (.090)	.025 (1.040)	-.442 (.917)	-1.121 (1.695)	178	.010	-.013
Hungary	-.051* (.022)	-.029 (.047)	-.073 (.664)	-1.510* (.719)	-1.501 (.908)	228	.045	.027
Ireland	-.053** (.018)	-.122 (.078)	-2.116 (1.296)	-2.525 (1.357)	.708 (1.005)	300	.047	.035
Italy	-.043** (.015)	.160* (.078)	.199 (1.181)	-3.092* (1.209)	-2.842* (1.240)	313	.047	.034

(continued)

TABLE B.4.3 (continued)

	Sentiment$_{t-1}$	Misery Index$_{t-1}$	Δ Misery Index$_t$ (Pos)	Δ Misery Index$_t$ (Neg)	Constant	N	Rsq	Adj Rsq
Netherlands	-.028*	.132	-3.189**	-.225	-1.201	313	.049	.036
	(.012)	(.139)	(1.193)	(1.193)	(.997)			
Poland	-.213***	-.533**	-1.413	-5.734*	4.830	117	.131	.100
	(.060)	(.200)	(1.950)	(2.857)	(2.518)			
Portugal	-.042*	.106	.008	-1.386	-2.022*	296	.032	.019
	(.017)	(.069)	(.934)	(.864)	(1.017)			
Spain	-.035*	.025	.425	-2.324*	-.709	296	.031	.018
	(.016)	(.053)	(.947)	(.984)	(.951)			
Sweden	-.160***	-.731**	.218	-.875	7.471**	184	.107	.087
	(.036)	(.252)	(.934)	(.884)	(2.298)			
UK	-.083***	-.225*	-.205	-2.084	1.602	313	.046	.034
	(.024)	(.098)	(1.041)	(1.105)	(.857)			

Cells contain OLS regression coefficients, with standard errors in parentheses. Data are the same as in Tables B.4.1 and B.4.2.
*p < .05; **p < .01; ***p < .001.

TABLE B.4.4. *Economic Sentiment and Presidential/Government Approval, United States and United Kingdom*

	DV: Δ Presidential Approval$_t$							
	Retrospective Egotropic		Prospective Egotropic		Retrospective Sociotropic		Prospective Sociotropic	
Levels								
Approval$_{t-1}$	−.090***	(.021)	−.093***	(.023)	−.071***	(.020)	−.064**	(.020)
Econ Sentiment$_{t-1}$	.077*	(.033)	.109*	(.049)	.018	(.013)	.003	(.033)
Changes								
Δ Sentiment$_t$ (Pos)	.178	(.100)	.157	(.129)	.056	(.085)	−.000	(.095)
Δ Sentiment$_t$ (Neg)	.324**	(.108)	.247*	(.124)	.075	(.080)	.279**	(.103)
Time								
Party (months)	−.284*	(.125)	−.286*	(.126)	−.288*	(.127)	−.309*	(.127)
Party (months) Sqrd	.006*	(.003)	.006*	(.003)	.006*	(.003)	.006*	(.003)
Govt (months)	−.133	(.072)	−.097	(.069)	−.107	(.073)	−.060	(.067)
Govt (months) Sqrd	.001	(.001)	.001	(.001)	.001	(.001)	.001	(.001)
Constant	6.297***	(1.743)	3.696*	(1.796)	5.648**	(1.760)	5.877***	(1.672)
N	364		364		364		364	
Rsq	.092		.076		.059		.069	
Adj Rsq	.072		.055		.038		.048	

(continued)

TABLE B.4.4 (continued)

	DV: Δ Government Approval_t			
	Retrospective Egotropic	Prospective Egotropic	Retrospective Sociotropic	Prospective Sociotropic
Levels				
Approval$_{t-1}$	−.188*** (.037)	−.181*** (.036)	−.210*** (.038)	−.184*** (.037)
Econ Sentiment$_{t-1}$	.080 (.041)	.051 (.047)	.066** (.023)	.052 (.035)
Changes				
Δ Sentiment$_t$ (Pos)	.181 (.202)	.180 (.175)	.400*** (.113)	.156 (.095)
Δ Sentiment$_t$ (Neg)	.273 (.166)	.323* (.158)	.117 (.118)	.199* (.097)
Time				
Party (months)	−.030 (.031)	−.040 (.031)	−.016 (.031)	−.033 (.031)
Party (months) Sqrd	−.000 (.000)	−.000 (.000)	−.000 (.000)	−.000 (.000)
Govt (months)	−.272* (.126)	−.255* (.128)	−.312* (.124)	−.235 (.131)
Govt (months) Sqrd	.005* (.002)	.005* (.002)	.006** (.002)	.004* (.002)
Constant	1.846 (1.968)	1.503 (2.139)	1.658 (2.005)	1.988 (2.023)
N	286	286	286	286
Rsq	.121	.124	.171	.133
Adj Rsq	.095	.099	.147	.108

Cells contain OLS regression coefficients, with standard errors in parentheses.
*p < .05; **p < .01; ***p < .001.

TABLE B.4.5. *Economic Sentiment, United States and EU Combined*

	DV: Retrospective Egotropic							
	Model 1		Model 2		Model 3		Model 4	
Levels								
Sentiment$_{t-1}$	−.058***	(.005)	−.057***	(.005)	−.058***	(.005)	−.059***	(.005)
Unemp$_{t-1}$	−.085**	(.032)	−.080*	(.032)	−.093**	(.032)	−.096**	(.032)
Inflation$_{t-1}$	−.041	(.021)	−.043*	(.021)	−.049*	(.022)	−.049*	(.022)
Changes								
Δ Unemp$_t$ (Pos)	3.537	(1.939)	.004	(.715)	.022	(.713)	−.844	(.878)
Δ Unemp$_t$ (Neg)	−4.392**	(1.415)	−3.415***	(.546)	−3.752***	(.567)	−4.088***	(.769)
Δ Inflation$_t$ (Pos)	−.251	(.242)	−.242	(.242)	−.310	(.248)	−.321	(.249)
Δ Inflation$_t$ (Neg)	−1.354***	(.255)	−1.351***	(.255)	−1.335***	(.261)	−1.322***	(.261)
Interactions[a]								
Δ Unemp$_t$ (Pos)* Unemp$_{t-1}$	−.422*	(.199)						
Δ Unemp$_t$ (Pos)* Low Unemp$_{t-1}$			−1.279	(.657)			3.752*	(1.582)
Δ Unemp$_t$ (Pos)* High Unemp$_{t-1}$					−1.578	(.912)	.080	(1.338)
Δ Unemp$_t$ (Neg)* Unemp$_{t-1}$	.111	(.148)						
Δ Unemp$_t$ (Neg)* Low Unemp$_{t-1}$			.067	(.373)			−.882	(1.192)
Δ Unemp$_t$ (Neg)* High Unemp$_{t-1}$					1.434*	(.679)	1.961	(1.119)
Constant	.389	(.274)	.363	(.274)	.486	(.275)	.502	(.275)
N	4,757		4,757		4,725		4,725	
Rsq (within, between)	.040	.021	.039	.021	.041	.021	.041	.021
Rsq (overall)	.011		.020		.076		.073	
sigma e, sigma u	3.948	.822	3.948	.806	3.950	.844	3.950	.857
rho	.042		.040		.044		.045	

(continued)

TABLE B.4.5 (continued)

	DV: Retrospective Egotropic							
	Model 1		Model 2		Model 3		Model 4	
Levels								
Sentiment$_{t-1}$	-.091***	(.006)	-.090***	(.006)	-.090***	(.006)	-.091***	(.006)
Unemp$_{t-1}$	-.087*	(.035)	-.080*	(.035)	-.098**	(.034)	-.101**	(.035)
Inflation$_{t-1}$	-.060*	(.025)	-.059*	(.025)	-.052*	(.026)	-.051*	(.026)
Changes								
Δ Unemp$_t$ (Pos)	3.025	(2.238)	-.299	(.826)	-.134	(.822)	-1.080	(1.011)
Δ Unemp$_t$ (Neg)	-3.258*	(1.630)	-2.517***	(.629)	-2.895***	(.651)	-2.740**	(.886)
Δ Inflation$_t$ (Pos)	-.384	(.279)	-.372	(.279)	-.421	(.286)	-.421	(.286)
Δ Inflation$_t$ (Neg)	-1.434***	(.294)	-1.443***	(.294)	-1.336***	(.301)	-1.326***	(.302)
Interactions[a]								
Δ Unemp$_t$ (Pos)* Unemp$_{t-1}$	-.372	(.230)	-.369	(.759)	-.774	(1.051)		
Δ Unemp$_t$ (Pos)* Low Unemp$_{t-1}$							3.170	(1.821)
Δ Unemp$_t$ (Pos)* High Unemp$_{t-1}$							1.040	(1.543)
Δ Unemp$_t$ (Neg)* Unemp$_{t-1}$	.074	(.172)	.565	(.430)	2.119**	(.783)		
Δ Unemp$_t$ (Neg)* Low Unemp$_{t-1}$							-2.490	(1.375)
Δ Unemp$_t$ (Neg)* High Unemp$_{t-1}$							1.808	(1.291)
Constant	1.166***	(.325)	1.104***	(.325)	1.243***	(.326)	1.267***	(.326)
N	4,757		4,757		4,725		4,725	
Rsq (within, between)	.050	.055	.050	.057	.050	.049	.050	.048
Rsq (overall)	.024		.024		.023		.023	
sigma e, sigma u	4.556	1.129	4.557	1.114	4.555	1.144	4.554	1.154
rho	.058		.056		.059		.060	

DV: Prospective Sociotropic

	Model 1		Model 2		Model 3		Model 4	
Levels								
Sentiment$_{t-1}$	−.032***	(.004)	−.031***	(.004)	−.032***	(.004)	−.032***	(.004)
Unemp$_{t-1}$	.170**	(.053)	.170**	(.053)	.108*	(.053)	.105*	(.053)
Inflation$_{t-1}$	−.097*	(.038)	−.101**	(.038)	−.110**	(.039)	−.109**	(.039)
Changes								
Δ Unemp$_t$ (Pos)	1.228	(3.493)	−3.293*	(1.309)	−2.900*	(1.301)	−3.689*	(1.595)
Δ Unemp$_t$ (Neg)	−9.770***	(2.555)	−5.415***	(.992)	−6.418***	(1.028)	−5.124***	(1.391)
Δ Inflation$_t$ (Pos)	−.970*	(.436)	−.954*	(.436)	−1.041*	(.447)	−1.010*	(.447)
Δ Inflation$_t$ (Neg)	−1.301**	(.458)	−1.300**	(.458)	−1.367**	(.469)	−1.365**	(.469)
Interactions[a]								
Δ Unemp$_t$ (Pos)* Unemp$_{t-1}$	−.547	(.358)	−1.961	(1.182)	−4.587**	(1.637)		
Δ Unemp$_t$ (Pos)* Low Unemp$_{t-1}$							6.634*	(2.833)
Δ Unemp$_t$ (Pos)* High Unemp$_{t-1}$							−3.082	(2.401)
Δ Unemp$_t$ (Neg)* Unemp$_{t-1}$	.480	(.267)	1.047	(.670)	5.272***	(1.219)		
Δ Unemp$_t$ (Neg)* Low Unemp$_{t-1}$							−7.770***	(2.140)
Δ Unemp$_t$ (Neg)* High Unemp$_{t-1}$							3.025	(2.010)
Constant	−1.827***	(.480)	−1.810***	(.481)	−1.226*	(.479)	−1.198*	(.479)
N	4,757		4,757		4,725		4,725	
Rsq (within, between)	.036	.012	.036	.003	.041	.003	.041	.003
Rsq (overall)	.026		.028		.034		.035	
sigma e, sigma u	7.097	.930	7.097	.768	7.092	.687	7.091	.682
rho	.017		.012		.009		.009	

(*continued*)

TABLE B.4.5 (continued)

	DV: Prospective Sociotropic			
	Model 1	Model 2	Model 3	Model 4
Levels				
Sentiment$_{t-1}$	-.090*** (.006)	-.089*** (.006)	-.090*** (.006)	-.090*** (.006)
Unemp$_{t-1}$	.141* (.059)	.109 (.059)	.084 (.058)	.078 (.058)
Inflation$_{t-1}$	-.069 (.044)	-.068 (.044)	-.068 (.045)	-.065 (.045)
Changes				
Δ Unemp$_t$ (Pos)	1.627 (3.977)	-3.678* (1.481)	-3.511* (1.476)	-4.863** (1.806)
Δ Unemp$_t$ (Neg)	-.253 (2.891)	-1.514 (1.106)	-1.835 (1.148)	.764 (1.562)
Δ Inflation$_t$ (Pos)	-1.063* (.495)	-1.030* (.495)	-1.027* (.508)	-.962 (.508)
Δ Inflation$_t$ (Neg)	-1.521** (.521)	-1.550** (.521)	-1.723** (.534)	-1.723** (.534)
Interactions[a]				
Δ Unemp$_t$ (Pos) * Unemp$_{t-1}$	-.623 (.407)	-1.783 (1.345)	-3.876* (1.867)	
Δ Unemp$_t$ (Pos) * Low Unemp$_{t-1}$				7.390* (3.230)
Δ Unemp$_t$ (Pos) * High Unemp$_{t-1}$				-1.307 (2.736)
Δ Unemp$_t$ (Neg) * Unemp$_{t-1}$	-.156 (.304)	1.047 (.763)	2.908* (1.392)	
Δ Unemp$_t$ (Neg) * Low Unemp$_{t-1}$				-7.917** (2.439)
Δ Unemp$_t$ (Neg) * High Unemp$_{t-1}$				-1.604 (2.292)
Constant	-1.877*** (.550)	-1.610** (.550)	-1.353* (.548)	-1.299* (.548)
N	4,757	4,757	4,725	4,725
Rsq (within, between)	.050 / .080	.050 / .093	.051 / .092	.053 / .094
Rsq (overall)	.036	.037	.038	.040
sigma e, sigma u	8.081 / 1.250	8.081 / 1.133	8.090 / 1.127	8.084 / 1.126
rho	.023	.019	.019	.019

*p < .05; **p < .01; ***p < .001. Cells contain GLS regression coefficients, with standard errors in parentheses, from a fixed-effects TSCS estimation. For time periods and variable specification, see preceding Appendix tables.

[a] Model 1 uses the continuous measure of unemployment in interactions; Model 2 uses the three-category measure of unemployment (lower quartile, interquartile range, upper quartile) in interactions; Model 3 uses the three-category measure of unemployment (lower quartile, interquartile range, upper quartile) in interactions; Model 4 uses separate binary variables, based on the three-category measure of unemployment, for (a) lower quartile and (b) upper quartile in interactions.

TABLE B.6.1. *News Content, Within-Respondent ANCOVA: Skin Conductance Levels*

	ANCOVA		
	Partial SS	df	F
Model	559.415	44	18.45**
Respondent	158.952	38	6.07**
Order (c)	4.584	1	6.65**
Time (c)	161.269	1	234.08**
Time2 (c)	68.072	1	98.80**
Negative	4.176	1	6.06*
Neg*Time	18.868	1	27.39**
Neg*Time2	20.400	1	29.61**
Residual	5,071.377	7,361	
Total	5,630.792	7,405	

$N = 240$.
$^*p < .05$, $^{**}p < .01$, $^{***}p < .001$.

TABLE B.6.2. *News Content, Within-Respondent ANCOVA: Heart Rate*

	ANCOVA		
	Partial SS	df	F
Model	954,600.833	44	566.25***
Respondent	935,232.136	38	642.35***
Order (c)	1,714.909	1	46.10***
Time (c)	1,027.469	1	26.82***
Time2 (c)	768.560	1	20.06***
Negative	1,108.093	1	28.92***
Neg*Time	537.598	1	14.03***
Neg*Time2	514.596		13.43***
Residual	279,618.277	7,298	
Total	1,234,219.11	7,342	

$N = 240$.
$^*p < .05$, $^{**}p < .01$, $^{***}p < .001$.

TABLE B.6.3. *Campaign Ads, Within-Respondent ANCOVA: Skin Conductance Levels*

	ANCOVA		
	Partial SS	df	F
Model	316.777	47	14.47***
Respondent	272.539	38	15.40***
Order (c)	4.480	1	9.62**
Time (c)	1.925	1	4.13*
Tone	10.453	2	11.22***
Tone*Time	20.149	2	21.64***
Party	11.523	3	8.25***
Residual	1,259.061	2,704	
Total	1,575.838	2,751	

$N = 2,752$.
$*p < .05, **p < .01, ***p < .001$.

TABLE B.6.4. *Campaign Ads, Within-Respondent ANCOVA: Heart Rate*

	ANCOVA		
	Partial SS	df	F
Model	629,567.459	48	73.01***
Respondent	588,354.501	39	83.97***
Order (c)	18.052	1	.10
Time (c)	500.847	1	2.79
Tone	796.065	2	2.22[a]
Tone*Time	1,169.363	2	3.25*
Party	1,128.515	3	2.09[a]
Residual	494,775.039	2,754	
Total	1,124,342.5	2,802	

$N = 2,752$.
[a]$p < .10, *p < .05, **p < .01, ***p < .001$.

Bibliography

Aalberg, Toril, Peter van Aelst, and James Curran. 2010. "Media System and the Political Information Environment: A Cross-National Comparison." *International Journal of Press/Politics* 15(3): 255–71.

Aarts, Kees, and André Blais. 2011. "Pull or Push? Positive and Negative Leader Evaluations and Vote Choice." In *Political Leaders and Democratic Elections*, ed. K. Aarts, A. Blais, and H. Schmitt. Oxford: Oxford University Press.

Aarts, Kees, André Blais, and Hermann Schmitt. 2011. *Political Leaders and Democratic Elections*. Oxford: Oxford University Press.

Abbe, O. G., P. S. Herrnson, D. B. Magleby, and K. Patterson. 2001. "Are Professional Campaigns More Negative?" In *Playing Hardball: Campaigning for the U.S. Congress*, ed. P. S. Hernson. Upper Saddle River, NJ: Prentice Hall.

Abbott, Eric A., and Lynn T. Brassfield. 1989. "Comparing Decisions on Releases by TV and Newspaper Gatekeepers." *Journalism Quarterly* 66: 853–56.

Abele, Andrea. 1985. "Thinking about Thinking: Causal, Evaluative, and Finalistic Cognitions about Social Situations." *European Journal of Social Psychology* 15: 315–32.

Abelson, Robert P., Donald R. Kinder, Mark D. Peters, and Susan T. Fiske. 1982. "Affective and Semantic Components in Political Person Perception." *Journal of Personality and Social Psychology* 42: 619–30.

Abizadeh, Arash. 2002. "The Passions of the Wise: Phronêsis, Rhetoric and Aristotle's Passionate Practical Deliberation." *The Review of Metaphysics* 56(2): 267–96.

Ahn, T. K., Elinor Ostrom, and James Walker. 2010. "A Common-Pool Resource Experiment with Postgraduate Subjects from 41 Countries." *Ecological Economics* 70: 1580–89.

Akhtar, Shumi, Robert Faff, Barry Oliver, and Avanidhar Subrahmanyam. 2011. "The Power of Bad: The Negativity Bias in Australian Consumer Sentiment Announcements on Stock Returns." *Journal of Banking and Finance* 35: 1239–49.

Alford, John, Carolyn Funk, and John R. Hibbing. 2005. "Are Political Orientations Genetically Transmitted?" *American Political Science Review* 99: 153–66.

Alford, John R., and John R. Hibbing. 2004. "The Origin of Politics: An Evolutionary Theory of Political Behavior." *Perspectives on Politics* 2: 707–23.

Alterman, Eric. 2003. *What Liberal Media? The Truth about Bias and the News*. New York: Basic Books.

Altheide, David L. 1985. *Media Power*. Beverly Hills, CA: Sage Publications.

Altheide, David L. 1997. "The News Media, the Problem Frame, and the Production of Fear." *Sociological Quarterly* 38(4): 647–68.

Altheide, David L., and Robert P. Snow. 1979. *Media Logic*. Beverly Hills, CA: Sage.

Altheide, David L., and Robert P. Snow. 1991. *Media Worlds in the Postjournalism Era*. Hawthorne, NY: Aldine de Gruyter.

Anderson, Norman H. 1965. "Averaging versus Adding as a Stimulus-Combination Rule in Impression Formation." *Journal of Personality and Social Psychology* 70(4): 394–400.

Andreevskaia, Alina, and Sabine Bergler. 2006. "Mining WordNet for Fuzzy Sentiment: Sentiment Tag Extraction from WordNet Glosses." In *Proceedings of the 11th Conference of the European Chapter of the Association for Computational Linguistics*, Trento, Italy.

Andreoni, James, William Harbaugh, and Lise Vesterlund. 2003. "The Carrot or the Stick: Rewards, Punishments, and Cooperation." *The American Economic Review* 93(3): 893–902.

Ansolabehere, Stephen, and Shanto Iyengar. 1995. *Going Negative: How Political Advertisements Shrink and Polarize the Electorate*. New York: Free Press.

Ansolabehere, Stephen, Shanto Iyengar, Adam Simon, and Nicholas Valentino. 1994. "Does Attack Advertising Demobilize the Electorate?" *American Political Science Review* 88(4): 829–38.

Anthony, Denise L., and John L. Campbell. 2011. "States, Social Capital and Cooperation: Looking Back on Governing the Commons." *International Journal of the Commons* 5(2): 284–302.

Apergis, Nicholas, and Stephen M. Miller. 2006. "Consumption Asymmetry and the Stock Market: Empirical Evidence." *Economics Letters* 93(3): 337–42.

Aragones, Enriqueta. 1997. "Negativity Effect and the Emergence of Ideologies." *Journal of Theoretical Politics* 9(2): 189–210.

Arch, Elizabeth. 1993. "Risk-Taking: A Motivational Basis for Sex Differences." *Psychological Reports* 73(3): 6–11.

Àries, Philippe. 1981. *The Hour of Our Death*. Trans. Helen Weaver. New York: Knopf.

Arkes, Hal R., and Catherine Blumer. 1985. "The Psychology of Sunk Cost." *Organizational Behavior and Decision Processes* 5: 124–40.

Averill, James R. 1980. "On the Paucity of Positive Emotions." In *Advances in the Study of Communication and Affect*, ed. K. R. Blankstein, P. Pliner, and J. Polivy. New York: Plenum.

Babbitt, Paul R., and Richard R. Lau. 1994. "The Impact of Negative Political Campaigns on Political Knowledge." Paper presented at the annual meeting of the Southern Political Science Association, Atlanta.

Ball-Rokeach, S. J., and M. L. DeFleur. 1976. "A Dependency Model of Mass-Media Effects." *Communication Research* 3: 3–21.

Banaji, Mahzarin R., and Curtis Hardin. 1994. "Affect and Memory in Retrospective Reports." In *Autobiographical Memory and the Validity of Retrospective Reports*, ed. Norbert Schwarz and Seymour Sudman. New York: Springer-Verlag.

Banerjee, Anindya, Juan Dolado, John Galbraith, and David F. Hendry. 1993. *Cointegration, Error Correction, and the Econometric Analysis of Non-Stationary Data*. Oxford: Oxford University Press.

Barlow, Melissa Hickman, David E. Barlow, and Theodore G. Chiricos. 1995. "Economic Conditions and Ideologies of Crime in the Media: A Content Analysis of Crime News." *Crime & Delinquency* 41(1): 3–19.

Bartels, Larry M. 1993. "Messages Received: The Political Impact of Media Exposure." *American Political Science Review* 87: 267–85.

Bartels, Larry M. 2002. "The Impact of Candidate Traits in American Presidential Elections." In *Leaders' Personalities and the Outcomes of Democratic Elections*, ed. Anthony King. Oxford: Oxford University Press.

Bartlett, Christopher, Jonathan Sterne, and Matthias Egger. 2002. "What Is Newsworthy? Longitudinal study of the Reporting of Medical Research in Two British Newspapers." *British Medical Journal* 325: 81–84.

Bartling, Björn, and Urs Fischbacher. 2011. "Shifting the Blame: On Delegation and Responsibility." *Review of Economic Studies* 79(1): 67–87.

Bartneck, Christoph, and Obaid, Mohammad. 2013. "Agents with Faces – What Can We Learn from Lego Minifigures?" Proceedings of the 1st International Conference on Human-Agent Interaction, Sapporo.

Bass, Abraham Z. 1969. "Refining the 'Gatekeeper' Concept: A UN Radio Case Study." *Journalism Quarterly* 46: 69–72.

Batchelor, Roy, and Pami Dua. 1992. "Survey Expectations in the Time Series Consumption Function." *The Review of Economics and Statistics* 74(4): 598–606.

Bateup, Helen S., Alan Booth, Elizabeth A. Shirtcliff, and Douglas A. Granger. 2002. "Testosterone, Cortisol, and Women's Competition." *Evolution and Human Behavior* 23(3): 181–92.

Baum, Lawrence. 1977. "Policy Goals in Judicial Gatekeeping: A Proximity Model of Discretionary Jurisdiction." *American Journal of Political Science* 21(1): 13–35.

Baumeister, Roy F., Ellen Bratslavsky, Catrin Finkenauer, and Kathleen D. Vohs. 2001. "Bad Is Stronger than Good." *Review of General Psychology* 5(4): 323–70.

Baumeister, Roy F., Todd F. Heatherton, and Dianne M. Tice. 1994. *Losing Control: How and Why People Fail at Self-Regulation*. San Diego, CA: Academic Press.

Baumeister, Roy F., and Leonard S. Newman. 1994. "Self-Regulation of Cognitive Inference and Decision Processes." *Personality and Social Psychology Bulletin* 20: 3–19.

Baumgartner, Frank R., and Bryan D. Jones. 1993. *Agendas and Instability in American Politics*. Chicago: University of Chicago Press.

Bean, Clive, and Anthony Mughan. 1989. "Leader Effects in Parliamentary Elections in Australia and Britain." *American Political Science Review* 83(4): 1165–79.

Behr, Roy, and Shanto Iyengar. 1985. "Television News, Real-World Cues, and Changes in the Public Agenda." *Public Opinion Quarterly* 49: 38–57.

Belsky, J., L. Steinberg, and P. Draper. 1991. "Childhood Experience, Interpersonal Development, and Reproductive Strategy: An Evolutionary Theory of Socialization." *Child Development* 62(4): 671–75.

Benoit, William L., Kevin A. Stein, and Glenn J. Hansen. 2005. "New York Times Coverage of Presidential Campaigns." *Journalism and Mass Communication Quarterly* 82(2): 356–76.

Berkowitz, Dan. 1990. "Refining the Gatekeeping Metaphor for Local Television News." *Journal of Broadcasting & Electronic Media* 34: 55–68.

Berkowitz, Dan. 1991. "Assessing Forces in the Selection of Local Television News." *Journal of Broadcasting & Electronic Media* 35: 245–51.

Berntson, Gary G., Sarah T. Boysen, and John T. Cacioppo. 1993. "Neurobehavioral Organization and the Cardinal Principle of Evaluative Bivalence." *Annals of the New York Academy of Science* 702: 75–102.

Beyer, Sylvia. 1998. "Gender Differences in Self-Perception and Negative Recall Biases." *Sex Roles* 1–2: 103–33.

Bidwell, Jr., Miles O., Bruce X. Wang, and J. Douglas Zona. 1995. "An Analysis of Asymmetric Demand Response to Price Changes: The Case of Local Telephone Calls." *Journal of Regulatory Economics* 8: 285–98.

Bittner, Amanda. 2011. *Platform or Personality? The Role of Party Leaders in Elections.* Oxford: Oxford University Press.

Blanz, Mathias, Amélie Mummendey, and Sabine Otten. 1997. "Normative Evaluations and Frequency Expectations Regarding Positive versus Negative Outcome Allocations between Groups." *European Journal of Social Psychology* 27: 165–76.

Bless, Herbert, David L. Hamilton, and Diane M. Mackie. 1992. "Mood Effects on the Organization of Person Information." *European Journal of Social Psychology* 22: 497–509.

Bloom, Howard S., and H. Douglas Price. 1975. "Voter Response to Short-Run Economic Conditions: The Asymmetric Effect of Prosperity and Recession." *American Political Science Review* 69: 1240–54.

Bohm, Michael. 2012. "Why Good News Is Bad News in Russia." *Moscow Times*, December 20, 2012.

Bolls, Paul D., Annie Lang, and Robert F. Potter. 2001. "The Effects of Message Valence and Listener Arousal on Attention, Memory, and Facial Muscular Responses to Radio Advertisements." *Communication Research* 28(5): 627–51.

Born, Richard. 1990. "Surge and Decline, Negative Voting, and the Midterm Loss Phenomenon: A Simultaneous Choice Analysis." *American Journal of Political Science* 34(3): 615–45.

Bowman, David, Deborah Minehart, and Matthew Rabin. 1999. "Loss Aversion in a Consumption-Savings Model." *Journal of Economic Behavior and Organization* 38: 155–78.

Boyd, Robert, Herbert Gintis, Samuel Bowles, and Peter J. Richerson. 2003. "The Evolution of Altruistic Punishment." *PNAS* 100(6): 3531–35.

Bradley, Brendan P., Karin Mogg, and Rachel Williams. 1995. "Implicit and Explicit Memory for Emotion-Congruent Information in Clinical Depression and Anxiety." *Behaviour Research and Therapy* 33: 755–70.

Bradley, M. M., J. Zack, and P. J. Lang. 1994. "Cries, Screams, and Shouts of Joy: Affective Responses to Environmental Sounds." *Psychophysiology* 31: S29.

Bradley, Margaret M., and Peter J. Lang. 1999. "Affective Norms for English Words (ANEW): Instruction Manual and Affective Ratings." Technical Report C-1, The Centre for Research in Psychophysiology, University of Florida.

Brauninger, Thomas, and Thomas Konig. 1999. "The Checks and Balances of Party Federalism: German Federal Government in a Divided Legislature." *European Journal of Political Research* 36: 207–34.

Brennan, T. 2005. *The Stoic Life*. Oxford: Oxford University Press.

Brewer, Marilynn B. 1996. "In-Group Favoritism: The Subtle Side of Intergroup Discrimination." In *Codes of Conduct: Behavioral Research Into Business Ethics*, ed. David M. Messick and Anne E. Tenbrunsel. New York: Russell Sage Foundation.

Brians, Craig L., and Martin P. Wattenberg. 1996. "Campaign Issue Knowledge and Salience: Comparing Reception from TV Commercials, TV News, and Newspapers." *American Journal of Political Science* 40: 172–93.

Brickman, P., D. Coates, and R. Janoff-Bulman. 1978. "Lottery Winners and Accident Victims: Is Happiness Relative?" *Journal of Personality and Social Psychology* 36: 917–27.

Brickman, P., and D. T. Campbell. 1971. "Hedonic Relativism and Planning the Good Society." In *Adaptation Level Theory*, ed. Appley. London: Academic Press.

Brinthaupt, Thomas M., Richard L. Moreland, and John M. Levine. 1991. "Sources of Optimism among Prospective Group Members." *Personality and Social Psychology Bulletin* 17: 36–43.

Brody, Richard A. 1991. *Assessing the President: The Media, Elite Opinion, and Public Support*. Stanford, CA: Stanford University Press.

Brosnan, Sarah F., Owen D. Jones, Susan P. Lambeth, March Catherine Mareno, Amanda S. Richardson, and Steven J. Schpiro. 2007. "Endowment Effects in Chimpanzees." *Current Biology* 17: 1704–07.

Buell, Emmett, and Lee Sigelman. 1985. "An Army That Meets Every Sunday?" *Social Science Quarterly* 66: 426–34.

Bullock, David A. 1994. "The Influence of Political Attack Advertising on Undecided Voters: An Experimental Study of Campaign Message Strategy." PhD dissertation. University of Arizona.

Busse, J. A., and T. C. Green. 2002. "Market Efficiency in Real Time." *Journal of Financial Economics* 65: 415–37.

Cacioppo, John T., and Gary G. Berntson. 1994. "Relationship between Attitudes and Evaluative Space: A Critical Review, with Emphasis on the Separability of Positive and Negative Substrates." *Psychological Bulletin* 115: 401–23.

Cacioppo, John T., Stephen L. Crites, Jr., and Wendi L. Gardner. 1996. "Attitudes to the Right: Evaluative Processing is Associated with Lateralized Late Positive Event-Related Brain Potentials." *Personality and Social Psychology Bulletin* 22: 1205–19.

Cacioppo, John T., Stephen L. Crites, Jr., Wendi L. Gardner, and Gary G. Berntson. 1994. "Bioelectrical Echoes from Evaluative Categorizations. I. A Late Positive Brain Potential that Varies as a Function of Trait Negativity and Extremity." *Journal of Personality and Social Psychology* 67(1): 115–25.

Cacioppo, John T., and Wendi L. Gardner. 1993. "What Underlies Medical Donor Attitudes and Behavior?" *Health Psychology* 12: 269–71.

Cacioppo, John T., and Wendi L. Gardner. 1999. "Emotion." *Annual Review of Psychology* 50: 191–214.

Cacioppo, John T., Wendi L. Gardner, and Gary G. Berntson. 1998a. "The Affect System: Form Follows Function." *Journal of Personality and Social Psychology* 76(5): 839–55.

Cacioppo, John T., Louis G. Tassinary, and Gary G. Berntson, eds. 1998b. *The Handbook of Psychophysiology*. New York: Cambridge University Press.

Cahill, L. 1996. "Neurobiology of Memory for Emotional Events: Converging Evidence from Infra-Human and Human Studies." *Cold Spring Harbor Symposia on Quantitative Biology* 61: 259–64.

Campbell, Angus, Philip E. Converse, Warren E. Miller, and Donald E. Stokes. 1960. *The American Voter*. New York: John Wiley and Sons.

Canli, T., Desmond, J. E., Zhao, Z., & Gabrieli, J. D. E. 2002. "Sex Differences in the Neural Basis of Emotional Memories." *Proceedings of the National Academy of Sciences of the United States of America* 99(16): 10789–95.

Cannon, W. B. 1932. *The Wisdom of the Body*. New York: Norton.

Cappella, Joseph N., and Kathleen Hall-Jamieson. 1997. *Spiral of Cynicism: The Press and the Public Good*. New York: Oxford University Press.

Carlsen, Fredrik. 2000. "Unemployment, Inflation and Government Popularity – Are There Partisan Effects?" *Electoral Studies* 19(2–3): 141–50.

Carlson, Earl R. 1966. "The Affective Tone of Psychology." *Journal of General Psychology* 75: 65–78.

Carlyle, Thomas. 1841. *Heroes: Hero-Worship and the Heroic in History*. New York: Charles Scribner and Sons.

Carmon, Ziv, and Dan Ariely. 2000. "Focusing on the Forgone: Why Value Can Appear So Different to Buyers and Seller." *Journal of Consumer Research* 27: 360–70.

Carpenter, Jeffrey P. 2006. "The Demand for Punishment." *Journal of Economic Behavior and Organization* 62: 522–42.

Carrithers, David W., Michael A. Mosher, and Paul A. Rahl, eds. 2001. *Montesquieu's Science of Politics: Essays on The Spirit of Laws*. Lanham, MD: Rowman & Littlefield.

Chan, W.S. 2003. "Stock Price Reaction to News and No-News: Drift and Reversal after Headlines." *Journal of Financial Economics* 70: 223–60.

Chen, C., T. Chiang, and M. So. 2003. "Asymmetrical Reaction to US Stock-Return News: Evidence from Major Stock Markets Based on a Double-Threshold Model." *Journal of Economics and Business* 55: 487–502.

Chermak, Steven, and Nicole M. Chapman. 2007. "Predicting Crime Story Salience: A Replication." *Journal of Criminal Justice* 35(4): 351–63.

Chermak, Steven M. 1994. "Body Count News: How Crime Is Presented in the News Media." *Justice Quarterly* 11(4): 561–82.

Chong, Denis, and James N. Druckman. "Framing Theory." *Annual Review of Political Science* 10: 103–26.

Chuliá, Helena, Martin Martens, and Dick van Dijk. 2010. "Asymmetric Effects of Federal Funds Target Rate Changes on S&P100 Stock Returns, Volatilities and Correlations." *Journal of Banking and Finance* 34: 834–39.

Citrin, Jack, and Donald Philip Green. 1986. "Presidential Leadership and the Resurgence of Trust in Government." *British Journal of Political Science* 16: 431–53.

Claggett, William. 1986. "A Reexamination of the Asymmetry Hypothesis: Economic Expansions, Contractions, and Congressional Elections." *Western Political Quarterly* 39(4): 623–33.

Clarke, Harold D., and Marianne C. Stewart. 1994. "Prospections, Retrospections, and Rationality: The 'Bankers' Model of Presidential Approval Reconsidered." *American Journal of Political Science* 38(4): 1104–23.

Clarke, Harold D., and Marianne C. Stewart. 1995. "Economic Evaluations, Prime Ministerial Approval and Governing Party Support: Rival Models Reconsidered." *British Journal of Political Science* 25(2): 145–70.

Clore, G. L., and A. Ortony. 1988. "The Semantics of Affective Lexicon." In *Cognitive Perspectives on Emotion and Motivation*, ed. V. Hamilton, G. H. Bower, and N. H. Frijda. NATO ASI Series D: Behavioural and Social Sciences vol. 44. Dordrecht, The Netherlands: Kluwer Academic.

Clutton-Brock, T. H., and G. A. Parker. 1995. "Punishment in Animal Societies." *Nature* 373: 209–16.

Coe, Kevin, David Tewksbury, Bradley J. Bond, Kristin L. Drogos, Robert W. Porter, et al. 2008. "Hostile News: Partisan Use and Perceptions of Cable News Programming." *Journal of Communication* 58(2): 201–19.

Coleman, Lerita M., Lee Jussim, and Jack Abraham. 1987. "Students' Reactions to Teachers' Evaluations: The Unique Impact of Negative Feedback." *Journal of Applied Social Psychology* 17(12): 1051–70.

Conover, Pamela J., and Stanley Feldman. 1986. "Emotional Responses to the Economy: I'm Mad as Hell and I'm Not Going to Take It Anymore." *American Journal of Political Science* 30: 50–78.

Constantini, Arthur F., and Kenneth L. Hoving. 1973. "The Effectiveness of Reward and Punishment Contingencies on Response Inhibition." *Journal of Experimental Child Psychology* 16(3): 484–94.

Cook, Timothy E. 1998. *Governing with the News: The News Media as a Political Institution*. Chicago: University of Chicago Press.

Cook, Timothy E. 2006. "The News Media as a Political Institution: Looking Backward and Looking Forward." *Political Communication* 23: 159–71.

Courtney, C. P. 2001. "Montesquieu and English Liberty." In *Montesquieu's Science of Politics: Essays on the Spirit of Laws*, ed. David W. Carrithers, Michael A. Mosher, and Paul A. Rahl. New York: Rowman and Littlefield.

Cover, Albert D. 1986. "Presidential Evaluations and Voting for Congress." *American Journal of Political Science* 30: 786–801.

Craig, Stephen. 1993. *The Malevolent Leaders*. Boulder, CO: Westview Press.

Croson, Rachel, and Uri Gneezy. 2009. "Gender Differences in Preferences." *Journal of Economic Literature* 47(2): 1–27.

Czapinski, Janusz. 1985. "Negativity Bias in Psychology: An Analysis of Polish Publications." *Polish Psychological Bulletin* 16(1): 27–44.

D'Alessio, Dave, and Mike Allen. 2000. "Media Bias in Presidential Elections: A Meta-Analysis." *Journal of Communication* 50(4): 133–56.

Daignault, Penelope, Stuart Soroka, and Thierry Giasson. 2013. "The Perception of Political Advertising During an Election Campaign: A Preliminary Study of Cognitive and Emotional Effects." *Canadian Journal of Communication* 28: 167–86.

Damasio, Antonio. 1994. *Descartes' Error: Emotion, Reason, and the Human Brain.* New York: Grossett/Putnam & Sons.

Danoff, Brian F. 2000. "Lincoln, Machiavelli, and American Political Thought." *Presidential Studies Quarterly* 30(2): 290–311.

Darwin, Charles. 1872. *The Expression of the Emotions in Man and Animals.* London: J. Murray.

Davey, Graham C.L. 1992. "An Expectancy Model of Laboratory Preparedness Effects." *Journal of Experimental Psychology: General* 121(1): 24–40.

David, James P., Peter J. Green, René Martin, and Jerry Suls. 1997. "Differential Roles of Neuroticism, Extraversion, and Event Desirability for Mood in Daily Life: An Integrative Model of Top-Down and Bottom-up Influences." *Journal of Personality and Social Psychology* 73(1): 149–59.

Davie, William R., and Jung Sook Lee. 1995. "Sex, Violence, and Consonance/Differentiation: An Analysis of Local TV News Values." *Journalism and Mass Communication Quarterly* 72(1): 128–38.

Davis, Michael. 1997. "The Neurophysiological Basis of Acoustic Startle Modulation: Research on Fear Motivation and Sensory Gating." In *Attention and Orienting*, ed. Peter J. Lang, Robert F. Simons, and Marie Balaban. Mahwah, NJ: Erlbaum.

Dawson, Michael E., Annie M. Schell, and Diane L. Filion. 2007. "The Electrodermal System." In *The Handbook of Psychophysiology*, ed. John Cacioppo, Louis G. Tassinary, and Gary G. Berntson. Cambridge: Cambridge University Press.

De Boef, Suzanna, and Paul M. Kellstedt. 2004. "The Political (and Economic) Origins of Consumer Confidence." *American Journal of Political Science* 48(4): 633–49.

de Quervain, Dominique J.-F., Urs Fischbacher, Valerie Treyer, Melanie Schellhammer, Ulrich Schnyder, et al. 2004. "The Neural Basis of Altruistic Punishment." *Science* 305: 1254–58.

Debré, Michel. 1959. "La nouvelle Constitution." *Revue français de science politique* 9(1): 7–29.

Debré, Michel. 1978. "La Constitution de 1958: Sa raison d'être, son évolution." *Revue français de science politique* 28(5): 817–39.

Dehaene, Stanislas, Michael I. Posner, and Don M. Tucker. 1994. "Localization of a Neural System for Error Detection and Compensation." *Psychological Science* 5: 303–05.

Diamond, Edwin. 1978. *Good News, Bad News.* Cambridge, MA: MIT Press.

Diamond, William D. 1988. "The Effect of Probability and Consequence Levels on the Focus of Consumer Judgments in Risky Situations." *Journal of Consumer Research* 15: 280–83.

Dickinson, David L. 2001. "The Carrot vs. the Stick in Work Team Motivation." *Experimental Economics* 4(1): 107–24.

Diener, Ed, Randy J. Larsen, Steven Levine, and Robert A. Emmons. 1985. "Intensity and Frequency: Dimensions Underlying Positive and Negative Affect." *Journal of Personality and Social Psychology* 48(5): 1253–65.

Dimmick, John. 1974. "The Gatekeeper: An Uncertainty Theory." *Journalism Monographs* 37: 1–39.

DeNisi, A. S., T. Cafferty, and B. Meglino. 1984. "A Cognitive View of the Performance Appraisal Process: A Model and Research Propositions." *Organizational Behavior and Human Performance* 33: 360–96.

Donohew, Lewis. 1967. "Newspaper Gatekeepers and Forces in the News Channel." *Public Opinion Quarterly* 31(1): 61–68.

Donohue, G. A., C. N. Olien, and P. J. Tichenor. 1989. "Structure and Constraints on Community Newspaper Gatekeepers." *Journalism Quarterly* 66: 807–12.

Donohue, George A., Phillip J. Tichenor, and Clarice N. Olien. 1972. "Gatekeeping: Mass Media Systems and Information Control." In *Current Perspectives in Mass Communication Research*, ed. F. G. Kline and P. Tichenor. Beverly Hills, CA: Sage.

Donsbach, Wolfgang. 1991. "Exposure to Political Content in Newspapers: The Impact of Cognitive Dissonance on Readers' Selectivity." *European Journal of Communication* 6(2): 155–86.

Dreber, Anna, and Moshe Hoffman. 2011. "Biological Basis of Sex Differences in Risk Aversion and Competitiveness." Unpublished manuscript.

Dua, Pami, and David J. Smyth. 1993. "Survey Evidence on Excessive Public Pessimism About the Future Behavior of Unemployment." *Public Opinion Quarterly* 57(4): 566–74.

Duch, Raymond M. 2008. *The Economic Vote: How Political and Economic Institutions Condition Election Results*. Cambridge: Cambridge University Press.

Duch, Raymond M., Harvey D. Palmer, and Christopher J. Anderson. 2000. "Heterogeneity in Perceptions of National Economic Conditions." *American Journal of Political Science* 44: 635–52.

Durr, Robert H. 1993. "What Moves Policy Sentiment?" *American Political Science Review* 87(1): 158–70.

Edelman, Murray. 1988. *Constructing the Political Spectacle*. Urbana: University of Illinois Press.

Edwards, George C. III, and B. Dan Wood. 1999. "Who Influences Whom? The President, Congress, and the Media." *American Political Science Review* 93(2): 327–44.

Edwards, Kimberly. 1996. "Prospect Theory: A Literature Review." *International Review of Financial Analysis* 5(1): 19–38.

Eichenberg, Richard C., and Richard J. Stoll. 2003. "Representing Defense: Democratic Control of the Defense Budget in the United States and Western Europe." *The Journal of Conflict Resolution* 47(4): 399–422.

Eisenger, Robert M., Loring R. Veenstra, and John P. Koehn. 2007. "What Media Bias? Conservative and Liberal Labeling in Major U.S. Newspapers." *Harvard International Journal of Press and Politics* 12: 17–36.

Ekman, Paul, and Richard J. Davidson, eds. 1994. *The Nature of Emotion: Fundamental Questions*. New York: Oxford University Press.

Eliade, M. 1982. *A History of Religious Ideas Vol. 2: From Gautama Buddha to the Triumph of Christianity*. Trans. W. Trask. Chicago: University of Chicago Press.

Eliade, M. 1985. *A History of Religious Ideas Vol. 3: From Muhammad to the Age of Reforms*. Trans. A. Hiltebeitel and D. Apostolos-Cappadona. Chicago: University of Chicago Press.

Ellis, Richard J. 1994. *Presidential Lightning Rods: The Politics of Blame Avoidance*. Lawrence: University of Kansas Press.

Ellsworth, P.C. 1994. "Some Reasons to Expect Universal Antecedents of Emotion." In *The Nature of Emotions: Fundamental Questions*, ed. Paul Ekman and Richard J. Davidson. New York: Oxford University Press.

Elster, Jon. 1999. *Alchemies of the Mind: Rationality and the Emotions*. Cambridge: Cambridge University Press.

Ericson, Richard, Patricia Baranek, and Janet Chan. 1987. *Visualizing Deviance: A Study of News Organization*. Toronto: University of Toronto Press.

Ericson, Richard V., Patricia M. Baranek, and Janet B. L. Chan. 1989. *Negotiating Control: A Study of News Sources*. Toronto: University of Toronto Press.

Erikson, Robert S., Michael B. MacKuen, and James A. Stimson. 2002. *The Macro Polity*. Cambridge: Cambridge University Press.

Evans, Geoffrey, and Robert Andersen. 2006. "The Political Conditioning of Economic Perceptions." *Journal of Politics* 68: 194–207.

Fallows, James. 1997. *Breaking the News*. New York: Vintage.

Farnsworth, Stephen J., and S. Robert Lichter. 2007. *The Nightly News Nightmare: Television's Coverage of U.S. Presidential Elections, 1988–2004*. Toronto: Rowman & Littlefield.

Fehr, Ernst, and Urs Fischbacher. 2004. "Third-Party Punishment and Social Norms." *Evolution and Human Behavior* 25: 63–87.

Fehr, Ernst, and Simon Gachter. 2000. "Cooperation and Punishment in Public Goods Experiments." *The American Economic Review* 90(4): 980–94.

Fehr, Ernst, and Simon Gachter. 2002. "Altruistic Punishment in Humans." *Nature* 415: 137–40.

Feldman, Sheldon. 1966. "Motivational Aspects of Attitudinal Elements and their Place in Cognitive Interaction." In *Cognitive Consistency: Motivational Antecedents and Behavioral Consequences*, ed. S. Feldman. New York: Academic Press.

Fiorina, Morris P. 1982. "Legislative Choice of Regulatory Forms: Legal Process or Administrative Process?" *Public Choice* 39(1): 33–66.

Fiorina, Morris P. 1986. "Legislator Uncertainty, Legislator Control and the Delegation of Legislative Power." *Journal of Law, Economics and Organization* 2: 133–51.

Fiorina, Morris P., and Kenneth A. Shepsle. 1989. "Is Negative Voting an Artifact?" *American Journal of Political Science* 33: 423–39.

Fischle, Mark. 2000. "Mass Response to the Lewinsky Scandal: Motivated Reasoning or Bayesian Updating?" *Political Psychology* 21: 135–59.

Fishman, Mark. 1978. "Crime Waves as Ideology." *Social Problems* 25(5): 531–43.

Fiske, Susan T. 1980. "Attention and Weight in Person Perception: The Impact of Negative and Extreme Behavior." *Journal of Personality and Social Psychology* 38(6): 889–906.

Flowers, Julianne F., Audrey A. Haynes, and Michael H. Crespin. 2003. "The Media, the Campaign, and the Message." *American Journal of Political Science* 47(2): 259–73.

Foersterling, F., and A. Groenvald. 1983. "Ursachzuschreibungen für ein Wahlergebnis: Eine Überprüfung von Hypothesen der Attributionstheorie in einer Feldstudie anhand die niedersachsischen Kommunalwahl [Attributions for election results: A study of attributional hypothesis in a field study of Lower Saxony community elections]." *Zeitschrift für Socialpsychologie* 14: 262–69.

Fogarty, Brian J. 2005. "Determining Economic News Coverage." *International Journal of Public Opinion Research* 17(2): 149–72.

Forgas, Joseph P. 1992. "Mood and the Perception of Unusual People: Affective Asymmetry in Memory and Social Judgments." *European Journal of Social Psychology* 22(6): 531–47.

Forgas, Joseph P. 1995. "Mood and Judgment: The Affect Infusion Model (AIM)." *Psychological Bulletin* 117(1): 39–66.

Fowler, James H. 2005. "Altruistic Punishment and the Origin of Cooperation." *PNAS* 102(19): 7047–49.

Fowler, James H., Christopher T. Dawes, and Nicholas A. Christakis. 2009. "Model of Genetic Variation in Human Social Networks." *Science* 106(6): 1720–24.

Frantzich, Stephen E. 1982. *Computers in Congress: The Politics of Information.* Beverly Hills, CA: Sage.

Frazer, James G. [1890] 1959. *The New Golden Bough: A Study in Magic and Religion (abridged).* New York: Macmillan.

Freedman, Paul, and Ken M. Goldstein. 1999. "Measuring Media Exposure and the Effects of Negative Campaign Ads." *American Journal of Political Science* 43(4): 1189–1208.

Fridkin, Kim Leslie, and Patrick J. Kenney. 2004. "Do Negative Messages Work? The Impact of Negativity on Citizens' Evaluations of Candidates." *American Politics Research* 32(5): 570–605.

Fridlund, Alan J. 1991. "Evolution and Facial Action in Reflex, Social Motive, and Paralanguage." *Biological Psychology* 32(1): 3–100.

Frijda, Nico H. 1993. "The Place of Appraisal in Emotion." *Cognition & Emotion* 7: 357–87.

Fukuyama, Francis. 1992. *The End of History and the Last Man.* New York: The Free Press.

Fuller, Jack. 2010. *What Is Happening to News: The Information Explosion and the Crisis in Journalism.* Chicago: University of Chicago Press.

Funk, Carolyn L. 1999. "Bringing the Candidate into Models of Candidate Evaluation." *The Journal of Politics* 61(3): 700–20.

Gächter, Simon, Eric J. Johnson, and Andreas Herrmann. 2007. "Individual-Level Loss Aversion in Riskless and Risky Choices." IZA Discussion Paper No. 2961, Institute for the Study of Labour, Bonn, Germany.

Gächter, Simon, Elke Renner, and Martin Sefton. 2008. "The Long-Run Benefits of Punishment." *Science* 322(5907): 1510.

Galbraith, John W. 1996. "Credit Rationing and Threshold Effects in the Relation between Money and Output." *Journal of Applied Econometrics* 11: 419–29.

Galtung, Johan, and Mari Holmboe Ruge. 1965. "The Structure of Foreign News." *Journal of Peace Research* 2(1): 64–90.

Gans, Herbert J. 1979. *Deciding What's News: A Study of CBS Evening News, NBC Nightly News, Newsweek and Time.* New York: Pantheon.

Ganzach, Yoav. 1995. "Negativity (and Positivity) in Performance Evaluation: Three Field Studies." *Journal of Applied Psychology* 80: 491–99.

Garcia, John, and Robert A. Koelling. 1966. "Relation of Cue to Consequence in Avoidance Learning." *Psychonomic Science* 4: 123–24.

Garofalo, James. 1981. "NCCD Research Review: Crime and the Mass Media: a Selective Review of Research." *Journal of Research in Crime and Delinquency* 18(2): 319–50.

Garrouste, Pierre, and Stavros Ioannides, eds. 2001. *Evolution and Path Dependence in Economic Ideas: Past and Present.* Cheltenham: Edward Elgar Publishing.

Geer, John G. 2006. *In Defense of Negativity: Attack Ads in Presidential Campaigns.* Chicago: University of Chicago Press.

Geer, John G., and Richard R. Lau. 1998. "A New Way to Model the Effects of Campaigns." Paper presented at the annual meeting of the American Political Science Association, Boston.

Gehring, William J., Brian Goss, Michael G. H. Coles, David E. Meyer, and Emanuel Donchin. 1993. "A Neural System for Error Detection and Compensation." *Psychological Science* 4(6): 385–90.

George, Mark S., Terence A. Ketter, Priti I. Parekh, Barry Horwitz, Peter Herscovitch, and Robert M. Post. 1995. "Brain Activity during Transient Sadness and Happiness in Healthy Women." *American Journal of Psychiatry* 152(3): 341–51.

Gerth, H. H. and C. Wright Mills, eds. 1991. *From Max Weber: Essays in Sociology.* Oxford: Routledge.

Gieber, W. 1964. "News Is What Newspaperman Make It." In *People, Society and Mass Communication,* ed. L. A. Dexter and D. M. White. New York: Free Press.

Gilbert, Avery Nelson, Alan J. Fridlund, and John Sabini. 1987. "Hedonic and Social Determinants of Facial Displays to Odors." *Chemical Senses* 12(2): 355–63.

Gilbert, D. T., Pinel, E. C., Wilson, T. D., Blumberg, S. J., and Wheatley, T. P. 1998. "Immune Neglect: A Source of Durability Bias in Affective Forecasting." *Journal of Personality and Social Psychology* 75: 617–38.

Gilovich, Thomas. 1983. "Biased Evaluation and Persistence in Gambling." *Journal of Social and Personal Psychology* 44(6): 1110–26.

Gilovich, Thomas. 1991. *How We Know What Isn't So.* New York: Free Press.

Goldberg, Bernard. 2002. *Bias: A CBS Insider Exposes How the Media Distort the News.* Washington, DC: Renergy.

Goldstein, K. M., J. S. Krasno, L. Bradford, and D. E. Seltz. 2001. "Going Negative: Attack Advertising in the 1998 Elections." In *Playing Hardball: Campaigning,* ed. Paul S. Herrnson. New York: Prentice Hall.

Goleman, Daniel. 1995. *Emotional Intelligence.* New York: Bantam.

Goreling, Tim, and Samuel Kernell. 1998. "Is Network News Coverage of the President Biased?" *Journal of Politics* 60(4): 1063–87.

Goren, Paul. 2002. "Character Weakness, Partisan Bias, and Presidential Evaluation." *American Journal of Political Science* 46(3): 627–41.

Gottman, John Mordechai. 1979. *Marital Interaction.* New York: Academic Press.

Gottman, John Mordechai. 1994. *Why Marriages Succeed or Fail.* New York: Simon & Schuster.

Grabe and Kamhawi. 2006. "Hard Wired for Negative News? Gender Differences in Processing Broadcast News." *Communication Research* 33(5): 346–69.

Graber, Doris A. 1980. *Crime News and the Public.* New York: Praeger Publishers.

Graziano, William G., Thomas Brothen, and Ellen Berscheid. 1980. "Attention, Attraction, and Individual Differences in Reaction to Criticism." *Journal of Personality and Social Psychology* 38: 193–202.

Groeling, Tim. 2008. "Who's the Fairest of Them All? An Empirical Test for Partisan Bias on ABC, CBS, NBC and Fox News." *Presidential Studies Quarterly* 38(4): 631–57.

Groeling, Tim, and Samual Kernell. 1998. "Is Network News Coverage of the President Biased?" *The Journal of Politics* 60(4): 1063–87.

Gurerk, Ozgur, Bernd Irlenbusch, and Bettina Rockenbach. 2006. "The Competitive Advantage of Sanctioning Institutions." *Science* 312: 108–11.

Habermas, Jurgen. 2003. *Truth and Justification*. Trans. B. Fultner. Cambridge, MA: MIT Press.

Hage, G. S., E. E. Dennis, A. H. Ismach, and S. Hartgen. 1976. *New Strategies for Public Affairs Reporting*. Englewood Cliffs, NJ: Prentice-Hall.

Hallin, Daniel C. 1992. "Sound Bite News: Television Coverage of Elections, 1968–1988." *Journal of Communications* 42(2): 5–24.

Hallin, Daniel C., and Paolo Mancini. 2004. *Comparing Media Systems: Three Models of Media and Politics*. Cambridge: Cambridge University Press.

Hamilton, David L., and Leroy J. Huffman. 1971. "Generality of Impression Formation Processes for Evaluative and Nonevaluative Judgments." *Journal of Personality and Social Psychology* 20(2): 200–07.

Haney López, Ian. 1996. *White by Law: The Legal Construction of Race*. New York: New York University Press.

Hansen, John Mark. 1985. "The Political Economy of Group Membership." *American Political Science Review* 79: 79–96.

Happy, J. R. 1982. "Voter Sensitivity to Economic Conditions: A Canadian-American Comparison." *Comparative Politics* 19(1): 45–56.

Happy, J. R. 1989. "Economic Performance and Retrospective Voting in Canadian Federal Elections." *Canadian Journal of Political Science* 22(2): 377–87.

Hardin, Garrett. 1968. "The Tragedy of the Commons." *Science* 162: 1243–48.

Harmon, Mark D. 1989. "Market Size and Local Television News Judgment." *Journal of Media Economics* 2(1): 15–29.

Harrington, David E. 1989. "Economic News on Television: The Determinants of Coverage." *Public Opinion Quarterly* 53(1): 566–74.

Harshman, Richard A., and Allan Paivio. 1987. "'Paradoxical' Sex Differences in Self-Reported Imagery." *Canadian Journal of Psychology* 41: 287–302.

Hart, R. P. 1984. *Verbal Style and the Presidency: A Computer-Based Analysis*. New York: Academic Press.

Hatemi, Peter K., Nathan A. Gillespie, Lindon J. Eaves, Brion S. Maher, Bradley T. Webb, et al. 2011. "A Genome-Wide Analysis of Liberal and Conservative Political Attitudes." *Journal of Politics* 73(1): 271–85.

Hatemi, Peter K., Carolyn Funk, Hermine Maes, Judy Silberg, Sarah Medland, et al. 2009. "Genetic Influences on Social Attitudes over the Life Course." *Journal of Politics* 71(3): 1141–56.

Hatemi, Peter K., J. R. Hibbing, S. E. Medland, M. C. Keller, J. R. Alford, et al. 2010. "Not by Twins Alone: Using the Extended Twin Family Designed to Investigate the Genetic Basis of Political Beliefs." *American Journal of Political Science* 54(3): 798–814.

Hatzivassiloglou, Vasileios, and Kathleen R. McKeown. 1997. "Predicting the Semantic Orientation of Adjectives." In *ACL '98 Proceedings of the 35th Annual Meeting of the Association for Computational Linguistics and Eighth Conference of the European Chapter of the Association for Computational Linguistics*. 174–81.

Headrick, Barbara, and David J. Lanoue. 1991. "Attention, Asymmetry, and Government Popularity in Britain." *Political Research Quarterly* 44(1): 67–86.

Helson, Harry. 1964. *Adaptation-Level Theory: An Experimental and Systematic Approach to Behavior*. New York: Harper.

Henrich, Joseph, Richard McElreath, Abigail Barr, Jean Ensminger, Clark Barrett, et al. 2006. "Costly Punishment across Human Societies." *Science* 312: 1767–70.

Herman, Edward S., and Noam Chomsky. 1988. *Manufacturing Consent: The Political Economy of the Mass Media*. New York: Pantheon Books.

Herwig, Uwe, Tina Kaffenberger, Thomas Buamgartner, and Luzt Jancke. 2007. "Neural Correlates of a 'Pessimistic' Attitude when Anticipating Events of Unknown Emotional Valence." *NeuroImage* 34: 848–58.

Hinckley, Barbara. 1981. *Congressional Elections*. Washington, DC: Congressional Quarterly Press.

Hitchon, Jacqueline C., and Chingching Chang. 1995. "Effects of Gender Schematic Processing on the Reception of Political Commercials for Men and Women Candidates." *Communication Research* 22(4): 430–58.

Hitchon, Jacqueline C., Chingching Chang, and Rhonda Harris. 1997. "Should Women Emote? Perceptual Bias and Opinion Change in Response to Political Ads for Candidates of Different Genders." *Political Communication* 14(1): 49–69.

Hobfoll, Stevan E. 1988. *The Ecology of Stress*. Washington, DC: Hemisphere.

Hodge, Mildred A., and Ruth J. Stocking. 1912. "A Note on the Relative Value of Punishment and Reward as Motives." *Animal Behavior* 2: 43–50.

Hodges, Bert H. 1974. "Effect of Valence on Relative Weighting in Impression Formation." *Journal of Personality and Social Psychology* 30(3): 378–81.

Hoffman, Moshe, Coren L. Apicella, Anna Dreber, Peter B. Gray, Anthony Little, and Benjamin C. Campbell. 2008. "Testosterone and Financial Risk Preferences." *Evolutionary Human Behavior* 29: 384–90.

Hofstetter, C. Richard, and David M. Dozier. 1986. "Useful News, Sensational News: Quality, Sensationalism and Local TV News." *Journalism Quarterly* 63(4): 815–53.

Holbrook, Allyson L., Jon A. Krosnick, Penny S. Visser, Wendi L. Gardner, and John T. Cacioppo. 2001. "Attitudes toward Presidential Candidates and Political Parties: Initial Optimism, Inertial First Impressions, and a Focus on Flaws." *American Journal of Political Science* 45(4): 930–50.

Holsti, Ole R. 1969. *Content Analysis for the Social Sciences and Humanities*. Reading, MA: Addison-Wesley.

Hood, Christopher. 2002. "The Risk Game and the Blame Game." *Government and Opposition* 37(1): 15–37.

Hood, Christopher. 2007. "What Happens when Transparency Meets Blame-Avoidance?" *Public Management Review* 9(2): 191–210.

Hoorens, Vera, and Bram P. Buunk. 1993. "Social Comparison of Health Risks: Locus of Control, the Person-Positivity Bias, and Unrealistic Optimism." *Journal of Applied Social Psychology* 23(4): 291–302.

Huckfeldt, Robert, and John Sprague. 1987. "Networks in Context: The Social Flow of Political Information." *American Political Science Review* 81(4): 1197–1216.

Huma, Bogdana. 2010. "Gender Differences in Impression Formation." *Journal of Comparative Research in Anthropology and Sociology* 1(1): 57–72.

Hunt, Pamela S., and Byron A. Campbell. 1997. "Autonomic and Behavioral Correlates of Appetitive Conditioning in Rats." *Behavioral Neuroscience* 111(3): 494–502.

Huston, Ted L., John P. Caughlin, Renate M. Houts, Shanna E. Smith, and Laura J. George. 2001. "The Connubial Crucible: Newlywed Years as Predictors of Marital Delight, Distress, and Divorce." *Journal of Personality and Social Psychology* 80(2): 281–93.

Huston, Ted L., and Anita L. Vangelisti. 1991. "Socioemotional Behavior and Satisfaction in Marital Relationships: A Longitudinal Study." *Journal of Personality and Social Psychology* 61(5): 721–33.

Isen, Alice M. 1984. "Toward Understanding the Role of Affect in Cognition." In *Handbook of Social Cognition Vol. 3*, ed. R. S. Wyer Jr. and T. K. Srull. Hillsdale, NJ: Erlbaum.

Isen, Alice M. 1987. "Positive Affect, Cognitive Processes, and Social Behavior." In *Advances in Experimental Social Psychology Vol. 20*, ed. L. Berkowitz. San Diego, CA: Academic Press.

Isen, Alice M., K. A. Daubman, and J. M. Gorgoglione. 1987. "The Influence of Positive Affect on Cognitive Organization." In *Aptitude, Learning and Instruction: Affective and Cognitive Processes, Vol. 3*, ed. R. Snow and M. Farr. Hillsdale, NJ: Erlbaum.

Ito, Tiffany A., and John T. Cacioppo. 2005. "Variations on a Human Universal: Individual Differences in Positivity Offset and Negativity Bias." *Cognition and Emotion* 19(1): 1–26.

Ito, Tiffany A., John T. Cacioppo, and Peter J. Lang. 1998. "Eliciting Affect using the International Affective Picture System: Trajectories through Evaluative Space." *Personality and Social Psychology Bulletin* 24(8): 855–79.

Iyengar, S., H. Norpoth, and K. S. Hahn. 2004. "Consumer Demand for Election News: The Horserace Sells." *Journal of Politics* 66(1): 157–75.

Iyengar, Shanto. 1991. *Is Anyone Responsible? How Television Frames Political Issues.* Chicago: University of Chicago Press.

Iyengar, Shanto, James Curran, Anker Brink Lund, Inka Salovaara-Moring, Kyu S. Hahn, and Sharen Cohen. 2010. "Cross-National versus Individual Differences in Political Information: A Media System Perspective." *Journal of Elections, Public Opinion and Parties* 20(3): 291–309.

Iyengar, Shanto, and Donald R. Kinder. 1987. *News That Matters.* Chicago: University of Chicago Press.

Iyengar, Shanto, Helmut Norpoth, and Kyu S. Hahn. 2004. "Consumer Demand for Election News: The Horserace Sells." *Journal of Politics* 66(1): 157–75.

Iyengar, Shanto, and Richard Reeves. 1997. *Do the Media Govern? Politicians, Voters and Reporters in America.* Thousand Oaks, CA: Sage.

Jain, Prem C. 1988. "Response of Hourly Stock Prices and Trading Volume to Economic News." *Journal of Business* 61(2): 219–31.

Jamieson, Kathleen Hall, and Paul Waldman. 2003. *The Press Effect: Politicians, Journalists, and the Stories That Shape the Political World.* New York: Oxford University Press.

Johnson, Martin, Paul Brace, and Kevin Arceneaux. 2005. "Public Opinion and Dynamic Representation in the American States: The Case of Environmental Attitude." *Social Science Quarterly* 86 (1): 87–108.

Johnston, Richard. 1999. "Business Cycles, Political Cycles and the Popularity of Canadian Governments, 1974–1998." *Canadian Journal of Political Science* 32(3): 499–520.

Johnstone, John W. C., Darnell F. Hawkins, and Arthur Michener. 1994. "Homicide Reporting in Chicago Dailies." *Journalism Quarterly* 71(4): 860–72.

Johnstone, John W. C., Edward J. Slawski, and William W. Bowman. 1972. "The Professional Values of American Newsmen." *Public Opinion Quarterly* 36(4): 522–40.

Jones, Bryan, Frank Baumgartner, Christian Breunig, Christopher Wlezien, Stuart Soroka, et al. 2009. "A General Empirical Law of Public Budgets: A Comparative Analysis." *American Journal of Political Science* 53(4): 855–73.

Jones, Bryan D. 2001. *Politics and the Architecture of Choice: Bounded Rationality and Governance.* Chicago: University of Chicago Press.

Jones, Robert L., Verling C. Troldahl, and J. K. Hvistendahl. 1961. "News Selection Patterns from a State TTS Wire." *Journalism Quarterly* 38: 303–12.

Jordan, Donald L. 1993. "Newspaper Effects on Policy Preferences." *Public Opinion Quarterly* 57(2): 191–204.

Jordan, Nehemiah. 1965. "The Asymmetry of Liking and Disliking: A Phenomenon Meriting Further Reflection and Research." *Public Opinion Quarterly* 29(2): 315–22.

Ju, Youngkee. 2008. "The Asymmetry in Economic News Coverage and Its Impact on Public Perception in South Korea." *International Journal of Public Opinion Research* 20(2): 237–49.

Just, Marion, Ann Crigler, Dean Alger, Timothy Cook, Montague Kern, and Darrell West. 1996a. *Crosstalk: Citizens, Candidates, and the Media in a Presidential Campaign.* Chicago: University of Chicago Press.

Just, Marion, Ann Crigler, and Tami Buhr. 1999. "Voice, Substance, and Cynicism in Presidential Campaign Media." *Political Communication* 16(1): 25–44.

Just, Marion R., Ann N. Crigler, and W. Russell Neuman. 1996b. "Cognitive and Affective Dimensions of Political Conceptualization." In *The Psychology of Political Communication*, ed. Ann N. Crigler. Ann Arbor: University of Michigan Press.

Kahn, Kim Fridkin, and Patrick J. Kenney. 1998a. "Negative Advertising and an Informed Electorate: How Negative Campaigning Enhances Knowledge of Senate Elections." Paper presented at the Conference on Political Advertising in Election Campaigns, Washington, DC.

Kahn, Kim Fridkin, and Patrick J. Kenney. 1998b. "Negative Advertising and an Informed Electorate: How Negative Campaigning Enhances Knowledge of Senate Elections." Paper presented at the Conference on Political Advertising in Election Campaigns, Washington, DC.

Kahn, Kim Fridkin, and Patrick J. Kenney. 1999. "Do Negative Campaigns Mobilize or Suppress Turnout? Clarifying the Relationship between Negativity and Participation." *American Political Science Review* 93(4): 877–89.

Kahneman, D., E. Diener, and N. Schwarz, eds. 1998. *Hedonic Psychology: Scientific Perspectives on Enjoyment, Suffering, and Well-Being.* New York: Cambridge University Press.

Kahneman, Daniel, Jack L. Knetsch, and Richard H. Thaler. 1990. "Experimental Tests of the Endowment Effect and the Coase Theorem." *Journal of Political Economy* 98(6): 1325–48.

Kahneman, Daniel, Jack L. Knetsch, and Richard H. Thaler. 1991. "Anomalies – The Endowment Effect, Loss Aversion, and the Status-Quo Bias." *Journal of Economic Perspectives* 5(1): 193–206.

Kahneman, Daniel, and Dan Lovallo. 1993. "Timid Choices and Bold Forecasts: A Cognitive Perspective on Risk Taking." *Management Science* 39(1): 17–31.

Kahneman, Daniel, and Richard Thaler. 1991. "Economic-Analysis and the Psychology of Utility – Applications to Compensation Policy." *American Economic Review* 81(2): 341–46.

Kahneman, Daniel, and Amos Tversky. 1979. "Prospect Theory: An Analysis of Decision under Risk." *Econometrica* 47(2): 263–92.

Kahneman, Daniel, and Amos Tversky. 1984. "Choices, Values, and Frames." *American Psychologist* 39(4): 341–50.

Kaid, Lynda Lee, Mike Chanslor, and Mark Hovind. 1992a. "The Influence of Program and Commercial Type on Political Advertising Effectiveness." *Journal of Broadcasting and Electronic Media* 36(3): 303–20.

Kaid, Lynda Lee, and Anne Johnston. 1991. "Negative versus Positive Television Advertising in U.S. Presidential Campaigns, 1960–1988." *Journal of Communication* 41(3): 53–64.

Kaid, Lynda Lee, Chris M. Leland, and Susan Whitney. 1992b. "The Impact of Televised Political Ads: Evoking Viewer Responses in the 1988 Presidential Campaign." *Southern Communication Journal* 57(4): 285–95.

Kamarck, Thomas W., Saul M. Shiffman, Leslie Smithline, Jeffrey L. Goodie, Jean A. Paty, et al. 1998. "Effects of Task Strain, Social Conflict, and Emotional Activation on Ambulatory Cardiovascular Activity: Daily Life Consequences of Recurring Stress in a Multiethnic Adult Sample." *Health Psychology* 17(1): 17–29.

Karnizova, Lilia, and Hashmat Khan. 2010. "The Stock Market and the Consumer Confidence Channel in Canada." Department of Economics, University of Ottawa Working Paper #1004E.

Karpen, Ulrich, ed. 1988. *The Constitution of the Federal Republic of Germany: Essays on the Basic Rights and Principles of the Basic Law with a Translation of the Basic Law*. Baden-Baden: Nomos Verlagsgesellschaft.

Katz, Elihu, and Paul Lazarsfeld. 1955. *Personal Influence: The Party Played by Individuals in the Flow of Mass Communication*. Glencoe, IL: Free Press.

Keech, William R. 1982. "Of Honeymoons and Economic Performance: Comment on Hibbs." *American Political Science Review* 76: 280–81.

Kerbel, Matthew. 1995. *Remote and Controlled*. Boulder, CO: Westview Press.

Kernell, Samuel. 1977. "Presidential Popularity and Negative Voting: An Alternative Explanation of the Midterm Congressional Decline of the President's Party." *American Political Science Review* 71(1): 44–66.

Kiewet, D. Roderick. 1983. *Macroeconomics and Micropolitics: The Electoral Effects of Economic Issues*. Chicago: University of Chicago Press.

Kinder, Donald, Robert Abelson, and Susan Fiske. 1979. "Developmental Research on Candidate Instrumentation: Results and Recommendations." Report submitted to

Board of Overseers, National Election Studies. Ann Arbor: University of Michigan Press.

Kinder, Donald, Mark Peters, Robert Abelson, and Susan Fiske. 1980. "Presidential Prototypes." *Political Behavior* 2(4): 315–37.

Kinder, Donald R. 1978. "Political Person Perception: The Asymmetrical Influence of Sentiment and Choice on Perceptions of Presidential Candidates." *Journal of Personality and Social Psychology* 36(8): 859–71.

Kinder, Donald R. 1983. "Presidential Traits." Pilot study report to the 1984 NES Planning Committee and NES Board, Washington, DC.

Kinder, Donald R. 1986. "Presidential Character Revisited." In *Political Cognition*, ed. Richard R. Lau and David O. Sears. Hillsdale, NJ: Lawrence Erlbaum.

Kinder, Donald R., and D. Roderick Kiewet. 1981. "Sociotropic Politics: The American Case." *British Journal of Political Science* 11(2): 129–61.

King, Anthony, ed. 2002. *Leaders' Personalities and the Outcomes of Democratic Elections*. Oxford: Oxford University Press.

King, Erika G., Robert W. Hendersen, and Hong C. Chen. 1998. "Viewer Response to Positive vs. Negative Ads in the 1996 Presidential Campaign." Paper presented at the annual meeting of the Midwest Political Science Association, Chicago, April 23–25.

Klar, Yechiel, and Eilath E. Giladi. 1997. "No-One in My Group Can Be Below the Group's Average: A Robust Positivity Bias in Favor of Anonymous Peers." *Journal of Personality and Social Psychology* 73(5): 885–901.

Klein, Jill. 1996. "Negativity in Impressions of Presidential Candidates Revisited: The 1992 Election." *Personality and Social Psychology Bulletin* 22(3): 288–95.

Klein, Jill G. 1991. "Negativity Effects in Impression Formation: A Test in the Political Arena." *Personality and Social Psychology Bulletin* 17: 412–18.

Klein, William M., and Ziva Kunda. 1992. "Motivated Person Perception: Constructing Justifications for Desired Beliefs." *Journal of Experimental Social Psychology* 28(2):145–68.

Knetch, Jack L. 1989. "The Endowment Effect and Evidence of Nonreversable Indifference Curves." *American Economic Review* 79(5): 1277–84.

Kommers, Donald P. 1989. *The Constitutional Jurisprudence of the Federal Republic of Germany*. Durham, NC: Duke University Press.

Krause, Sharon. 2000. "The Spirit of Separate Powers in Montesquieu." *The Review of Politics* 62(2): 231–65.

Kunda, Ziva. 1990. "The Case for Motivated Reasoning." *Psychological Bulletin* 108: 480–98.

Kuo, Biing-Shen, and Ching-Ting Chung. 2002. "Is Consumption Liquidity Constrained? The Asymmetric Impact." *Business Cycles, Academia Economic Papers* 30(4): 443–72.

Kurov, Alexander. 2010. "Investor Sentiment and the Stock Market's Reaction to Monetary Policy." *Journal of Banking and Finance* 34(1): 139–49.

Lane, Richard D., Eric M. Reiman, Geoffrey L. Ahern, Gary E. Schwartz, and Richard J. Davidson. 1997. "Neuroanatomical Correlates of Happiness, Sadness, and Disgust." *American Journal of Psychiatry* 154(7): 926–33.

Lang, Annie. 1990. "Involuntary Attention and Physiological Arousal Evoked by Structural Features and Emotional Content in TV Commercials." *Communication Research* 17: 275–99.

Lang, Annie. 1991. "Emotion, Formal Features, and Memory for Televised Political Advertisements." In *Television and Political Advertising, Vol. 1*, ed. Frank Biocca. Hillsdale, NJ: Lawrence Erlbaum.

Lang, Annie. 1995. "What Can the Heart Tell Us about Thinking?" In *Measuring Psychological Responses to Media*, ed. Annie Lang. Hillsdale, NJ: Lawrence Erlbaum.

Lang, Annie, Paul Bolls, Robert F. Potter, and Karlynn Kawahara. 1999. "The Effects of Production Pacing and Arousing Content on the Information Processing of Television Messages." *Journal of Broadcasting and Electronic Media* 43(4): 451–75.

Lang, Annie, Kulijinder Dhillon, and Qingwen Dong. 1995. "The Effects of Emotional Arousal and Valence on Television Viewers' Cognitive Capacity and Memory." *Journal of Broadcasting and Electronic Media* 39(3): 313–27.

Lang, Annie, John Newhagen, and Byron Reeves. 1996. "Negative Video as Structure: Emotion, Attention, Capacity, and Memory." *Journal of Broadcasting and Electronic Media* 40(4): 460–77.

Lang, Annie, Shuhua Zhou, Nancy Schwartz, Paul D. Bolls, and Robert F. Potter. 2000. "The Effects of Edits on Arousal, Attention, and Memory for Television Messages: When an Edit Is an Edit Can an Edit Be Too Much?" *Journal of Broadcasting & Electronic Media* 44(1): 94–109.

Lang, Peter J., Margaret M. Bradley, and Bruce N. Cuthbert. 1990. "Emotion, Attention, and the Startle Reflex." *Psychological Review* 97(3): 377–95.

Lanoue, David J. 1987. "Economic Prosperity and Presidential Popularity: Sorting Out the Effects." *Western Political Quarterly* 40(2): 237–45.

Larsen, Randy J., and Edward Diener. 1992. "Promises and Problems with the Circumplex Model of Emotion." In *Review of Personality and Social Psychology, Vol. 13*, ed. Margaret S. Clark. Newbury Park, CA: Sage.

Lasswell, Harold D. 1949. "Style in the Language of Politics." In *The Language of Politics: Studies in Quantitative Semantics*, ed. Harold D. Lasswell, Nathan Leites, Raymond Fadner, Joseph M. Goldsen, Alan Grey, et al. New York: George Stewart.

Lau, Richard R. 1982. "Negativity in Political Perception." *Political Behavior* 4(4): 353–77.

Lau, Richard R. 1984. "Dynamics of the Attribution Process." *Journal of Personality and Social Psychology* 46(5): 1017–28.

Lau, Richard R. 1985. "Two Explanations for Negativity Effects in Political Behavior." *American Journal of Political Science* 29(1): 119–38.

Lau, Richard R., and David P. Redlawsk. 1997. "Voting Correctly." *American Political Science Review* 91(3): 585–98.

Lau, Richard R., and David P. Redlawsk. 2006. *How Voters Decide: Information Processing during Election Campaigns*. Cambridge: Cambridge University Press.

Lau, Richard R., Lee Sigelman, Caroline Heldman, and Paul Babbitt. 1999. "The Effects of Negative Political Advertisements: A Meta-Analytic Assessment." *American Political Science Review* 93(4): 851–76.

Lazarus, Richard S. 1991. *Emotions and Adaptation*. New York: Oxford University Press.

Lazarus, Richard S. 1994. "Universal Antecedents of the Emotions." In *The Nature of Emotion: Fundamental Questions*, ed. Paul Ekman and Richard J. Davidson. New York: Oxford University Press.

LeDoux, Joseph E. 1995. "Emotion: Clues from the Brain." *Annual Review of Psychology* 46: 209–35.

LeDoux, Joseph E., Lizabeth Romanski, and Andrew Xagoraris. 1989. "Indelibility of Subcortical Emotional Memories." *Journal of Cognitive Neuroscience* 1(3): 238–43.

Levy, Jack S. 2003. "Applications of Prospect Theory to Political Science." *Synthese* 135(2): 215–41.

Lewin, Kurt. 1951. *Field Theory in Social Science: Selected Theoretical Papers*. Ed. Dorwin Cartwright. New York: Harper.

Lewis-Beck, Michael S. 1988. *Economics and Elections: The Major Western Democracies*. Ann Arbor: University of Michigan Press.

Lewis-Beck, Michael S., and Mary Stegmaier. 2007. "Economic Models of the Vote." In *The Oxford Handbook of Political Behavior*, ed. Russell Dalton and Hans-Dieter Klingemann. Oxford: Oxford University Press.

Lichtenstein, Sarah, Baruch Fischhoff, and Lawrence D. Phillips. 1982. "Calibration of Probabilities: The State of the Art to 1980." In *Judgment under Uncertainty: Heuristics and Biases*, ed. Daniel Kahneman, Paul Slovic, and Amos Tversky. Cambridge and New York: Cambridge University Press.

Lichter, S. Robert and Richard Noyes. 1995. *Good Intentions Make Bad News*. Lanham, MD: Rowman and Littlefield.

Lindblom, Charles E. 1959. "The Science of 'Muddling Through.'" *Public Administration Review* 19(2): 79–88.

Lindblom, Charles E. 1975. *The Policy-Making Process*. Englewood Cliffs, NJ: Prentice Hall.

Lodge, Milton, and Charles Taber. 2000. "Three Steps toward a Theory of Motivated Political Reasoning." In *Elements of Reason: Cognition, Choice, and the Bounds of Rationality*, ed. Arthur Lupia, Mathew D. McCubbins, and Samuel L. Popkin. New York: Cambridge University Press.

Lowry, Dennis T., Tarn Ching Josephine Nio, and Dennis W. Leither. 2003. "Setting the Public Fear Agenda: A Longitudinal Analysis of Network TV Crime Reporting, Public Perceptions of Crime, and FBI Crime Statistics." *Journal of Communication* 53(1): 61–73.

Lutz, Donald S. 2000. "Thinking about Constitutionalism at the Start of the Twenty-First Century." *Publius* 30(4): 115–35.

Luu, Phan, Paul Collins, and Don M. Tucker. 2000. "Mood, Personality, and Self-Monitoring: Negative Affect and Emotionality in Relation to Frontal Lobe Mechanisms of Error Monitoring." *Journal of Experimental Psychology: General* 129(1): 43–60.

Machiavelli, Niccolò. [1532] 2003. *The Prince*. London: Penguin Classics.

MacKuen, Michael B., Robert S. Erikson, and James A. Stimson. 1992. "Peasants or Bankers? The American Electorate and the U.S. Economy." *American Political Science Review* 86(3): 597–611.

Mahl, George F. 1952. "Relationship between Acute and Chronic Fear and the Gastric Acidity and Blood Sugar Levels in Macaca Mulatta Monkeys." *Psychosomatic Medicine* 14(3): 182–210.

Matlin, Margaret W., and David J. Stang. 1978. *The Pollyanna Principle: Selectivity in Language, Memory, and Thought*. Cambridge, MA: Schenkman Publishing Company.

Mansfield, Jr., Harvey C. 1989. *Taming the Prince: The Ambivalence of Modern Executive Power*. New York: The Free Press.

March, James G. and Johan P. Olsen. 1984. "The New Institutionalism: Organizational Factors in Political Life." *American Political Science Review* 78(3): 734–49.

March, James G., and Johan P. Olsen. 2006. "Elaborating the 'New Institutionalism'." In *The Oxford Handbook of Political Institutions*, ed. R.A.W Rhodes, Sarah A. Binder and Bert A. Rockman. Oxford: Oxford University Press.

Marco, Christine A., and Jerry Suls. 1993. "Daily Stress and the Trajectory of Mood: Spillover, Response Assimilation, Contrast, and Chronic Negative Affectivity." *Journal of Personality and Social Psychology* 64(6): 1053–63.

Marcus, George E. 2002. *The Sentimental Citizen: Emotion in Democratic Politics*. University Park: Pennsylvania State University Press.

Marcus, George E., and Michael MacKuen. 1993. "Anxiety, Enthusiasm and the Vote: The Emotional Underpinnings of Learning and Involvement during Presidential Campaigns." *American Political Science Review* 87: 688–701.

Marcus, George E., Michael MacKuen, Jennifer Wolak, and Luke Keele. 2006. "The Measure and Mismeasure of Emotion." In *Feeling Politics: Emotion in Political Information Processing*, ed. David Redlawsk. New York: Palgrave Macmillan.

Marcus, George E., W. Russell Neuman, and Michael B. MacKuen. 2000. *Affective Intelligence and Political Judgment*. Chicago: University of Chicago Press.

Marcus, George E., John L. Sullivan, Elizabeth Theiss-Morse, and Sandra L. Wood. 1995. *With Malice toward Some: How People Make Civil Liberties Judgments*. Cambridge: Cambridge University Press.

Marshall, Linda L., and Robert F. Kidd. 1981. "Good News or Bad News First?" *Social Behavior and Personality* 9: 223–26.

Martindale, Colin. 1975. *Romantic Progression: The Psychology of Literary History*. Washington, DC: Hemisphere.

Martindale, Colin. 1990. *The Clockwork Muse: The Predictability of Artistic Change*. New York: Basic Books.

Martinez, Michael D., and Tad Delegal. 1990. "The Irrelevance of Negative Campaigns to Political Trust: Experimental and Survey Results." *Political Communication and Persuasion* 7(1): 25–40.

Matlin, Margaret W., and David J. Stang. 1978. *The Pollyanna Principle: Selectivity in Language, Memory, and Thought*. Cambridge, MA: Schenkman Publishing Company.

Mauss, Marcel. [1902.] 1972. *A General Theory of Magic*. New York: W. W. Norton.

May, Anthony D. 2010. "The Impact of Bond Rating Changes on Corporate Bond Prices: New Evidence from the Over-the-Counter Market." *Journal of Banking and Finance* 34(11): 2822–36.

Mayer, John D., and Peter Salovey. 1993. "The Intelligence of Emotional Intelligence." *Intelligence* 17(4): 433–42.

McCombs, Maxwell E., and Lee B. Becker. 1979. *Using Mass Communication Theory*. Englewood Cliffs, NJ: Prentice-Hall.

McCormick, John P. 2003. "Machiavelli against Republicanism: On the Cambridge School's 'Guicciardinian Moments.'" *Political Theory* 31(5): 615–43.

McDermott, Rose. 1994. "Prospect Theory in International Relations: The Iranian Hostage Rescue Mission." In *Avoiding Losses/Taking Risks: Prospect Theory and International Conflict*, ed. Barbara Farnham. Ann Arbor: University of Michigan Press.

McDermott, Rose. 1998. *Risk-Taking in International Politics: Prospect Theory in American Foreign Policy*. Ann Arbor: University of Michigan Press.

McDermott, Rose. 2004. "Prospect Theory in Political Science: Gains and Losses from the First Decade." *Political Psychology* 25(2): 289–312.

McDermott, Rose, James H. Fowler, and Oleg Smirnov. 2008. "On the Evolutionary Origin of Prospect Theory Preferences." *The Journal of Politics* 29(2): 335–50.

McDermott, Rose, and Jacek Kugler. 2001. "Comparing Rational Choice and Prospect Theory Analyses: The US Decision to Launch Operation 'Desert Storm.'" *Journal of Strategic Studies* 24(3): 49–85.

McEvoy, James. 1971. *Radicals or Conservatives: The Contemporary American Right*. Chicago: Rand McNally.

McGraw, Kathleen M. 1991. "Managing Blame: An Experimental Test of the Effects of Political Accounts." *American Political Science Review* 85(4): 1133–57.

McGuire, Kevin T., and Barbara Palmer. 1996. "Issues, Agendas, and Decision Making on the Supreme Court." *American Political Science Review* 90(4): 853–65.

McQueen, Grant, Michael Pinegar, and Steven Thorley. 1996. "Delayed Reaction to Good News and the Cross-Autocorrelation of Portfolio Returns." *Journal of Finance* 51(3): 889–919.

Meffert, Michael F., Sungeun Chung, Amber J. Joiner, Leah Waks, and Jennifer Garst. 2006. "The Effects of Negativity and Motivated Information Processing During a Political Campaign." *Journal of Communication* 56(1): 27–51.

Meigs, Anna S. 1984. *Food, Sex, and Pollution: A New Guinea Religion*. New Brunswick, NJ: Rutgers University Press.

Mercer, Jonathan. 2005. "Prospect Theory and Political Science." *Annual Review of Political Science* 8: 1–21.

Mergenthaler, Erhard. 1996. "Emotion-Abstraction Patterns in Verbatim Protocols: A New way of Describing Psychotherapeutic Processes." *Journal of Consulting and Clinical Psychology* 64(6): 1306–15.

Mergenthaler, Erhard. 2008. "Resonating Minds: A School-Independent Theoretical Conception and its Empirical Application to Psychotherapeutic Processes." *Psychotherapy Research* 18: 109–26.

Merrill, John C., and Ralph L. Lowenstein. 1971. *Media, Messages and Men: New Perspectives in Communication*. New York: McKay.

Meyer, William J., and Stuart I. Offenbach. 1962. "Effectiveness of Reward and Punishment as a Function of Task Complexity." *Journal of Comparative and Physiological Psychology* 55(4): 532–34.

Meyrowitz, Joshua. 1985. *No Sense of Place: The Impact of Electronic Media on Social Behavior*. New York: Oxford University Press.

Meyrowitz, Joshua. 1994. "Visible and Invisible Candidates: A Case Study in 'Competing Logics' of Campaign Coverage." *Political Communication* 11(2): 145–64.

Miller, Arthur. 1974. "Political Issues and Trust in Government: 1964–1970." *American Political Science Review* 68(3): 951–72.

Miller, Arthur, Anne Hindreth, and Grace Simmons. 1986. "The Political Implications of Gender Group Consciousness." Paper presented at the annual meeting of the Midwest Political Science Association, Chicago.

Miller, Arthur H., Edie N. Goldberg, and Lutz Erbring. 1979. "Type-Set Politics: Impact of Newspapers on Public Confidence." *American Political Science Review* 73(1): 67–84.

Miller, N. E. 1961. "Some Recent Studies on Conflict Behavior and Drugs." *American Psychology* 16: 12–24.

Miltner, Wolfgang H. R., Cristoph H. Braun, and Michael G. H. Coles. 1997. "Event-Related Brain Potentials Following Incorrect Feedback in a Time-Estimation Task: Evidence for a 'Generic' Neural System for Error Detection." *Journal of Cognitive Neuroscience* 9(6): 788–98.

Mueller, John E. 1973. *War, Presidents and Public Opinion*. New York: John Wiley and Sons.

Mulder, G., and L. J. Mulder. 1981. "Information Processing and Cardiovascular Control." *Psychophysiology* 18(4): 392–402.

Nadeau, Richard, Richard G. Niemi, and Timothy Amato. 1994. "Expectations and Preferences in British General Elections." *American Political Science Review* 88(2): 371–83.

Nadeau, Richard, Richard G. Niemi, and Timothy Amato. 1995. "Emotions, Issue Importance, and Political Learning." *American Journal of Political Science* 39(3): 558–74.

Nadeau, Richard, Richard G. Niemi, and Timothy Amato. 1996. "Prospective and Comparative or Retrospective and Individual? Party Leaders and party Support in Great Britain." *British Journal of Political Science* 26(2): 245–58.

Nadeau, Richard, Richard G. Niemi, David P. Fan, and Timothy Amato. 1999. "Elite Economic Forecasts, Economic News, Mass Economic Judgments, and Presidential Approval." *Journal of Politics* 61(1): 109–35.

Nannestad, Peter, and Martin Paldam. 1997. "The Grievance Asymmetry Revisited: A Micro Study of Economic Voting in Denmark, 1986–92." *European Journal of Political Economy* 13(1): 81–99.

Newhagen, John E., and Byron Reeves. 1991. "Emotion and Memory Responses for Negative Political Advertising: A Study of Television Commercials Used in the 1988 Presidential Election." In *Television and Political Advertising, Vol. 1*, ed. Frank Biocca. Hillsdale, NJ: Lawrence Erlbaum.

Niedenthal, Paula M., and Shinobu Kitayama. 1994. *The Heart's Eye: Emotional Influences in Perception and Attention*. San Diego, CA: Academic Press.

Niederle, Muriel, and Lise Vesterlund. 2007. "Do Women Shy Away from Competition? Do Men Compete Too Much?" *Quarterly Journal of Economics* 122(3): 1067–1101.

Niven, David. 2000. "The Other Side of Optimism: High Expectations and the Rejection of Status Quo." *Political Behavior* 22(1): 71–88.

Niven, David. 2001. "Bias in the News: Partisanship and Negativity in Media Coverage of Presidents George Bush and Bill Clinton." *Harvard International Journal of Press and Politics* 6(3): 31–46.

Niven, David. 2002. *Tilt? The Search for Media Bias*. New York: Praeger.

Norpoth, Helmut. 1987. "Guns and Butter and Government Popularity in Britain." *American Political Science Review* 81(3): 949–59.

North, Douglass C., and Barry R. Weingast. 1989. "Constitutions and Commitment: The Evolution of Institutions Governing Public Choice in Seventeenth-Century England." *The Journal of Economic History* 49(4): 803–32.

Oesterreich, Traugott K. 1974. *Possession and Exorcism: Among Primitive Races, in Antiquity, the Middle Ages, and Modern Times*. New York: Causeway Books.

Öhman, Arne. 1993. "Fear and Anxiety as Emotional Phenomena: Clinical Phenomenology, Evolutionary Perspectives, and Information-Processing Mechanisms." In Michael Lewis, Jeannette M. Haviland-Jones, Lisa Feldman Barrett, eds., *Handbook of Emotions*. New York: Guildford Press.

Öhman, Arne, Alfons Hamm, and Kenneth Hugdahl. 2000. "Cognition and the Autonomic Nervous System: Orienting, Anticipation, and Conditioning." In John T. Cacioppo, Louis G. Tassinary, Gary G. Berntson, eds., *Handbook of Psychophysiology*, 2nd ed. New York: Cambridge University Press.

Öhman, Arne, Daviel Lundqvist, and Francisco Esteves. 2001. "The Face in the Crowd Revisited: A Threat Advantage with Schematic Stimuli." *Journal of Personality and Social Psychology* 80(3): 381–96.

Oliver, Pamela. 1980. "Rewards and Punishments as Selective Incentives for Collective Action: Theoretical Investigations." *American Journal of Sociology* 85(6): 1356–75.

Olson, Mancur. 1965. *The Logic of Collective Action: Public Goods and the Theory of Groups*. Cambridge, MA: Cambridge University Press.

Ostrom, Elinor. 1990. *Governing the Commons: The Evolution of Institutions for Collective Action*. Cambridge: Cambridge University Press.

Ostrom, Elinor. 2002. "Common-Pool Resources and Institutions: Toward a Revised Theory." In *Handbook of Agricultural Economics, Volume 2*, ed. Bruce L. Gardner and Gordon C. Rausser. Amsterdam: Elsevier Science.

Ottati, Victor C., Marco R. Steenbergen, and Ellen Riggle. 1992. "The Cognitive and Affective Components of Political Attitudes: Measuring the Determinants of Candidate Evaluations." *Political Behavior* 14(4): 423–42.

Owen, Andrew. 2008. "The Negativity Bias and the Effect of Policy Change on Evaluations of Political Incumbents." Paper presented at the Annual Meeting of the Canadian Political Science Association, June 3–6, 2008, Vancouver, BC.

Oxley, Douglas R., Kevin B. Smith, John R. Alford, Matthew V. Hibbing, Jennifer L. Miller, et al. 2008. "Political Attitudes Vary with Physiological Traits." *Science* 321(5896): 1667–70.

Page, Scott E. 2006. "Essay: Path Dependence." *Quarterly Journal of Political Science* 1: 87–115.

Pancer, S. Mark, Steven D. Brown, and Cathy Widdis Barr. 1999. "Forming Impressions of Political Leaders: A Cross-National Comparison." *Political Psychology* 20(2): 345–68.

Patterson, Kerry D. 1993. "The Impact of Credit Constraints, Interest Rates and Housing Equity Withdrawal on the Intertemporal Pattern of Consumption – A Diagrammatic Analysis." *Scottish Journal of Political Economy* 40(4): 391–407.

Patterson, Thomas. 1994. *Out of Order*. New York: Vintage.

Patty, John W. 2006. "Loss Aversion, Presidential Responsibility, and Midterm Congressional Elections." *Electoral Studies* 25(2): 227–47.

Peeters, Guido. 1991. "Evaluative Influence in Social Cognition: The Roles of Direct versus Indirect Evaluation and Positive-Negative Asymmetry." *European Journal of Social Psychology* 21(2): 131–46.

Peeters, Guido, and Janusz Czapinski. 1990. "Positive-Negative Asymmetry in Evaluations: The Distinction between Affective and Informational Negativity Effects." *European Review of Social Psychology* 1(1): 33–60.

Pennebaker, James W., Martha E. Francis, and Roger J. Booth. 2001. *Linguistic Inquiry and Word Count: LIWC 2001.* Mahwah, NJ: Lawrence Erlbaum.

Penney, R. K., and A. A. Lupton. 1961. "Children's Discrimination Learning as a Function of Reward and Punishment." *Journal of Comparative and Physiological Psychology* 54(4): 449–51.

Penney, Ronald K. 1968. "Effect of Reward and Punishment on Children's Orientation and Discrimination Learning." *Journal of Experimental Psychology* 75(1): 140–42.

Perry, David K. 2003. *Roots of Civic Journalism: Darwin, Dewey, and Mead.* Lanham, MD: Rowman and Littlefield.

Phelps, Elizabeth A., and Adam K. Anderson. 1997. "Emotional Memory: What Does the Amygdala Do?" *Current Biology* 7(5): R311–R314.

Pierce, Patrick A. 1993. "Political Sophistication and the Use of Candidate Traits in Candidate Evaluation." *Political Psychology* 14(1): 21–35.

Pierson Paul. 1994. *Dismantling the Welfare State? Reagan, Thatcher, and the Politics of Retrenchment.* New York: Cambridge University Press.

Pierson, Paul. 1996. "The New Politics of the Welfare State." *World Politics* 48: 143–79.

Pierson, Paul. 2000. "Increasing Returns, Path Dependence, and the Study of Politics." *American Political Science Review* 94(2): 251–67.

Pierson, Paul, and Theda Skocpol. 2002. "Historical Institutionalism in Contemporary Political Science." In *Political Science: State of the Discipline*, ed. Ira Katznelson and Helen V. Milner. New York: W. W. Norton.

Placek, Paul J. 1974. "Direct Mail and Information Diffusion: Family Planning." *Public Opinion Quarterly* 38(4): 548–61.

Powell, G. Bingham, and Guy D. Whitten. 1993. "A Cross-National Analysis of Economic Voting: Taking Account of the Political Context." *American Journal of Political Science* 37(2): 391–414.

Price, Michael E., Leda Cosmides, and John Tooby. 2002. "Punitive Sentiment as an Anti-Free Rider Psychological Device." *Evolution and Human Behavior* 23(3): 203–31.

Price, Simon, and David Sanders. 1993. "Modeling Government Popularity in Postwar Britain: A Methodological Example." *American Journal of Political Science* 37(1): 317–34.

Pulford, Briony D., and Andrew M. Colman. 1996. "Overconfidence, Base Rates and Outcome Positivity/Negativity of Predicted Events." *British Journal of Psychology* 87(3): 431–45.

Pyszczynski, Tom, and Jeff Greenberg. 1987. "Toward an Integration of Cognitive and Motivational Perspectives on Social Inference: A Biased Hypothesis Testing Model." In *Advances in Experimental Social Psychology, Volume 20*, ed. Leonard Berkowitz. New York: Academic Press.

Quirk, Gregory J., J. Christoher Repa, and Joseph E. LeDoux. 1995. "Fear Conditioning Enhances Short-Latency Auditory Responses of Lateral Amygdala Neurons: Parallel Recordings in the Freely Behaving Rat." *Neuron* 15(5): 1029–39.

Rand, David G., Anna Dreber, Tore Ellingsen, Drew Fudenberg, and Martin A. Nowak. 2009. "Positive Actions Promote Public Cooperation." *Science* 325(5945): 1272–75.

Ravaja, Niklas. 2004. "Contributions of Psychophysiology to Media Research: Review and Recommendations." *Media Psychology* 6(2): 193–235.

Redlask, David P. 2006. *Feeling Politics: Emotion in Political Information Processing.* New York: Palgrave Macmillan.

Reefmann, Nadine, Franziska Bütikofer Kaszàs, Beat Wechsler, and Lorenz Gygax. 2009. "Ear and Tail Postures and Indicators of Emotional Valence in Sheep." *Applied Animal Behaviour Science* 118(3–4): 199–207.

Regan, Pamela C., Mark Snyder, and Saul M. Kassin. 1995. "Unrealistic Optimism: Self-Enhancement or Person Positivity?" *Personality and Social Psychology Bulletin* 21(10): 1073–82.

Resnick, Philip. 1987. "Montesquieu Revisited, or the Mixed Constitution and the Separation of Powers in Canada." *Canadian Journal of Political Science* 20(1): 97–115.

Richardson, George P. 1983. "The Feedback Concept in American Social Science, with Implications for System Dynamics." Paper presented at the International System Dynamics Conference, Chestnut Hill, MA, July 27–30.

Roberts, Marilyn S. 1995. "Political Advertising: Strategies for Influence." In *Presidential Campaign Discourse: Strategic Communication Problems*, ed. Kathleen E. Kendall. Albany: SUNY Press.

Robinson, John, and Michael Levy. 1985. *The Main Source: Learning from Television News.* Beverly Hills, CA: Sage.

Roget, Peter M. 1911. *Roget's Thesaurus of English Words and Phrases, 1911 Edition.* Via Lisle, IL: Project Gutenberg.

Ronis, David L., and Edmund R. Lipinski. 1985. "Value and Uncertainty as Weighting Factor in Impression Formation." *Journal of Experimental Social Psychology* 21(1): 47–60.

Roper, Burns W. 1982. "The Predictive Value of Consumer Confidence Measures." *Public Opinion Quarterly* 46(3): 361–67.

Roseman, Ira J. 1996. "Appraisal Determinants of Emotions: Constructing a more Accurate and Comprehensive Theory." *Cognition & Emotion* 10(3): 241–77.

Rosen, Jay. 1999. *What Are Journalists For?* New Haven, CT: Yale University Press.

Rosenblatt-Wisch, Rina. 2008. "Loss Aversion in Aggregate Macroeconomic Time Series." *European Economic Review* 52: 1140–59.

Ross, Dennis. 1984. "Risk Aversion in Soviet Decisionmaking." In *Soviet Decisionmaking for National Security*, ed. J. Valenta and W. Potter. London: Allen & Unwin.

Rothstein, Bo. 1998. *Just Institutions Matter: The Moral and Political Logic of the Universal Welfare State.* Cambridge: Cambridge University Press.

Rowe, Patricia M. 1989. "Unfavorable Information and Interview Decisions." In *The Employment Interview: Theory, Research, and Practice*, ed. Robert W. Eder and Gerald R. Ferris. Newbury Park. CA: Sage.

Rozin, Paul, Linda Millman, and Carol Nemeroff. 1986. "Operation of the Laws of Sympathetic Magic in Disgust and Other Domains." *Journal of Personality and Social Psychology* 50(4): 703–12.

Rozin, Paul, and Carol Nemeroff. 1990. "The Laws of Sympathetic Magic: A Psychological Analysis of Similarity and Contagion." In *Cultural Psychology: Essays on Comparative Human Development*, ed. James W. Stigler, Richard A. Shweder, and Gilbert Herdt. Cambridge: Cambridge University Press.

Rozin, Paul, Carol Nemeroff, Marcia Wane, and Amy Sherrod. 1989. "Operation of the Sympathetic Magical Law of Contagion in Interpersonal Attitudes among Americans." *Bulletin of the Psychonomic Society* 27(4): 367–70.

Rozin, Paul, and Edward B. Royzman. 2001. "Negativity Bias, Negativity Dominance, and Contagion." *Personality and Social Psychology Review* 5(4): 296–320.

Rudolph, Thomas J., Amy Gangl, and Dan Stevens. 2000. "The Effects of Efficacy and Emotions on Campaign Involvement." *Journal of Politics* 62(4): 1189–97.

Rusbult, Caryl E., Dennis J. Johnson, and Gregory D. Morrow. 1986. "Impact of Couple Patterns of Problem Solving on Distress and Nondistress in Dating Relationships." *Journal of Personality and Social Psychology* 50(4): 744–53.

Russell, James A. 1980. "A Circumplex Model of Affect." *Journal of Personality and Social Psychology* 39(6): 1161–78.

Russell, James A., José-Miguel Fernandez-Dols, Antony S. R. Manstead, and J. C. Wellenkamp, eds. 1995. "Everyday Conceptions of Emotion: An Introduction to the Psychology, Anthropology, and Linguistics of Emotion." In *Behavioral and Social Sciences, Vol. 81.* Dordrecht, The Netherlands: Kluwer Academic.

Ryfe, David Michael. 2006. "New Institutionalism and the News." *Political Communication* 23(2): 135–44.

Ryu, Jung S. 1982. "Public Affairs and Sensationalism in Local TV News Programs." *Journalism Quarterly* 59(1): 74–77, 137.

Sabato, Larry. 1991. *Feeding Frenzy: How Attack Journalism Has Transformed American Politics.* New York: Free Press.

Sacco, Vincent F. 1995. "Media Constructions of Crime." *Annals of the American Academy of Political and Social Science* 539: 141–54.

Sanders, David. 1996. "Economic Performance, Management Competence and the Outcome of the Next General Election." *Political Studies* 64: 203–31.

Sanders, David. 1999. "Conservative Incompetence, Labour Responsibility and the Feelgood Factor: Why the Economy Failed to Save the Conservatives in 1997." *Electoral Studies* 18(2): 251–70.

Sanders, David, David Marsh, and Hugh Ward. 1993. "The Electoral Impact of Press Coverage of the British Economy, 1979–87." *British Journal of Political Science* 23(2): 175–210.

Sanders, Elizabeth. 2006. "Elaborating the 'New Institutionalism.'" In *The Oxford Handbook of Political Institutions*, ed. R. A.W. Rhodes, Sarah A. Binder, and Bert A. Rockman. Oxford: Oxford University Press.

Sanghera, M. K., E. T. Rolls, and A. Roper-Hall. 1979. "Visual Responses of Neurons in the Dorsolateral Amygdala of the Alert Monkey." *Experimental Neurology* 63(3): 610–26.

Scharz, Norbert. 1990. "Feelings as Information: Informational and Motivational Functions of Affective States." In *Handbook of Motivation and Cognition: Foundations of*

Social Behavior, Vol. 2, ed. Tory E. Higgins and Richard M. Sorrentino. New York: Guilford Press.

Schaubroeck, John, and Elaine Davis. 1994. "Prospect Theory Predictions When Escalation Is Not the Only Chance to Recover Sunk Costs." *Organizational Behavior and Human Decision Processes* 57(1): 59–82.

Schell, Anne M., Michael E. Dawson, and Ksenija Marinkovic. 1991. "Effects of Potentially Phobic Conditioned Stimuli on Retention, Reconditioning, and Extinction of the Conditioned Skin Conductance Response." *Psychophysiology* 28(2): 140–53.

Scherer, Klaus R. 1997. "Profiles of Emotion-Antecedent Appraisal: Testing Theoretical Predictions across Cultures." *Cognition & Emotion* 11(2): 113–50.

Schiffer, Adam J. 2006. "Assessing Partisan Bias in Political News: The Case(s) of Local Senate Election Coverage." *Political Communication* 23: 23–39.

Schudson, Michael. 2002. "The News Media as Political Institutions." *Annual Review of Political Science* 5: 249–69.

Schwarz, Norbert. 1990. "Feelings as Information: Informational and Motivational Functions of Affective States." In *The Handbook of Motivation and Cognition: Foundations of Social Behavior, Vol. 2*, ed. E. T. Higgins and R. M. Sorrentino. New York: Guilford Press.

Schwarz, Norbert, and Gerald L. Clore. 1996. *Feelings and Phenomenal Experiences.* New York: Guilford.

Schweller, Randall L. 1996. "Neorealism's Status Quo Bias: What Security Dilemma?" *Security Studies* 5(3): 90–121.

Scott, James C. 1977. *The Moral Economy of the Peasant: Rebellion and Subsistence in Southeast Asia.* New Haven, CT: Yale University Press.

Sears, David O. 1969. "Political Behavior." In *Handbook of Social Psychology, Revised Edition, Vol. 5*, ed. Gardner Lindzey and Elliot Aronson. Reading, MA: Addison-Wesley.

Sears, David O. 1983. "The Person-Positivity Bias." *Journal of Personality and Social Psychology* 44(2): 233–49.

Seymour, Ben, Tania Singer, and Ray Dolan. 2007. "The Neurobiology of Punishment." *Nature Reviews: Neuroscience* 8: 300–11.

Shapiro, Michael A., and Robert H. Rieger. 1992. "Comparing Positive and Negative Political Advertising on Radio." *Journalism Quarterly* 69(1): 135–45.

Shea, John. 1995. "Myopia, Liquidity Constraints, and Aggregate Consumption: A Simple Test." *Journal of Money, Credit, and Banking* 27(3): 798–805.

Sheldon, Kennon M., Richard Ryan, and Harry T. Reis. 1996. "What Makes for a Good Day? Competence and Autonomy in the Day and in the Person." *Personality and Social Psychology Bulletin* 22(12): 1270–79.

Sheley, Joseph F., and Cindy D. Ashkins. 1981. "Crime, Crime News, and Crime Views." *Public Opinion Quarterly* 45(4): 492–506.

Sherif, M., and C. W. Sherif. 1967. "Attitudes as the Individual's Own Categories: The Social Judgement Approach to Attitude Change." In *Attitude, Ego Involvement, and Change*, ed. C. W. Sherif and M. Sherif. New York: Wiley.

Shirvani, Hassan, and Barry Wilbratte. 2000. "Does Consumption Respond More Strongly to Stock Market Declines than to Increases?" *International Economic Journal* 14(3): 41–49.

Shizgal, Peter. 1998. "On the Neural Computation of Utility: Implications from Studies of Brain Stimulation Reward." In *Hedonic Psychology: Scientific Perspectives on Enjoyment, Suffering, and Well-Being,* ed. D. Kahneman, E. Diener, and N. Scwarz. New York: Cambridge University Press.

Shklar, Judith H. 1987. *Montesquieu.* Oxford: Oxford University Press.

Shoemaker, Pamela J. 1991. *Gatekeeping.* Newburry Park, CA: Sage Publications.

Shoemaker, Pamela J. 1996a. "Hard Wired for News: Using Biological and Cultural Evolution to Explain the Surveillance Function." *Journal of Communication* 46(3): 32–47.

Shoemaker, Pamela J. 1996b. "Media Gatekeeping." In *An Integrated Approach to Communication Theory and Research,* ed. Michael B Salwen and Don W. Stacks. Mahwah, NJ: Lawrence Erlbaum.

Shoemaker, Pamela J., T. Change, and N. Bredlinger. 1987. "Deviance as a Predictor of Newsworthiness." In *Communication Yearbook 10,* ed. M. McLaughlin. Beverly Hills, CA: Sage.

Shoemaker, Pamela J., Lucig H. Danielian, and Nancy Brendlinger. 1991. "Deviant Acts, Risky Business and U.S. Interests: The Newsworthiness of World Events." *Journalism & Mass Communication Quarterly* 68(4): 781–95.

Shoemaker, Pamela J., Martin Eichholz, Eunyi Kim, and Brenda Wrigley. 2001. "Individual and Routine Forces in Gatekeeping." *Journalism and Mass Communication Quarterly* 78(2): 233–46.

Shoemaker, Pamela J., and Howard C. Kunreuther. 1979. "An Experimental Study of Insurance Decisions." *The Journal of Risk and Insurance* 46(4): 603–18.

Shoemaker, Pamela J., and Tim P. Vos. 2009. *Gatekeeping Theory.* New York: Routledge.

Sigal, L. V. 1973. *Reporters and Officials: The Organization and Politics of Newsgathering.* Lexington, MA: Heath.

Sigmund, Karl. 2007. "Punish or Perish? Retaliation and Collaboration among Humans." *Trends in Ecology and Evolution* 22(11): 593–600.

Sigmund, Karl, Christoph Hauert, and Martin A. Nowak. 2001. "Reward and Punishment." *PNAS* 98(19): 10757–62.

Simons, Robert F., Benjamin H. Detenber, Thomas .M. Roedema, and Jason E. Reiss. 1999. "Emotion Processing in Three Systems: The Medium and the Message." *Psychophysiology* 36(5): 619–27.

Singh, Ramadhar, and Jennifer Boon Pei Teoh. 2000. "Impression Formation from Intellectual and Social Traits: Evidence for Behavioural Adaptation and Cognitive Processing." *British Journal of Social Psychology* 39(4): 537–54.

Skowronski, John J., and Donal E. Carlston. 1987. "Social Judgment and Social Memory: The Role of Cue Diagnosticity in Negativity, Positivity, and Extremity Biases." *Journal of Personality and Social Psychology* 52(4): 689–99.

Skowronski, John J., and Donal E. Carlston. 1989. "Negativity and Extremity Biases in Impression Formation: A Review of Explanations." *Psychological Bulletin* 105(1): 131–42.

Small, William J. 1972. *Political Power and the Press.* New York: Norton.

Smirnov, Oleg. 2007. "Altruistic Punishment in Politics and Life Sciences: Climbing the Same Mountain in Theory and Practice." *Perspectives on Politics* 5(3): 489–501.

Smith, Kevin B., Levente Littvay, Chris Larimer, and John R. Hibbing. 2007. "Evolutionary Theory and Political Leadership: Why Certain People Do Not Trust Decision Makers." *Journal of Politics* 69(2): 285–99.

Smith, N. Kyle, John T. Cacioppo, Jeff T. Larsen, and Tanya L. Chartrand. 2003. "May I Have Your Attention, Please: Electrocortical Responses to Positive and Negative Stimuli." *Neuropsychologia* 41(2): 171–83.

Sniderman, Paul M., Richard A. Brody, Jonathan W. Siegel, and Percy H. Tannenbaum. 1982. "Evaluative Bias and Issue Proximity." *Political Behavior* 4(2): 115–31.

Sondrol, Paul C. 1991. "Totalitarian and Authoritarian Dictators: A Comparison of Fidel Castro and Alfredo Stroessner." *Journal of Latin American Studies* 23(3): 599–620.

Soroka, Stuart. 2002. *Agenda-Setting Dynamics in Canada*. Vancouver: University of British Columbia Press.

Soroka, Stuart. 2003. "Media, Public Opinion and Foreign Policy." *Harvard International Journal of Press and Politics* 8(1): 27–48.

Soroka, Stuart. 2006. "Good News and Bad News: Asymmetric Responses to Economic Information." *The Journal of Politics* 68(2): 372–85.

Soroka, Stuart. 2012. "The Gatekeeping Function: Distributions of Information in Media and the Real World." *The Journal of Politics* 74(2): 514–28.

Soroka, Stuart, and Blake Andrew. 2009. "Media Coverage of Canadian Elections: Horse-Race Coverage and Negativity in Election Campaigns." In *Mediating Canadian Politics*, ed. Linda Trimble and Shanon Sampert. Toronto: Pearson.

Soroka, Stuart, Marc Andre Bodet, Lori Young, and Blake Andrew. 2009. "Campaign News and Vote Intentions." *Journal of Elections, Public Opinion and Parties* 19(4): 359–76.

Soroka, Stuart, and Stephen McAdams. N.d. "News, Politics and Negativity." Forthcoming in *Political Communication*.

Soroka, Stuart, and Christopher Wlezien. 2004. "Opinion Representation and Policy Feedback: Canada in Comparative Perspective." *Canadian Journal of Political Science* 37(3): 531–60.

Soroka, Stuart, and Christopher Wlezien. 2005. "Opinion-Policy Dynamics: Public Preferences and Public Expenditure in the UK." *British Journal of Political Science* 35: 665–89.

Soroka, Stuart, and Christopher Wlezien. 2010. *Degrees of Democracy: Politics, Public Opinion and Policy*. Cambridge: Cambridge University Press.

Sparrow, Bartholomew. 1999. *Uncertain Guardians: The News Media as a Political Institution*. Baltimore, MD: The Johns Hopkins University Press.

Spense, J. T., and L. L. Segner. 1967. "Verbal vs. Nonverbal Reinforcement Combinations in the Discrimination Learning of Middle and Lower Class Children." *Child Development* 38: 29–38.

Staton, J. J. 1984. "Acquired Practical Reasoning through Teacher-Student Interactions in Dialogue Journals." Unpublished doctoral dissertation, University of California, Los Angeles.

Stevenson, H. N. C. 1954. "Status Elevation in the Hindu Caste System." *Journal of the Royal Anthropological Institute of Great Britain and Ireland* 84: 45–65.

Stevenson, Randolph T. 2001. "The Economy and Policy Mood: A Fundamental Dynamic of Democratic Politics?" *American Journal of Political Science* 45(3): 620–33.

Stone, Philip J., Dexter C. Dumphy, Marshall S. Smith, and Daniel M. Ogilvie. 1966. *The General Inquirer: A Computer Approach to Content Analysis.* Cambridge, MA: MIT Press.

Strapparava, Carlo, and Alessandro Valitutti. 2004. "WordNet-Affect: An Affective Extension of WordNet." In *Proceedings of the Fifth International Conference on Language Resources and Evaluation*, Lisbon.

Subasic, Pero, and Alison Huettner. 2001. "Affect Analysis of Text Using Fuzzy Semantic Typing." *IEEE Transactions on Fuzzy Systems* 9(4): 483–96.

Sulfaro, Valerie A. 1998. "Political Sophistication and the Presidential Campaign: Citizen Reactions to Campaign Advertisements." Paper presented at the annual meeting of the Midwest Political Science Association, Chicago.

Sulitzeanu-Kenan, Raanan. 2010. "Reflection in the Shadow of Blame: When Do Politicians Appoint Commissions of Inquiry?" *British Journal of Political Science* 40: 613–34.

Swank, O. H. 1993. "Popularity Functions Based on the Partisan Theory." *Public Choice* 75(4): 339–56.

Tarnopolsky, Christina. 2004. "Prudes, Perverts and Tyrants: Plato and the Contemporary Politics of Shame and Civility." *Political Theory* 32(4): 468–94.

Tarnopolsky, Christina. 2010. *Prudes, Perverts and Tyrants: Plato's Gorgias and the Politics of Shame.* Princeton, NJ: Princeton University Press.

Taylor, Shelley E. 1983. "Adjustment to Threatening Events: A Theory of Cognitive Adaptation." *American Psychologist* 38(11): 1161–73.

Taylor, Shelley E. 1991. "Asymmetrical Effects of Positive and Negative Events: The Mobilization-Minimization Hypothesis." *Psychological Bulletin* 110(1): 67–85.

Tewksbury, David. 2005. "The Seeds of Audience Fragmentation: Specialization in the Use of Online News Sites." *Journal of Broadcasting and Electronic Media* 49(3): 332–48.

Thaler, Richard. 1980. "Toward a Positive Theory of Consumer Choice." *Journal of Economic Behavior & Organization* 1(1): 39–60.

Thaler, Richard H., Amos Tversky, Daniel Kahneman, and Alan Schwartz. 1997. "The Effect of Myopia and Loss Aversion on Risk Taking: An Experimental Test." *The Quarterly Journal of Economics* 112(2): 647–61.

Thomas, D. L., and Diener, E. 1990. "Memory Accuracy in the Recall of Emotions." *Journal of Personality and Social Psychology* 59: 291–97.

Thompson, C. Bradley. 1995. "John Adams's Machiavellian Moment." *The Review of Politics* 57(3): 389–417.

Thompson, Charles P. 1985. "Memory for Unique Personal Events: Effects of Pleasantness." *Motivation and Emotion* 9(3): 277–89.

Thorson, Esther, William G. Christ, and Clarke Caywood. 1991. "Selling Candidates Like Tubes of Toothpaste: Is the Comparison Apt?" In *Television and Political Advertising, Vol. 1*, ed. Frank Biocca. Hillsdale, NJ: Lawrence Erlbaum.

Tidmarch, Charles M. 1985. "Covering Congress." *Polity* 17(3): 463–83.

Tindall, Robert C., and Richard G. Ratliff. 1974. "Interaction of Reinforcement Condi-
    tions and Developmental Level in a Two-Choice Discrimination Task with Children."
    Journal of Experimental Child Psychology 18(2): 183–89.
Tsebelis, George. 2002. *Veto Players*. Princeton, NJ: Princeton University Press.
Tufte, Edward R. 1978. *Political Control of the Economy*. Princeton, NJ: Princeton
    University Press.
Turney, Peter, and M. L. Littman. 2002. "Unsupervised Learning of Semantic Orien-
    tation from a Hundred-Billion-Word Corpus." Technical Report ERC-1094 (NRC
    44929), National Research Council of Canada.
Tversky, Amos, and Daniel Kahneman. 1981. "The Framing of Decisions and the
    Psychology of Choice." *Science* 211(4481): 453–58.
Tversky, Amos, and Daniel Kahneman. 1986. "Rational Choice and the Framing of
    Decisions." *Journal of Business* 59(4): S251–S278.
Tversky, Amos, and Daniel Kahneman. 1991. "Loss Aversion in Riskless Choice: A
    Reference dependent Model." *Quarterly Journal of Economics* 106(4): 1039–61.
Tversky, Amos, Paul Slovic, and Daniel Kahneman. 1990. "The Causes of Preference
    Reversal." *The American Economic Review* 80(1): 204–17.
Twight, Charlotte. 1991. "From Claiming Credit to Avoiding Blame: The Evolution
    of Congressional Strategy for Asbestos Management." *Journal of Public Policy* 11:
    153–86.
van Atteveldt, Wouter, Jan Kleinnijehuis, Nel Rugrok, and Stefan Schlobach. 2008.
    "Good News or Bad News? Conducting Sentiment Analysis on Dutch Text to Distin-
    guish Between Positive and Negative Relations." *Journal of Information Technology
    & Politics* 5(1): 73–94.
Van der Pligt, Joop, and J. Richard Eiser. 1980. "Negativity and Descriptive Extremity
    in Impression Formation." *European Journal of Social Psychology* 10(4): 415–19.
Van Goozen, Stephanie, and Nico H. Frijda. 1993. "Emotion Words Used in Six Euro-
    pean Countries." *European Journal of Social Psychology* 23(1): 89–95.
Vogel, Lean, Jan-Oliver Menz, and Ulrich Fritsche. 2009. "Prospect Theory and Infla-
    tion Perceptions – An Empirical Assessment." Department Economics and Politcs
    (DEP) Discussion Papers, Macroeconomics and Finance Series, Universitat Hamburg,
    March.
Vonk, Roos. 1993. "The Negativity Effect in Trait Ratings and in Open-Ended Descrip-
    tion of Persons." *Personality and Social Psychology Bulletin* 19(3): 269–78.
Vonk, Roos. 1996. "Negativity and Potency Effects in Impression Formation." *Euro-
    pean Journal of Social Psychology* 26(6): 851–65.
Wagenaar, Willem A. 1986. "My Memory: A Study of Autobiographical Memory over
    Six Years." *Cognitive Psychology* 18(2): 225–52.
Wang, Juan. in progress. *The Sinews of State Power: Intra-State Cohesion in Rural
    China*. Book manuscript.
Warden, Carl J., and Mercy Aylesworth. 1927. "The Relative Value of Reward and
    Punishment in the Formation of a Visual Discrimination Habit in the White Rat."
    Journal of Comparative Psychology 7(2): 117–27.
Watson, David, and Auke Tellegen. 1985. "Toward a Consensual Structure of Mood."
    Psychological Bulletin 98(2): 219–35.
Way, Baldwin M., and Roger D. Masters. 1996. "Political Attitudes: Interactions of
    Cognition and Affect." *Motivation & Emotion* 20(3): 205–36.

Weaver, R. Kent. 1986. "The Politics of Blame Avoidance." *Journal of Public Policy* 6(4): 371–98.

Weaver, R. Kent. 2010. "Paths and Forks or Chutes and Ladders? Negative Feedbacks and Policy Regime Change." *Journal of Public Policy* 30(2): 137–62.

Weinberg, Gerald M. 1975. *An Introduction to General Systems Thinking.* New York: Wiley.

Weiner, Bernard. 1985. "'Spontaneous' Causal Thinking." *Psychological Bulletin* 97(1): 74–84.

Weingast, Barry R. 1995. "The Economic Role of Political Institutions: Market-Preserving Federalism and Economic Development." *Journal of Law, Economics and Organization* 11(1): 1–31.

Weisberg, Herbert F., and Arthur H. Miller. 1979. "Evaluation of the Feeling Thermometer." A Report to the National Election Study Board Based on Data from the 1979 Pilot Survey.

Wells, Jennifer D., Stevan E. Hobfoll, and Justin Lavin. 1999. "When It Rains, It Pours: The Greater Impact of Resource Loss Compared to Gain on Psychological Distress." *Personality and Social Psychology Bulletin* 25(9): 1172–82.

Westley, Bruce H., and Malcolm S. MacLean, Jr. 1957. "A Conceptual Model for Communications Research." *Journalism Quarterly* 34(1): 31–38.

Weyland, Kurt G. 2002. *The Politics of Market Reform in Fragile Democracies: Argentina, Brazil, Peru, and Venezuela.* Princeton, NJ: Princeton University Press.

Weyland, Kurt G. 2004. "Neoliberalism and Democracy in Latin America: A Mixed Record." *Latin American Politics and Society* 46(1): 135–57.

Whissell, C. M. 1989. "The Dictionary of Affect in Language." In *Emotion: Theory, Research, and Experience*, ed. R. Plutchik and H. Kellerman. New York: Academic Press.

White, David Manning. 1950. "The 'Gate Keeper': A Case Study in the Selection of News." *Journalism Quarterly* 17(4): 383–90.

White, Richard T. 1982. "Memory for Personal Events." *Human Learning* 1: 171–83.

Wilcox, Clyde, Lee Sigelman, and Elizabeth Cook. 1989. "Some Like It Hot: Individual Differences in Responses to Group Feeling Thermometers." *Public Opinion Quarterly* 53(2): 246–57.

Wildavsky, Aaron B. 1984. *The Politics of the Budgetary Process, 4th Edition.* Boston: Little Brown.

Wlezien, Christopher. 1995. "The Public as Thermostat: Dynamics of Preferences for Spending." *American Journal of Political Science* 39(4): 981–1000.

Wlezien, Christopher. 1996. "Dynamics of Representation: The Case of US Spending on Defence." *British Journal of Political Science* 26(1): 81–103.

Wlezien, Christopher. 2004. "Patterns of Representation: Dynamics of Public Preferences and Policy." *Journal of Politics* 66(1): 1–24.

Wlezien, Christopher, Mark Franklin, and Daniel Twiggs. 1997. "Economic Perceptions and Vote Choice: Disentangling the Endogeneity." *Political Behavior* 19(1): 7–17.

Wlezien, Christopher, and Stuart Soroka. 2011. "Federalism and Public Responsiveness to Policy." *Publius: The Journal of Federalism* 41(1): 31–52.

Wlezien, Christopher, and Stuart Soroka. 2012. "Political Institutions and the Opinion-Policy Link." *West European Politics* 35(6): 1407–32.

Ybarra, Oscar, and Walter G. Stephan. 1996. "Misanthropic Person Memory." *Journal of Personality and Social Psychology* 70(4): 691–700.

Young, Lori, and Stuart Soroka. 2012. "Affective News: The Automated Coding of Sentiment in Political Texts." *Political Communication* 29: 205–231.

Zajonc, Robert B. 1980. "Feeling and Thinking: Preferences Need no Inferences." *American Psychologist* 35(2): 157–93.

Zajonc, Robert B. 1998. "Emotions." In *Handbook of Social Psychology*, ed. Daniel T. Gilbert, Susan T. Fiske, and Lindzey Gardner. New York: Oxford University Press.

Zucker, Harold G. 1978. "The Variable Nature of News Media Influence." In *Communication Yearbook* 2, ed. Brent D. Ruben. New Brunswick, NJ: Transaction Books.

Index

Books in the Series